FINAL REPORT

MICHAEL D. COE

FINAL REPORT

An Archaeologist
Excavates His Past

with 41 illustrations

Thames & Hudson

To my children and grandchildren

First published in the United Kingdom in 2006 by
Thames & Hudson Ltd, 181A High Holborn, London WC1V 7QX

www.thamesandhudson.com

British Library Cataloguing-in-Publication Data
A catalogue record for this book is available from the British Library

ISBN-13: 978-0-500-05143-6
ISBN-10: 0-500-05143-7

Printed and bound in Slovenia by MKT Print d.d.

CONTENTS

Preface

ϗ

"Who dares to teach should never cease to learn."

I've never been able to discover who originated this sentence, but it was inscribed in stone over the entrance doorway to the local high school in the Long Island town where I spent part of my boyhood. It may have disconcerted some of the teachers there, but I've never forgotten it.

The most famous autobiography ever written by an American is called *The Education of Henry Adams*, and in a large way my own memoirs are all about my own education, which began in the year of the great stock market crash, and will end only with my demise. I've learned from my parents and grandparents, from parents-in-law, from my teachers and from my students, from my colleagues, from fishing guides in many countries, and from my friends (and even from some enemies!). But my teachers have also included long-vanished peoples, who have allowed me to look into their minds and actions, even though "through a glass darkly" – the ancient farmers and fishers of the Guatemalan coast, the Olmecs of Veracruz, the Classic Maya, the Khmer of Angkor, and mid-18th-century Yankee soldiers on the Massachusetts frontier.

In the school where I learned most, the motto was in Latin: Poteris Modo Velis, "you can if you will," in other words, "if you want to, you can do it." I've found out that this is true, but sometimes it takes more than a bit of luck. And in a profession like archaeology, where what one is seeking is by definition hidden below ground or otherwise out of sight, it helps to have the Goddess of Fortune on one's side. I once knew a prehistorian in a country to the south of the U.S. who had the greatest technical knowledge in the world, but never found anything of importance. He sounded impressive, though!

7

Some individuals can claim that the trajectory of their life has been absolutely straight, that they knew from childhood that they would be a general, a fireman, a lawyer, a doctor, a minister, a college professor, and so forth. My own life, and I suspect that of most people in what is called "the developed world," has been bounced around by profoundly random, unforeseeable events. For example, as you will see, the chance infatuation of a high-school biology teacher for a lady-love deflected me from a career in biology or biochemistry. Neither I, nor anyone who knew me as an adolescent, would ever have predicted that I'd end up teaching anthropological archaeology at Yale, digging up dead civilizations, and writing about them.

The saddest thing about writing one's memoirs in what are euphemistically called "the golden years" is that most of the people in it are no longer alive. That's the downside. The up side is that one's memory of long-dead persons and past events actually sharpens with old age, and one has a lot more to recall than if the autobiography were prematurely written at age 30 or 40. And one can say about them what one likes without fear of contradiction or libel suits! Curiously, what remains the longest in the mind is the sound of people's voices, and I can still hear those of each and every one of the individuals mentioned in this book as though they were still speaking to me.

Almost everyone who has read Henry Adams's *Education* has been struck by the fact that he never once mentions his wife. This I cannot understand. A large part of my life, both professional and personal, was bound up with that of my late wife Sophie Dobzhansky Coe. She was the companion of almost four decades who taught me the most of what I know as a human being. Without her support and love, and that of our five children, I would have been nothing.

Why is this a "Final Report"? Because that is what archaeologists are supposed to produce at the end of a project, but (I regret to say) often don't. I've been digging into my own past, and this is my report on what I've found.

Rome
New Haven

CHAPTER 1

A Silver Spoon

My mother gave birth to me on 14 May 1929, in Miss Lippincott's Lying-in Hospital, on Manhattan's East Side. This very posh sanitarium was located just above the old Colony Restaurant; rather than having to eat hospital cuisine (a genuine oxymoron), the patients could have gourmet dishes sent up from downstairs. According to my mother, my parents' friend, the large-nosed comedian Jimmy Durante, sent up a wreath for me with the inscription "Good Luck." There is little doubt that I was born with a silver spoon in my mouth, but I could just as easily have been born in a place and at a time when my destiny would have been not to eat with silver spoons, but to polish them at regular intervals, as my not-so-distant ancestors once did in the old country from which we Coes came.

Like nearly all affluent American families high up in the social scale (we were regularly listed in the New York Social Register), the Coes were not always so well-off. I always knew that the family had come to America from England some time in the late 19th century, and that my great-grandfather Frederick Augustus Coe was the one who had brought over his Scottish wife Margaret Robertson and their nine children, among whom was my grandfather William Robertson Coe, then a 14-year-old boy.

I have a relative who loves to construct elaborate Coe family trees, complete with armorial bearings; the truth is that our race is more reminiscent of Charles Dickens' Chuzzlewit family, which

… undoubtedly descended in a direct line from Adam and Eve; and was, in the very earliest times, closely connected with the agricultural interest.

The surname Coe is of Norse origin and originally meant "jackdaw," a noisy but intelligent member of the crow family. The name is particularly widespread in East Anglia, which was settled by Norsemen from Denmark; a glance at the Cambridge telephone directory will disclose pages of Coes, although it is a relatively rare name elsewhere in England. So, we must have originated as tillers of the soil in the rural fen country of eastern England.

The very first ancestral Coe that I can be sure of is my great-great-great-grandfather Robert Coe (we will call him Robert Coe I), who was born in 1752, but we don't know where. He died in 1834, and is buried with his wife Martha Saunders in the lovely churchyard of All Souls Church, on the south bank of the upper Thames in the village of Bisham, Berkshire. A local newspaper notice of his decease described him as "many years butler to George Vansittart of Bisham Abbey." Other records describe him as a house steward, the top category for "upper servants." Enthusiasts of the macabre know Bisham Abbey as the haunt of one of England's most famous ghosts, that of Lady Elizabeth Hoby, who is supposed to have killed her own son in a fit of rage when the unfortunate boy blotted his lesson for the day. Originally an establishment of the Knights Templar, then following the Dissolution the home of the Hoby family, the Abbey passed into the hands of George Vansittart, member of a line of distinguished naval and military men, and parliamentarians. Today it is the National Sports Centre.

Robert I must have had to coexist uneasily with Lady Hoby's spectral presence while he carried on with his duties below stairs and upstairs. Martha may well have been the Vansittart housekeeper, a common arrangement. A son, also named Robert, was born to them in 1792; this Robert II was my great-great-grandfather, and he, too, is buried in the Bisham churchyard alongside his wife Alice Cass. At first he made his living as a brewer, across the river in High Wycombe; he then migrated to London, where he also became a butler to a parliamentary family of Welsh origin, the Gwynne-Holfords, at 31 Grosvenor Square – a building demolished after World War II to make way for Eero Saarinen's gigantic American Embassy. This Robert died there in 1863, the kindly owners having let the old man spend the final part of his life in the place he knew best.

10

It was his son Frederick Augustus Coe, my great-grandfather, who delivered us out of the world of higher servants, who brought us upstairs from downstairs. Born on 14 April 1838, two-and-a-half months before the coronation of Queen Victoria, he died in Philadelphia on 5 December 1929. On my christening, he presented me with a small silver cup inscribed with his name. A handsome, white-haired man with a Van Dyck beard, my father told me that he liked to hold me and say "I'll button back your ears and swallow you," but of course I don't remember this or him.

At some point Frederick turned his back on his father's profession and left High Wycombe for the industrial Midlands, becoming paymaster and eventually manager of the Brettell Iron Works. He became prosperous enough to have a house in Kingswinford, to the west of Birmingham. I have no idea of how he met my Presbyterian great-grandmother, Margaret Robertson of Edinburgh, but the two of them were married in 1861, in London at St. George's Church on Hanover Square – this very same church had seen the weddings of his butler father and grandfather, and had once been the place of worship of George Frederick Handel.

Frederick and Margaret were true winners in the Darwinian sweepstakes, producing 11 children, nine of whom survived to adulthood; except for my maiden great-aunts Maud and Margaret, most of these also were genetically prolific. Even if not all of the Coes have been financially successful, we have done very well in the biological line – I have more than a hundred identifiable cousins on my father's side of the family. An old group photograph from the Kingswinford days shows that the two progenitors were prosperous enough to have servants. Among the children in that image is a small boy who can be none other than my grandfather William Robertson Coe. Born in June 1869, he became by far the wealthiest Coe ever and, as will be seen, had a great deal to do with my early life.

But Frederick had bigger ideas for himself, his wife, and large brood. Armed with a letter of recommendation from his employer Mr. Brettell, in the winter of 1883 he left Cardiff with his family for America in the S.S. *Rhodora*, a small cargo vessel owned by Margaret's brother George Robertson. After a very rough crossing, they settled in Cinnaminson, New Jersey, just east of Philadelphia. There is a family tradition that my great-grandfather continued his profession as ironworks manager within Andrew Carnegie's steel empire, but I have never found proof for this. Curiously, my grandfather hardly ever mentioned his father or told me what he did, a reticence that more naturally extended to his butler forebears.

The 14-year-old Will, along with his younger brother George, attended a Quaker academy in Cinnaminson, but was soon apprenticed as an office boy in the Philadelphia branch of Johnson & Higgins, the marine insurers. He must have done much more there than "polish up the handle on the big front door," for he rapidly rose through the ranks, specializing in marine adjusting. There came a time in his middle age when my grandfather became the company's president and eventually chairman of the board, a true American success story – not exactly rags to riches, but certainly lower middle class to upper class.

There were some odd postscripts to his career with Johnson & Higgins. The first happened in 1911; being a good friend of Bruce Ismay, the chairman of the White Star Line, my grandfather was one of the insurers of the *Titanic*'s "unsinkable" hull. On the morning of 15 April 1912, he was the first person in America to learn of the disaster, having been woken by an emergency telephone call. He had first-class tickets for his entire family (including my father) on the ill-fated liner's return journey, which was scheduled to leave five days later for Southampton. These were of course cancelled, but the family subsequently made a number of trips between the U.S. and England on the *Titanic*'s nearly identical sister ship, the *Olympic*.

The second postscript was when I had dinner with him in his Manhattan duplex apartment in January 1952, shortly before my departure for a two-year government assignment in Taiwan (then generally known to outsiders as Formosa).

"Watch out for cannibals when you get to Formosa, young man!"

This made no sense to me at all, until he explained that a Japanese ship insured by his firm had been wrecked on the island's east coast in the late 1880s, and the crew killed and supposedly eaten by the local aboriginal population. In retrospect, I now know that the cannibalism part was probably untrue, but until the end of World War II the Formosan aborigines were enthusiastic and often successful headhunters, the hated Japanese being favorite targets. Each of the crewmen would almost certainly have been "shortened by a head," as the saying goes.

❧

My grandfather married three times. His first wife was the daughter of a Savannah judge, but she died after a few years. Then he met the young Mai Rogers on a transatlantic voyage, and they were wed in New York on 4 June 1900. For William Robertson Coe and all of his descendants, including myself, this was an incredible windfall, for Mai was the daughter of Henry Huttleston Rogers, one of the great "robber barons" of that freewheeling age, an organizer of the Standard Oil Trust, and according to a Forbes survey one of the 25 richest men who has ever lived in the United States. In spite of my grandfather's claim, often made to me, that he (WRC) had risen to his present prosperity through his own hard work, I know for a fact – Federal tax documents prove it – that in the early 1920s Mai's income was four times her husband's.

The Rogerses were a far more ancient and respectable family than the Coes. The part-Cherokee humorist Will Rogers, not related to us in any way, once said: "My forefathers didn't come over on the *Mayflower*, but they met the boat." But in 1620 Mai's ancestors actually were on that boat – these were Thomas Rogers, the ship's carpenter and a native of Devon, and his son. The family naturally settled first in Plymouth, then moved to the southeastern part of Massachusetts, to the tiny Puritan settlements lying along the coast of Buzzard's Bay, and to Martha's Vineyard.

By the early decades of the 19th century, this region had greatly prospered from the whaling trade. Fairhaven, on the eastern side of New Bedford Harbor, was one of these whaling ports, and all of its leading whaling families, people like the Giffords, Delanos, and Winslows, had intermarried over and over. The young H. H. Rogers, son of a Fairhaven grocer, was born in 1840, and originally intended to ship out on a whaler like other young men of the town, but he later changed his mind and traded dreams of whale oil for visions of "rock oil," that is, petroleum.

In this venture he was joined by his young wife Abbie Palmer Gifford, daughter of the prominent whaling captain Peleg Gifford. Capt. Gifford was a spade-bearded Yankee who had made many long voyages on the seas of the world, and I have often wondered whether Herman Melville, who shipped out from Fairhaven, didn't get the name of Ahab's friend Peleg from this particular ancestor. Capt. Gifford was also one of the redoubtable skippers who in 1861 sailed 16 old whaling ships ("The Great Stone Fleet") laden with blocks of granite to Charleston and scuttled them to blockade the harbor.

By 1862 H. H. Rogers and Abbie had established themselves in Titusville, Pennsylvania, where three years earlier "Colonel" Edwin Drake had brought in the world's first oil well. Rogers and his partner Charles Pratt at first were in competition with John D. Rockefeller, son of an itinerant patent-medicine quack, but eventually the wily Rockefeller brought them into his organization. Rogers was the brains behind the creation of the great financial machine that became known as Standard Oil. While in Titusville, he invented the oil pipeline, as a way to circumvent the rapacious railroads that were hugely overcharging the producers for transportation of their oil-laden barrels.

Rogers's rise in the dog-eat-dog world of laissez-faire capitalism was truly meteoric. From Standard Oil's New York offices he managed to get control of all Staten Island's transportation, along with more extensive holdings such as Montana's Anaconda Copper Company. His Wall Street manipulations were so ferocious that he became known as "Hell Hound" Rogers. A favorite target of the "yellow press" and muckraking reporters of the day such as Ida Tarbell (who liked him as a person), H. H. Rogers had many enemies, including J.P. Morgan and Rockefeller himself. Eventually, after a bitter confrontation with Rockefeller, he cashed in his Standard Oil interests to construct the Virginian Railway Company, a highly profitable line that brought coal from West Virginia to Norfolk.

Sensational journalists applied to him the epithet "the Jekyll and Hyde of Wall Street," suggesting that there were two totally different sides to my great-grandfather – a devil who could ruin competitors, and a saint, combined in the same man. This was certainly true. A strikingly handsome man with many warm friends, especially those from his childhood days in Fairhaven, he was immensely kind to his family and a major benefactor to his native town, where he continued to spend his summer holidays. His lasting claim to fame, though, was his close friendship with Mark Twain, whom he saved from financial ruin at a critical moment in the great writer's life. In his autobiography, Twain states "He is not only the best friend I've ever had, but the best man I've ever met." At the latter's urging, Rogers secretly paid for the blind and deaf Helen Keller's Radcliffe education and was the principal financial backer of black educator and reformer Booker T. Washington's Tuskegee Institute.

Twain was a frequent visitor to the Rogers and Coe families (when a boy, my father often heard him tell stories), and frequently traveled on the Kanawha, my great-grandfather's luxurious, steam-driven yacht, then the world's fastest. There is a wonderful surviving correspondence between Rogers and Twain, making it plain that their friendship often involved good drink, good cigars, and ribald stories – all those things that drew the detestation and ire of the puritanical, psalm-singing Rockefeller.

It is said that one day Mark Twain was walking down a New Bedford street with a censorious lady who exclaimed to him, "Mr. Clemens, I don't see how you can associate yourself with a man like Henry Rogers. Don't you know that his money is tainted?" "You're right, madame," he replied, "t'aint yours and t'aint mine."

With the presidency of the crusading Theodore Roosevelt, H. H. Rogers became a major target of the United States government's trust-busting efforts, and the strain of his defense along with the worries attendant upon the completion of his railroad were too much for his health. He died of a stroke in 1909, leaving a very large estate to his four children. The Rogerses and the Coes have been freely spending their heritage ever since, with the tax authorities taking a hefty bite with the passing of each generation. There is a very American mantra which goes "overalls to overalls in five generations." In the case of the Coes, it might yet prove to be true.

~

My grandparents, William and Mai, had four children, three boys and a girl. The eldest was my father, William Rogers Coe, born in 1901. Unlike his younger siblings, he was the only one who stayed close to home all his life, and who made a dutiful effort to follow his father's stern instructions (often unsuccessfully). He was the only one who entered the world of Wall Street, finally settling as Vice President and Treasurer of the Virginian – the family railroad. His younger brother Robert had an overseas life in the Foreign Service, retiring eventually to Cannes; another brother, Henry – the charming black sheep of the family – settled in Cody, Wyoming (of which more later); and Natalie, the youngest, married an Italian diplomat and spent most of her life in Italy.

My father had a wonderful boyhood, but it must be admitted that his academic career was checkered. He didn't do badly at all in posh day schools in New York City. He liked to recount the time when Col. William Frederick Cody, by that time a close family friend, brought his famous Wild West show to New York. The young Billy and his brother Bob were given tickets by Buffalo Bill for themselves and as many of their school chums that they wished to bring. After the performance had begun, the great showman invited the two Coe boys to ride in the storied Deadwood Stagecoach during a simulated attack by hostile Indians. They got in, and the stagecoach took off, careening around the arena; when a throng of whooping red men (who not long before had been real "hostiles") came after it, the terrified Billy and Bob dropped down to the bottom of the vehicle, clinging to the slats for dear life, and wishing that they were somewhere else.

The connection with Buffalo Bill was a happy one for the family. My grandfather was an avid hunter, and had a particularly successful trip in Montana, shooting elk and mountain sheep. Like many other transplanted Englishmen of the era, he was drawn to the Rockies and wanted to have a place where he, Mai, and the children could summer. A mutual friend introduced him to the great scout, and in 1910 he purchased Irma Lake Lodge, Buffalo Bill's hunting lodge on Carter Mountain, southwest of Cody, Wyoming. This was the paradise where I spent the happiest days of my youth. The lake was named for the colonel's dipsomaniac daughter. From the house that my grandfather built there, one could see over 100 miles north to the snow-covered Beartooth Mountains of Montana. But more about the ranch later in my story.

In 1913, my grandfather, at that time president of Johnson & Higgins, bought a large house and extensive property in Oyster Bay, on Long Island's North Shore – with Mai's money, of course. Adding adjacent farms to his estate, he named it "Planting Fields," and his family divided their time between it, a New York town house, and Wyoming.

When it came to his children's upbringing and education, my grandfather was an unsuccessful micromanager. My father, along with Uncle Bob, was sent to St. Paul's School, an Episcopalian boarding school in Concord, New Hampshire; every fortnight, both of them had to send their grades back to their father, but my father was no great academic achiever. Here is an extract from one of my grandfather's many stern letters to Billy, sent when he was just 14 and in the Second Form:

Your mother and I are very much disgusted with the way you are going on. Just think of it! You are number 13 in a division of 14, and your younger brother is number 4! You ought to be ashamed of yourself. You will remember the talk we had with you before you went to school. We offered you certain presents for any prizes you got. In looking at the report I see that sixty demerits during the entire school term prevents your getting any testimonials and you have already gotten thirty-four in only six weeks! ... If you continue the way you are going I can see one thing ahead of you. You will be dropped to the first form and ultimately expelled from the school. If that should happen you will regret it all your life.

However, he did manage to graduate from the school, unlike so many of my relatives who for one reason or another actually were expelled from St. Paul's. It wasn't until I was in college myself that I learned from my grandfather that my father had once been a freshman at Princeton, but had been asked by the authorities not to return after a year largely spent going to Gatsbyesque parties in New York. In due course, after much private tutoring, he was accepted into the U.S. Naval Academy, but dropped out after three years.

His father was not pleased by this fecklessness, but, as I later found out in my own relations with my grandfather, his bark was far worse than his bite, and his anger didn't last very long. The upshot was that the young Bill was sent on an around-the-world tour in 1922, complete with African safari. To keep him out of trouble, he was accompanied by a British cicerone and duenna, one Col. Gibson, an old colonial hand. On his return, my father began life on Wall Street on the bottom rung of the investment firm E. H. Harriman & Company (the railroad tycoon Harriman had been a business associate of H. H. Rogers).

But my father once more got into hot water, this time far more serious. In March of 1923 he eloped with my mother Clover Simonton, a young dress designer; the couple was secretly married in New York City on Easter Sunday. His parents were outraged, as this was a woman they had never even met, and probably had never even heard of. It would be many months before even the more open-minded Mai would speak to either of the newly-weds, but at last they relented. In a way this was ironic, because before she married WRC, Mai herself had once eloped with a complete bounder and fortune-hunter, a crisis that was resolved when H. H. Rogers had the union annulled. Eventually, Mai and my mother became the closest of friends, but I don't think that my grandfather ever warmed to her. Nonetheless, this was the happiest of marriages, and my parents were true lovebirds all their life, until my father's death 48 years later.

I am smothered in information about the Coes and Rogerses, but I know remarkably little about the Simontons, about whom my mother was quite elusive. She told me that the family was originally from Charleston, and owned the Sword Gate House, still a tourist landmark in that beautiful city, and implied that they had lost everything at the close of the Civil War. This romantic scenario is highly unlikely, as records show that her grandfather Thomas Campbell Simonton, Sr., was a mining engineer living in New York State's Dutchess County on the date of his marriage.

My maternal grandfather, Thomas Campbell Simonton, Jr., was a well-known lawyer in Paterson, New Jersey, and for a long time its city attorney. A very handsome man with rakish mustachios, he was also something of a bon vivant and rake – according to a maternal cousin of mine, he suffered a classic death in the arms of his mistress. At one time, he came very close to being Attorney General of the United

States, as his Paterson law partner and fellow Republican, Garet A. Hobart, was elected as McKinley's Vice-President, and had every intention of nominating Simonton to that post. As luck would have it, however, Hobart died of a heart attack before he could carry this out (and was replaced by Teddy Roosevelt).

My mother's parents both died when she was still a girl, and she was raised by her elder sisters Dallas and Louise, the family by that time having moved to Manhattan's Upper West Side. Aunt Louise was a wonderfully kind, eccentric and delightful person; she called herself "Mrs. Louise Morgan" and sometimes "Mrs. Webb Morgan," I suppose from some rotter of a husband who had seemingly left her long before I was born. She was a true innocent – years later, when I was at Harvard, a rental apartment that she owned turned out to be a male brothel, but I don't think she ever realized the true nature of her rather odd tenants. There were a host of brothers also left orphaned by the death of Thomas and his wife, but I don't think I ever heard my mother mention their names.

Like my father's family, the Simontons were all devout Episcopalians, and my mother was educated in the day school of Saint Mary the Virgin, a very "high" church famed in Manhattan for its sung mass, incense, and magnificent music. She never went to college – few young women in her day did – but soon gravitated into the world of fashion and dress design, at which she was very good. While still in her early 20s, she made two trips to Paris, and she was already a success in that very competitive world. Then, she met my father at a party, and her life was changed. Four years after she was married my brother Bill was born, and two-and-a-half years after that, I appeared, only a few months before the great stock market crash and the beginning of the Great Depression.

My very earliest memory is one of my happiest, in spite of its arising from a near-death experience. When I was only a few months old, my father moved his young family from New York City to the North Shore of Long Island, where we lived in an ever-changing series of rented houses. In spite of changed economic conditions, they kept their heads well above water (my Grandfather Coe was reputed to have made a large amount of money on the Crash), and they had servants and even a chauffeur, until my mother learned how to drive her own car. When I was three years old, we lived in Glen Head, in a converted 18th century barn complete with still-occupied pigeon cotes. This property also had a swimming pool, and I was allowed to dabble in it under Aunt Louise's supervision. As a precaution, I was outfitted with water wings, paired inflated balloons attached to my back. But all did not go according to plan. When my aunt wasn't looking, I tumbled into the water, but on my back rather than my belly – so that my head was actually looking up, but completely underwater.

For me it was truly beautiful, for I could see through the surface the wavy, refracted image of blue sky, fluffy white clouds, and, in the distance, our white house. I felt at total peace and contentment, even though I was drowning. All this came to a shattering end as I was fished from the water by a shrieking Aunt Louise, who was soon joined by my panicked mother and other adults. The whole experience came to a humiliating end for me, since after they had dried me off, to my immense displeasure I was put into a small girl's dress instead of the usual buttoned-up male sun suit I had been wearing on this summer day. I never did understand what all the fuss had been about.

But there was another kind of panic in the air. This was the year 1932; in March the infant son of Charles Lindbergh had been kidnapped from his New Jersey home and murdered, and all well-off parents on Long Island, mine among them, feared for their own children. That summer saw the installation of prison-like bars on my bedroom window and presumably on my brother's, too.

These precautions were wasted, since by the next year we had moved to another rented house in Glen Head – my mother couldn't bear staying in the same place very long. This upscale residential community was called "High Farms," for until recently it had been cultivated land, and it abutted several working farms. In fact, most of Long Island to the east of Queens was then primarily agricultural, rather than the intensely urbanized landscape of today. As a consequence, during the hot Long Island summer, houseflies were ubiquitous; in every kitchen strips of flypaper hung stickily from the ceiling.

$$\mathcal{Q}$$

In our class, for those who could afford it, a live-in governess was de rigueur for pre-school children, and even for those in the first grade or two. My brother and I had a whole series of these, most of them unsatisfactory for one reason or another. A choleric German governess lasted only a few months, to be followed by an equally short-lived French mademoiselle. Next in line was an English nanny named Ann, who not only stayed several years but whose influence in one direction proved to be disastrous.

It became quite clear to me, small though I was, that she far preferred my brother Bill, on whom she doted. Right then and there I determined to strike out on my own regardless of her disapproval, and it was something of a triumph when, on my fourth birthday, I completely dressed myself without Ann's help, right down to tying my shoes. But what was truly insidious is that bit by bit she weaned my brother's affections away from his mother. This came to a head one day when my mother dressed down the six-year-old Bill for some act of childish rebellion. I listened in awe as he screamed "I don't love you! I hate you! I hate you! I love Ann!" Not surprisingly, it was not long before this particular nanny was fired for insubordination. But the hatred lingered and grew worse with every succeeding year, even through adolescence and into manhood, and eventually came to settle on me. The ways of the human mind are strange indeed.

The only governess whom I really liked was the final one, a kindly Norwegian. Although she was young, blonde, and pretty, her boyfriend persuaded her that her looks would be improved by having all her teeth extracted and replaced with dentures. I was horrified when she showed me her now toothless gums, crisscrossed with black suture thread. I think she eventually married this man and left our service, but by this time I was seven and on the verge of going off to boarding school, so no replacement was needed.

❦

Regardless of where we lived, we were never very far from Planting Fields, and constantly at the beck and call of my grandfather, the family patriarch whose wishes were law – at least, that is what he thought. Mai Rogers, my grandmother, had died in 1924, leaving an immense fortune to her children and husband. Some time prior to her death, my grandfather had met a recently divorced Southerner, Caroline Graham Slaughter, and they were often seen together at race courses and other stylish venues. A society gossip columnist had unkindly dubbed the two of them "Cash and Carry," and it was pretty obvious to all observers that they were having an affair; my mother, who adored Mai, was certain that my grandmother died of a broken heart. Two years later, Will and Caroline were married.

Caroline must have had a hard row to hoe, as she never won the hearts of her stepchildren, least of all that of my mother. Nonetheless, she was a good wife for my grandfather, for she knew exactly how to handle him. A very intelligent woman with a wicked sense of humor, she often laughed at his pontifications and, I think, made him a better person. Caroline was a wonderful step-grandmother, and I must say that because of her I always looked forward to our frequent command-performance attendances at their lunches.

Let me describe Planting Fields, which is now part of the New York State parks system. Covering 409 acres, it is a fair recreation of that kind of English estate that the ancestral Coes had worked for, but never owned. At its heart is a 65-room Tudor-Elizabethan mansion completed in 1922. Surrounded by huge lawns dotted with magnificent specimen trees, and by gardens and greenhouses and outbuildings, it was at once a country home and a working farm. To a small child like myself, it was a wonderland. Arrival at Planting Fields was an event in itself. At its entrance were the magnificent, wrought-iron Carshalton Gates, the oldest and finest gates in America, bought in England by my grandfather and removed to Planting Fields over Parliamentary protests. One then drove through fields covered in daffodils (in springtime), up through woodlands and azaleas and rhododendrons, past huge copper beeches, and finally to the great front door of the house.

One of the most memorable events of my childhood took place at

Planting Fields. This was the marriage in 1934 of my aunt Natalie with an Italian diplomat, Count Leonardo Vitetti. For this, Natalie had not only to be converted to Catholicism, but papal permission had to be obtained for the rite to be conducted in a secular setting. A very large contribution to the Church's coffers settled the matter, my grandfather even receiving a signed photograph from Pope Pius XI congratulating him for "having knelt humbly at the feet of His Holiness" – something that it was inconceivable for my grandfather to do for anyone, let alone a pope. It was a very impressive affair. Not only was the entire Italian diplomatic corps based in Washington present, with all their uniforms, medals, and decorations, but the marriage was conducted by the Papal Nuncio, with Count Galeazzo Ciano (Mussolini's son-in-law) as a witness in absentia.

According to my cousin George Coe (and I have no reason to doubt him), my grandfather planted a private detective in the stateroom adjacent to the one occupied by the newly-weds on their return voyage to Italy, to check up on whether this foreign son-in-law was treating his beloved daughter well. His report back was said to be, "Mr. Coe, I wouldn't be sorry for *her*, I'd be sorry for *him!*" Leonardo had married an heiress with money, all right, but one who was headstrong, outspoken, and very much used to having her own way in all matters, large and small. I thought she was wonderful, and I still do.

In the summer of 1936 my parents traveled to Europe, and my brother and I were left with Caroline and my grandfather at Planting Fields, along with the usual governess (I can't remember which). My father's goal was to attend Hitler's Olympics in Berlin. For me this was a kind of dream, for I had free reign to wander all over the paradise of Planting Fields. I was then deeply in puppy love with Linda Payson, a fellow grade schooler, and I think she with me (somewhere I still have her Valentine card childishly inscribed to "cute little Mickey"), and I was allowed to invite her over one day for a platonic tryst in the gardens and play house of Planting Fields. I doubt if she was overawed by the magnificence of Planting Fields – the beautiful little Linda lived on the even grander Whitney estate in Manhasset.

But the most memorable excitement that summer was a night in late June when a cat burglar climbed up to the terrace of my grandpar-

23

ents' bedrooms, entered silently, and stole $400,000 worth of diamonds, pearls, and other valuables. The next morning Planting Fields was crawling with detectives, with whose procedures I was fascinated. I was joined by my best friend (male) Vicky McCuaig in watching these cigar-chewing sleuths make casts of the miscreant's footprints left in the soft flower beds below the terrace. Of course, they never did catch the culprit – most of the jewel robberies on the "Gold Coast" of Long Island were inside jobs, and that one probably was, too. But I'm sure that my grandfather, as an insurance magnate himself, would have fully insured everything he owned.

Meantime, among all these diversions and comparative comfort and luxury (compared to the deprivations of most American children during the Depression), I had to get educated.

CHAPTER 2

"Stop Walking on Your Knees": A Small Boy's Education

I pretty much learned how to read on my own, having watched and listened as my mother taught that skill to my brother, so by the time I was sent to the first grade at the Greenvale School, the lessons there were basically a recapitulation of what I already knew. Greenvale was the private elementary school of choice for the offspring of the North Shore elite, and no one could have been more elite than the 11-year-old Gloria Vanderbilt, who arrived and left each day in a large, black, chauffeur-driven limousine. Also on hand was her bodyguard, since the little heiress had been the object of a bitter and much publicized custody dispute between her mother and her aunt, the sculptress Gertrude Vanderbilt Whitney.

At the close of that school year, it was decided to promote me into the third grade, but I remember very little of *that* year either. Throughout my boyhood and early adolescence, I was not only small for my age, but having skipped the second grade, I was always one year younger than my classmates. Taunts such as "Hey, shorty! Stop walking on your knees!" were all too frequent. Accordingly, I occasionally had to fight back, with wits when necessary, and with fists as a last resort. So, with the encouragement of my parents, I took boxing lessons in the third grade at the Greenvale School. It must have been a ridiculous sight, two not very big boys outfitted with enormous padded gloves flailing away at each other, but I greatly enjoyed these bouts even though I often lost them.

I was seven years old when my father, who considered himself an Annapolis alumnus (even though he had dropped out of the Naval Academy), took my mother and myself to the Army-Navy football game in Philadelphia. It was a cold, grey day in November of 1936 when we boarded the Pennsylvania Railroad train to that city. We traveled in style on a private car that had been leased by my father's friend Col. Edgar Garbisch, who had been a near-legendary captain of the West Point football team and a member of Walter Camp's All-American team. The colonel was very well-heeled, especially since his marriage to Bernice Chrysler and her automobile fortune. By the time we boarded, the car was filled with tobacco smoke and, although it was still late morning, with the smell of whiskey and other drinks being dispensed from a well-stocked bar.

There were no other children in the car, so I was feeling rather out of it all, when one of the Garbisch guests, a ruddy-faced gentleman who had obviously been sharing in the colonel's liquid hospitality, approached and asked me what sports I liked to play in school. On my replying that I had taken up boxing, he suddenly dropped into a fighting crouch, bringing his face down to my own level, and his arms up in defense.

"Go ahead sonny, let's see your punch. Give me a punch."

"Do you really mean that?"

"Yes, hit me as hard as you can."

I made my fist into a ball and put all my effort into a right hook. This unknown person had not been quite quick enough, and my small fist landed in his right eye socket. He stood up, staggering.

"That was a good one, sonny," he muttered, as he retreated to the bar.

My father later told me who this was. I had given a bit of a black eye to Gene Tunney, victor over Jack Dempsey and retired heavyweight champion of the world,.

It was all downhill after that. We had hard, cold seats on the Navy side of the stadium. The wind blew and there were even a few snow flurries. I was shivering throughout most of the game, but the adults in our party not only had heavy overcoats (the wives, of course, were in furs), but sustained themselves with frequent nips of brandy from silver hip flasks. Although my father tried to explain to me what was going on down on the field, the action seemed to me to be incomprehensible, slow, and endless. The Navy team won a 14–0 victory, and my father was elated, but all I cared about was getting home.

I vowed then and there never to go to another football game for the rest of my life, and I never have.

Ϟ

There are two places that I often revisit in my dreams, or in those last nighttime moments before I drop off to sleep, walking around them in my mind's eye and resurrecting the sights, sounds, and especially the smells of those distant times. One of these is my grandfather's ranch in Wyoming (of which more anon), with its perfume of damp conifers and pungent sagebrush. The other is the small New England boarding school in which I spent some of my formative years, and its pervasive odor of floor wax.

Two months following my encounter with Gene Tunney and that chilly football game, I was shipped off to this school. I was only seven. For years I believed that I must have been the youngest child ever to enter the Fay School in Southborough, Massachusetts, but I now know that in the 19th century they took in some boys at the ripe age of five! For the first few months I was quite naturally overwhelmed by home-sickness. The only emotion that remotely resembles homesickness is grief, also the consequence of temporary or permanent separation from those one knows and loves best.

My introduction to this new world of boarding schools, which I was to know until I entered Harvard ten years later, took place in my school's locker room a few days after my arrival. One of the older boys came up to me and gave me an order.

"You see that guy over there? Go tell him he's a son of a bitch."

Now this was a term that I'd heard my father shout while listening to the radio during a fireside speech of Franklin Delano Roosevelt (a distant cousin), but I had no idea of what it meant. Naively, I did so, and was immediately knocked to the floor. I soon learned how to adapt to this particular subculture, a process that involved taking a host of such loaded epithets into my vocabulary. I quickly learned the basic rules of boarding school life, which were:

- Don't snitch on your schoolmates, no matter what.
- Don't ever cry openly, no matter what.

27

- Don't boast about anything.
- Call the masters "Sir," but don't suck up to them.

Actually, Fay was a wonderful place; it is one of the oldest private boarding schools in the country, and if my parents were a bit thoughtless in sending me into exile at such a tender age, they had nevertheless chosen well. Founded in 1861, in my day Fay had between 50 and 60 boys as boarders. Its kindly headmaster was Edward Winchester Fay, a tall man with a definite physical resemblance to Neville Chamberlain. Our main contacts with "Eddie" Fay were firstly, lining up in the study hall every morning before breakfast, and presenting our hands so that he could inspect for dirt under the fingernails, and secondly, when he personally countersigned our checks (each of us actually had a minuscule checking account!). One of the boys was permanently grubby, and no matter how much he scrubbed his fingers with pumice stone, the grime just wouldn't come off – always greasy-skinned and disheveled, we called him "Captain Filthy."

Besides our "bank account," we also had an overly generous weekly candy allowance. Vast quantities of Milky Ways, Baby Ruths, Tootsie Rolls, Charleston Chews and other sweets were dispensed to the boys over the school year. No one then had any idea of how disastrous this would be to the children's teeth. Naturally, I developed some cavities, and these were treated by an aged dentist in Southborough; his drill was operated by a foot pump, and the closest thing to an anesthetic was a red liquid that he called "bug juice," the main ingredient of which was oil of cloves. The pain was unimaginable.

Except for the sixth formers, who had their own rooms above the dining hall, the rest of us lived cheek by jowl in dormitories. As in the English public schools (i.e. private schools) on which New England boarding schools were modeled, the boys then slept in a variant of wooden barracks. Each so-called "alcove" in the dormitory was a cubicle closed off by a plain curtain, not a door, and the wooden walls came up only about eight feet, with no ceiling. There was no furniture beyond an iron bed, a bureau, and a wooden chair; there was thus no privacy whatever, and the master in charge of the dormitory had it pretty much in control – or thought he did.

Again, as in English schools, we were not divided into grades but into "forms," Because I didn't even fit into the First Form, I was inserted into a newly created "Sub-First Form," and put into the hands of a special teacher, a middle-aged widow named Elizabeth Benzaquin. She was the best teacher I have ever known. In the space of about two years, Mrs. Benzaquin gave me a good portion of the mental skills that I would need for the rest of my life. These included not only such practical matters as long division, but how to write an English sentence (she was a strict grammarian), how to write essays and stories, and – perhaps most importantly – how to read texts with understanding and make outlines or précis from them. Little did I know that she was preparing me not just for school, but for college and graduate study as well.

The school library was small but good, an oak-panelled room that one entered by a bronze bust of Alfred, Lord Tennyson. There were several oak tables where one could read by lamps with green glass shades, and upholstered side nooks. Week after week Mrs. Benzaquin guided me through the world of books, and I gained there a lasting love of such classics as the great adventure novels of Jules Verne, especially *Journey to the Center of the Earth* (which I have re-read many times), the Sherlock Holmes and Professor Challenger stories of Conan Doyle, and Arthur Ransome's "Swallows and Amazons" series.

In time, I was weaned from Mrs. Benzaquin's supervision and introduced to the old-fashioned but very good classical education that Fay had to offer. We called the masters "Sir," and they taught us English, Latin, French, geography, mathematics, and all the rest of what made up an education in those days. Most of them were very good at it, some indifferent, and a few bad. I particularly disliked the athletics instructor, thanks to my almost total, lifelong distaste for team sports, especially football. This red-faced, choleric gentleman was a dorm master, and seemed to spend an inordinate amount of time with the boys in the obligatory communal shower that we all had to take every afternoon. One evening he announced to the dorm that there was a lot of misguided talk about sex going around; if any boy wanted personal guidance on this subject, he could come to his room after lights out. I never learned whether any of his charges took him up on this.

As in boarding schools around the world, the less-than-popular masters sometimes received scathing nicknames from the boys. Chief among these was Mr. Park, who also ran a summer camp on Lake Winnipesaukee in New Hampshire. He was known as "Pluto" through his frequent extolling of a venerable and supposedly powerful patent laxative called "Pluto Water." His wife should, of course, have been known as "Persephone," but instead was misguidedly dubbed "Venus." According to Pluto's philosophy, boys were by nature savage animals (not so far off the mark, actually); what they had to do was to "learn how to live," a refrain that he repeated over and over in study hall, while he rubbed his forehead to a fiery red color. One day, an older and quite hotheaded boy challenged him, and refused to show him a piece of cardboard that he was drawing upon rather than studying. The two of them got into a real brawl in the schoolroom, Pluto kicking him savagely once he had gotten the revolutionist down on the floor. For this show of bad sportsmanship, he was despised even more than before.

In truth, this boy was a real daredevil, and would do just about anything on a bet; he would even eat earthworms if enough onlookers would each pay him ten cents. The ultimate in such foolhardiness was reached when he recruited another boy, the best golfer in the school (we had a somewhat primitive nine-hole golf course), to drive a golf ball off his face while he lay on the ground holding the tee in his teeth. Many of us paid 25 cents each to witness this spectacle.

Occasionally I got in trouble, too, and my parents received more than a few transcripts from the school mentioning fistfights (always with the same enemy, a hateful fellow student with little pig eyes and freckles).

These were of course all punishable offenses, but the discipline at Fay School was relatively relaxed and quite humane for an institution of this kind. "Marks," that is, demerits for infractions of various sorts, could actually be worked off by going on extensive disciplinary walks in the beautiful countryside around the school. They were under the direction of Mr. Jones, who unfortunately for a runt like me had very long legs, so it was usually not long before I had a stitch in my side. But Mr. Jones was a man of great kindness, letting us rest from time to time, and looking the other way when we filched apples and sickel pears from local farmers' orchards.

While this wasn't a church school in the strict sense, most of us were Episcopalians and were expected to attend Sunday services in St. Mark's Church on Southborough's Main Street, where I sang in the choir. From my vantage point, I could watch the blind church organist slumbering or twiddling his thumbs through the rector's long sermons.

Like some South American primitive tribe studied by anthropologists, the student body was divided into moieties, the Whites and the Reds. These competed against each other in games and other activities, and had their own cheers to challenge the other side. I was a White because my wild Uncle Henry had been one before he was expelled from the school. Our club cheer was taken from Aristophanes' *The Frogs: Brekekekex, ko-ax, ko-ax*!

Unlike many schools, Fay did not force one to take the loathed football as a sport. Instead I went in for soccer, which I far preferred, along with "one-on-one" sports like tennis.

Not all learning went on in the classroom. Every Saturday night there was a guest lecture in the gymnasium, even the faculty wives attending. All of these talks were instructive, and some were downright terrifying. I especially remember the speleologist who regaled us with hand-colored lantern slides showing the last days of his friend Floyd Collins; in 1925 Collins had become stuck while crawling through a Kentucky cave and died *in situ* several weeks later in the midst of a media frenzy. This presentation gave me instant claustrophobia, and in my later archaeological career I have always avoided digging caves. Another memorable figure was one of the survivors of the *Shenandoah* dirigible catastrophe of the same year; his jaw was crushed in the disaster, but was put together with silver wire, which made his lecture slightly incomprehensible. Then there was the young man who could have been a double of Clark Gable. His specialty was radioactivity and Mme. Curie, and he came complete with several glass tubes filled with some kind of radium salt that he kept in his vest pocket. I seriously doubt that he survived into middle age.

Also unforgettable was the herpetologist who lectured on snakes, and who had brought along a live one in a gunnysack. After assuring the audience that a snake held up by its tail could never lose its stomach contents, it did just that as he passed it over the faculty ladies in the front row.

31

ↄ

No hurricane had struck New England since the days of the early Colony, and the masters and boys at Fay were somewhat disbelieving when we were told one late September day in 1938 that such a storm was headed this way and was due to pass over central Massachusetts that night. Even though the skies were turning grey and ominous, and the wind was picking up, for much of that afternoon we continued blithely on with whatever we were doing. I was roller skating on the concrete outside the schoolhouse without paying much attention to the weather.

By the time of our after-supper study hall, the old school building was starting to shake from time to time. My desk was in the farthest row to the left, just in front of a large plate glass window which gave a view out to the tennis courts and the landscape to the south. The sky outside was now indeed black. To my horror, with each successive gust the glass began to bend in towards me and my fellows – I had not realized until then that glass could actually bend. It did not take much of this to convince me that the window was about to blow in, and I put my hand up.

"Sir, I think the window is going to break."

Somewhat reluctantly, the master in charge of the study evacuated the two rows nearest the window, and we were led to a small classroom in the back of the building and told to wait there.

Within what probably was an interval of 15 minutes, I heard a huge crash, and doors slamming all over the schoolhouse. The window had finally imploded, and jagged pieces of plate glass skimmed across the study. Miraculously, only one boy suffered any damage, my friend Willie Stevenson (whom I was to encounter many years later in Washington, as you shall see), a glass fragment badly cutting the back of his hand; but a student could easily have been decapitated.

When we arose from our dormitory beds the next morning, it was a very different world. In the brilliant sunshine one could see a totally devastated landscape. Of the magnificent elms and sugar maples around the school and down on the athletic grounds, hardly one had survived the storm. Mr. Fay wisely gave us all the day off, and we had an absolutely wonderful time playing in the branches of the toppled giants, hardly at all affected by the great 1938 hurricane, the greatest disaster in terms of lives lost and destruction ever to hit New England in all of its history – in fact, as unthinking children we had rather enjoyed the excitement of it all.

But one of our fellow-students did not join in our frolics. His family owned a large summer house in Rhode Island, on the spit of land known as Watch Hill. Battered by 125-mile-an-hour winds and 20-foot tidal surges, the entire structure was carried off in the huge surf, with his mother and two sisters inside, and all three perished. I'm not sure whether their bodies were ever recovered, but the boy temporarily left school.

♌

Fair moon, to thee I sing,
Bright regent of the heavens,
Say, why is everything
Either at sixes or at sevens?

And there I was singing solo in my soprano voice, on a darkened stage and gazing up at a yellowish spotlight – a ridiculously small Captain Corcoran in *H.M.S. Pinafore.*

For me, the high point of the school year was the Gilbert & Sullivan operetta that was given each May in the gymnasium. I was in the chorus or performed as a principal in all five G&S works presented while I was at Fay. For the principals, once they had learned their parts, there was a very special treat: we would be driven to Boston to take in a performance by the wonderful D'Oyly Carte Company. With luck, this would be the same operetta that we were playing in, and we would have a chance to see how seasoned troupers handled their roles. Of course, we didn't have an orchestra, only the upright piano played by Mr. Smith, our director, and our sets were simple compared to those of the D'Oyly Carte, but we had plenty of enthusiasm, along with an appreciative audience of parents and fellow students.

Our excitement picked up with the arrival on opening day of a professional husband-and-wife team of makeup artists from Boston, with their suitcases full of wigs, whiskers, and marvelous-smelling greasepaint. We were transformed physically and mentally, carried into a make-believe world that endured until we took off our costumes, cleaned our faces with cold cream, and returned to our Spartan dormitories.

Fay was where I received at least 75 percent of my education, and it was a classical one. Once a week we were drilled in Spencerian penmanship, writing over and over such sentences as "Time and tide wait for no man." We studied Latin from such texts as "Ritchie's First Steps" and "Ritchie's Second Steps," and I must say that I loved this language. I will unblushingly say that I did well in all of these subjects, and was often either at the top of the school or number two in grade average. The outcome of this was that I was allowed to leave for vacation a day or two earlier than the other boys.

But there was another kind of education in those days, for the comic book had just been invented. We Fay boys could buy these at the "Spa," an eatery in Southborough to which we also repaired for hamburgers and "frappes" (milk shakes). It did not take long for me and my friends to lose ourselves in the heady, exciting world of Superman, Batman, Captain Marvel, Flash Gordon, and other superheroes. In my final year at Fay, my parents had given me a portable radio, which I was allowed to have in the dormitory, so every evening before "lights out" we boys gathered around it to hear such classic adventure programs as "I Love a Mystery," "The Lone Ranger," "Jack Armstrong, the All-American Boy," and the like. My education had become two-track: a classical one, and one centered on what we would now call pop culture. I enjoyed them both.

My father having long ago decided that I should enter preparatory school (St. Paul's) in that school's Second Form, I graduated at age 12 from Fay at the close of my Fifth Form year with very mixed feelings, as on the one hand I looked forward to a new, more adult world, but on the other I had really loved the school and my life there.

CHAPTER 3

Life with Grandfather

⊱

My grandfather – whom I called "Granddaddy" – loomed very large in my early life, not only because he had most of the money in the family, and because we lived near him, but also because I seem to have been his favorite grandchild – for a time at least, until I was supplanted by my Italian cousin Tino Vitetti, and he in turn by our Wyoming cousin Hank Coe. But while his philosophy may have been that his word must always be obeyed, it really didn't work out that way. If you stood up to him, you gained his respect and even affection. A tall blue-eyed, white-haired man with the accent and somewhat beaky nose of a true Britisher, he could be formidable in his wrath, but it didn't last long. I liked him very much, as I did his wife Caroline. With his many servants he was strict but fair – they may have called him "The Iron Duke" behind his back, but they very seldom left his service to seek new employment. Caroline and his many old friends called him "Will."

Yes, it's true that in theory he was Chairman of the Board of Johnson & Higgins (the insurance firm for which he had begun working while still a teenager), but I don't think he had time to do very much for them. He had an office in the Chrysler Building in New York, but he was seldom there. In reality, thanks to Mai's immense wealth, he led a life that can only be compared to the famous "progresses" of the first Queen Elizabeth about her realm. Here is how his annual program worked.

During the autumn months he would be in residence at Planting Fields. There his staff would include about a dozen servants within the house, and as many as 50 or 60 men outside it, tending his gardens, hothouses, lawns, riding horses, and farm animals. When the snow really began to fall in earnest, he and Caroline would usually be found in their duplex apartment high up in the River House, overlooking the bridges and boats in Manhattan's East River.

By the month of March they would have transferred to Cherokee Plantation, his 60,000-acre shooting estate in Yemassee, South Carolina. He had bought this for Caroline in 1930 (I have already told you that he made money on the Crash) from the impoverished Blake family, who had gotten it as a royal grant in 1710, and who there had raised long-grained Carolina rice with a small army of black slaves. Then in April or May they would once more be back in Planting Fields.

Finally, by about the first of July, it was time to go to Wyoming, where at one time he had about a quarter of a million acres devoted to cattle ranching and sheep farming; this included of course the ranch at Irma Lake, Buffalo Bill Cody's old shooting lodge high up in the mountains. This would entail a complex move by train with a small contingent of servants from Planting Fields – including Nat and Hattie (a black brother-sister team of cooks, two of the best I have ever known), Jocelyn (the butler, a former Tommie from the trenches of World War I), and several maids; before the train left Pennsylvania Station for Chicago, a supply of fresh vegetables from Planting Fields would be put aboard. One would have to change trains in Chicago.

I vividly remember one crisis when I was traveling with my grandparents on the western leg of the trip, via the Burlington Line. We were in the dining car for evening dinner, but crossing a partially "dry" state (Minnesota?) which had a rule about bringing liquor into eating establishments. My grandfather always traveled with a fitted leather case containing flasks of his favorite whiskeys. He asked the black waiter for a split of soda water to mix with it. He said "No, sir, you'll have to ask the steward." When this gentleman (a white man) arrived, my grandfather was told "under no circumstances." My grandfather was furious, fixed the steward with his steely gaze, and icily stated "Young man, I (pause) don't (pause) like you, and I will take this up with my friend Mr. Budd." Mr. Budd owned the railroad. My grandfather got his soda.

Before the first snows fell at the ranch in early September, the entire entourage was once more at Planting Fields, to start a new cycle of what anthropologists call "patterned nomadism."

$\mathcal{Q}$

From the age of eight on, I spent part of every summer at the Cody ranch, mostly without my brother as our parents and grandparents must have already detected more than a whiff of sibling rivalry. That arrangement was all right with me.

We would arrive by train at the old Burlington Depot in Cody; this was the jumping off place for the yellow tourist buses that took dudes up to Yellowstone Park, and it was where we were met by my grandfather's first cousin Edward V. Robertson. "E.V." was the manager of his ranches, the owner of the Cody Trading Company, and during World War II, the Republican Senator from Wyoming. During his one term of office, E.V. was voted by the Washington press corps the worst person in Congress! He was also something of a crook, as it turned out later. Then we were driven up the South Fork of the Shoshone River, and up the long, winding dirt road to the ranch, 7,500 feet high.

The house was covered in brown shingles with white trim, and was built in 1912 in the rustic style typical of the Adirondacks. It was filled with Indian artifacts of all sorts, including what most experts believed was the finest Crow war bonnet in existence. Thanks to Mai, it was also stocked with a fine library, including a great illustrated set of one of my favorite authors, Jules Verne. Tragically, it burned completely to the ground in the winter of 1939–40, but my grandfather immediately had it rebuilt on a design by my Uncle Bob's old friend from Harvard days, John Woods.

My idol in those days was Bill Pawley, the ranch foreman and the very essence of the western cowboy. With weather-beaten face burned red by the sun, he bore a distinct resemblance to Will Rogers. Even while on horseback, by using one hand and his gold-capped teeth, he could roll a cigarette from the packet of Bull Durham that he carried in his shirt pocket. Bill was a champion rodeo rider and performer, and in our family it was believed that he was the original model for the bucking horse-and-rider on the Wyoming license plate. "Teach me to spin a rope, Bill," I pleaded, and that he did. He could also pull my leg: one day he convinced me that if you put a horse hair in a jar of water, and screwed down the lid, it would eventually turn into a snake. But Bill was not just a cowhand, he was a literate one. It was he who introduced me to the novels of the author-artist Will James, himself a cowboy who had been part of the last great cattle drive from Texas to Montana.

As you can see, I wanted to be a cowboy when I grew up, and never leave Wyoming.

Bill also knew how to deal with my grandfather. Every morning the "old man" obliged all of us – family and guests alike – to go on a long horseback ride, returning somewhat saddle sore by lunchtime. About every two weeks these would be all-day rides, covering as much as 25 miles through the ranch lands or up into the far reaches of Carter Mountain to altitudes of over 10,500 feet, far above tree line. The order of march along the trail was always with my grandfather in front, with Bill Pawley taking up the rear, only riding ahead to open and close gates. While returning from one of these long excursions late one afternoon, we came to a fork in the trail near what are known as the Hoodoo Springs. My grandfather insisted that we take the left hand fork. Bill was just as insistent that the correct way home was the right fork. As the argument grew heated, Bill said "Mr. Coe, I don't give a damn where you're going, I'm going my way."

So, the old man went his way, followed by the other guests. I went with Bill. It was not long before my grandfather appeared, somewhat crestfallen, along with the other dudes. But he respected Bill even more after this confrontation.

Being with my grandfather on those summer vacations from school turned me into a lifelong outdoorsman. My father was a fine bird shot, and my mother excelled at skeet, but I was never inducted into that particular world. But at the ranch I could fish as much as I wanted to for the huge rainbow trout that swam in the lake; I often paddled the old man around the lake at sundown, while he caught fish after rising fish with his split cane fly rod – the same H. L. Leonard rod that I inherited on his death in 1955, and which in some ways changed my life. As a

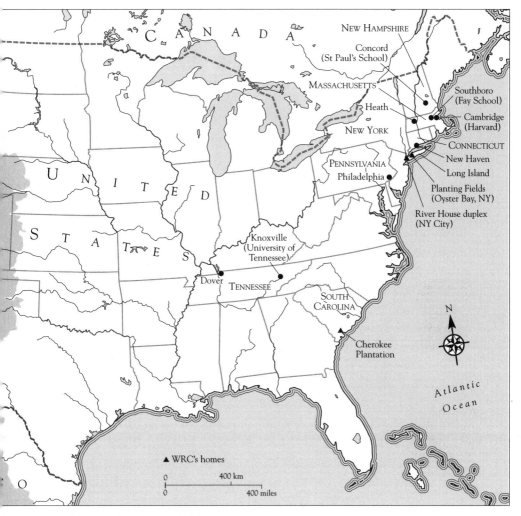

The geography of my early life.

teenager, I learned to hunt for deer, elk, and pronghorn antelope, but fishing was always foremost.

Bill Pawley literally died in the saddle. Many years later, after most of the family's ranches had been sold to the legendary Texas oilman H. L. Hunt, Bill continued to work as a cowpuncher for the Hunt interests. During one severe winter blizzard, a search party found Bill dead on the ground by his horse, felled by a heart attack. His dog sat nearby, faithfully guarding the body of his master. It was right out of a Will James story.

When my grandparents purchased their plantation in South Carolina, then known as Broadhouse, they immediately renamed it "Cherokee," for the wild Cherokee roses that grew there. Long after their deaths it passed into the hands of Robert Evans, then the CEO of American Motors; he liked it so much that he named his new version of the time-honored Jeep for the place. It is now a private club with a one million dollar entrance fee.

It was terribly run down when it passed into Coe hands in 1930, and the blacks who lived on the place – the descendants of the plantation's slaves – were in a state of destitution, probably worse off than they had been before Emancipation. A new brick mansion in "southern Georgian" style was built, a landscape laid out by the Olmsted firm (who had also landscaped Planting Fields), and decent but hardly luxurious new housing constructed for the black population. These people were true ebony black in color, with none of the white or Indian admixture so common in the rest of the African-American population of my country. Among themselves they spoke rapid-fire Gitchi-Gullah, a West African language, and the women characteristically smoked corncob pipes. This was all very exotic to me.

I began to spend Easter vacations from Fay down in Cherokee. It was a beautiful place, already balmy in the southern spring. The back swamps that had provided water for the irrigated rice fields of the Blakes were silent, mysterious places, crowded with large cypress trees shrouded in Spanish moss. To teach me how to ride, I was put into the hands of Ike, Cherokee's black groom and the South Carolinan counterpart of Bill Pawley. At first they gave me a Shetland pony, a notoriously mean breed. When riding out one day with Ike in attendance, this creature shied at a culvert it didn't like, and I was bucked off, landing on my face. Furious, I roundly cussed out the pony with all the swear words that I had picked up at Fay. Ike, a very religious man, was horrified, and told Caroline, "Mis' Coe, that boy got the *devil* in him!"

Through the years of my childhood, I came to know some of Cherokee's blacks, besides Ike. It seems difficult to believe, but three of these had been born into slavery. There was the old couple, "Old Sol" and his pipe-smoking wife, both supposed to be over a hundred years of age. But the one I knew best was Francis, who had been a ten-year old boy when the slaves were freed by Lincoln. What we, who came from totally different worlds, had in common was a love of fishing. It was Francis who taught me how to hook carp and catfish from the Combahee River, which lazily meandered through the plantation on its way to the sea.

But this was the South – the *deep* South – and certain facts of southern American life slowly intruded themselves into my childish mind. As the southbound train left Washington, I began to see in the stations along the way separate drinking fountains marked "White" and "Colored," respectively. At breakfast in the dining car, I couldn't understand why "colored" people had to sit at the rear end, shielded from all of us by a drawn curtain. Segregation of the races was accepted by all once you were in Dixie, but it still seemed strange to me, and became even more disturbing by the time I was in preparatory school and fell in love with Dixieland jazz and its practitioners.

I still blush with shame to think of one spring visit to Cherokee. The year was 1942, I was a Second Former at St. Paul's, and the country was at war. In fact, the United States along with its allies was then losing that war. I traveled alone, but in New York I was handed onto the train and shown to my Pullman compartment not by a mere porter but by the conductor and brakeman. Most of the other passengers were troops passing south to Florida on their way to their respective assignments.

Instead of letting me out in Walterboro, the nearest stop to Yemassee, by prearrangement the entire train came to a halt at the red dirt crossing leading up to the Cherokee plantation house. Waiting there was a shiny black Chrysler limousine, and a liveried black chauffeur. As I was handed out the train by the conductor and helped into the car, I could see the faces of the soldiers pressed to the window, staring in wonder at this spectacle. I have never felt more ashamed.

CHAPTER 4

A Little Rebellion
in a Big School

As I've said, it was a foregone conclusion that I'd be sent to St. Paul's, a very strict Episcopalian church school in Concord, New Hampshire – this was where my father, Uncle Bob, and various other relatives had gone, not all of them lasting till graduation. My brother went there, too, only to be expelled at the end of his Fifth Form year. When I say "strict," I mean exactly that: in my five years at SPS, I had exactly one weekend off (in my Sixth Form year). And when I say "church," I mean that, too: chapel every morning, twice on Sunday, and a minimum of three hours attendance on Good Friday to hear non-stop sermons on the Seven Last Words. My mother wanted me to go to Groton, but on this subject my father got his way – not always the case, as my mother "wore the pants" in our family.

In a way, I was prepared and I *wasn't* prepared for life there. I found myself in familiar surroundings – a Second Form dormitory not very different from those of Fay, with the basic rules of the jungle also in effect. But SPS had about 500 boys, whereas Fay had only one tenth as many. I had starred at Fay, but that was not to be the case here.

This was the autumn of 1941, and World War II began to intrude here in a very big way. There was a large contingent of upper class, even noble, refugees from various European countries, and these brought a level of sophistication and worldliness previously unheard of in New England preparatory schools. Speaking French among themselves, they generally refused to join in such "manly" sports as American football (I admired them for this), but went out for fencing and the like.

Among these, I found an especial friend in my own Second Form dormitory. This was Emmanuel de Crussol, eldest son of the late Duke of Uzès, and in the candidateship for inheriting the French throne, at least in theory. Although he was then 14, Emmanuel looked about 18, and could tell stories about his life in France that matched his apparent age, and fascinated and astonished a 12-year-old innocent like myself, such as his account of how he had consummated his passion for a young lady in the back of a Paris taxicab. He lived in one of France's great castles, and claimed he had the formula for making nitroglycerine, and could manufacture it when he wished. But when he boasted about his prowess with dagger and hatchet, the other boys challenged him to prove it.

Now we had to clean our own alcoves, and in each was a long-handled dust mop clipped to the wood partition. Emmanuel, standing at one end of the long dormitory and holding in his hand the hatchet that he had illegally concealed in his bureau (weapons of any sort were banned at SPS), demanded that a mop handle be clipped to the wall of the alcove at the other end. "Now watch," he said, and the hatchet flew end over end to strike the handle, instantly splitting it in two longitudinal halves. No one questioned his veracity after that display.

Emmanuel had a special enmity for the other foreigner in our dorm. This was George Ortiz, the grandson of Simon I. Patiño, the near-legendary "tin king" of Bolivia; George had actually never lived in that Andean country, but had grown up in Paris, in the grandiose Patiño mansion on the Avenue Foch near the Place de l'Étoile. Today he is known as the world's foremost collector of antiquities. It is no news that boarding school children can be cruel, and we certainly were so to George. At one point we gave him the Eskimo blanket toss, the poor boy being flung as high as the dorm's rafters. He only increased our glee when he fell to his knees after he was let down, praying out loud, "Lord forgive them, for they know not what they do." Years later, when we were both at Harvard, George told me that de Crussol had once cornered him in the dorm's lavatory and held a dagger to his throat, and that his heart had temporarily stopped beating.

My friend Emmanuel was expelled at the end of the Second Form year. It couldn't have mattered much to him, because he became the 15th Duke of Uzès when his uncle died in 1943.

❧

Once the United States entered the war on 7 December 1941, the already Spartan life of the school became even more Spartan. Before that date, uniformed maids had waited on the tables, now we did. We were assigned work details of varying difficulties, the stoking of coal in the heating plant being the least desirable. But for me the worst of all was that during the long, severe New Hampshire winters, for reasons of economy the school went on "Double Daylight Savings Time," which meant that we were woken in the dark by a noisy bell at 6:50 AM, went to breakfast in the dark, then to chapel in the dark, and after that for morning assembly in the dark. I promised myself then and there that if I ever got out of SPS, I'd never get up in the dark again – a vow unfortunately never fulfilled.

Like other church schools, St. Paul's was headed by a rector, and the then incumbent was the Rev. Norman Burdett Nash. Nash was an imposing, almost a scary, figure. During chapel, he sat alone in a stall on the left of the nave, his beady dark eyes peering out from steel-rimmed glasses and from the pious gloom that surrounded him. He was a strange, cold person whom I couldn't help but associate with the school's eponymous saint, the St. Paul who had taken the charisma out of Christianity and imposed a strict discipline on all of the Founder's followers. Norman Nash was obsessed with discipline, and I, along with many of the boys, began to dislike him with a passion. After chapel each morning, during assembly, he seemed to take a perverse delight in reading out the delinquencies that had been committed during the previous 24 hours, and meting out the appropriate punishments, from a few demerits up to a disciplinary "red list" and even to expulsion.

Like all martinets, he didn't always have it his way. In my Fourth Form year, *Forever Amber*, Kathleen Winsor's notorious "bodice-ripper" set in Restoration England, had appeared and been banned in Boston by the Watch and Ward Society. The rector immediately informed us that its mere possession would be severely punished, as a result of which most boys tried to obtain a copy by one means or another, and many of them did.

Decades later, when Nash had been made Bishop of Massachusetts and I was a Harvard undergraduate, I used to see him and his wife from time to time in one Boston restaurant or another. He no longer looked ten feet tall or had fangs, and was even cordial. And one day while I was lunching in Cambridge with the great Mayanist Eric Thompson, I had the pleasure of introducing him to my old bête noire. Eric was clearly elated, as he was a devout Anglican.

♌

I don't think my grandparents ever went to church, and am none too sure that they were even believers – but my father and mother definitely were. At home on Long Island, we regularly attended the posh little St. John's of Lattingtown, which had been built with J. P. Morgan, Jr.'s money. Mr. Morgan himself passed the plate for the Sunday offering, and one Sunday, in place of the quarter coin that my parents had given me, I slipped in a piece of Chinese cash that had come with a packet of "jackass" firecrackers. When my father found this out he was mortified, and went to see the church's verger. "Oh, Mr. Coe, don't worry! Mr. Morgan gets a very good rate of exchange."

In the spring term of my first year at SPS, I and a group of my young classmates spent a week in retreat for instruction in the Anglican catechism, to culminate with our Confirmation by the Rt. Rev. Dallas, Bishop of New Hampshire. I was then a true believer, and while kneeling at the altar rail during the evening service really felt dedicated to the love of God when the bishop laid his hands on my head, intoning in his rolling Irish brogue, "Bless O Lord this thy child." The entire school was in attendance at these annual rites, with a certain number of proud parents and other guests present in the visitors' gallery above the nave's entrance. A few years later there was a considerable stir among the sex-starved boys in the chapel when someone spotted the glamorous Dorothy Lamour in the front row of the gallery: she turned out to be the stepmother of one of the neophyte communicants.

Before my voice changed from soprano to tenor, I also sang in the choir. The choirmaster, organist, and director of music at SPS was Channing Lefebvre, a remarkable musician and teacher. We sang not only the standard hymns, but compositions by Bach, Handel, Brahms,

Sibelius, and other greats; it was my introduction to fine music, and stayed with me throughout life. Every Sunday night following even-song, there would be an organ recital by Mr. Lefebvre, and choir boys who wished could actually go into the organ loft and watch him per-form. I was fascinated. Looking back, I should have stayed in the choir, but I was growing more and more loutish as I grew older.

Sacred Studies was an obligatory course for every form, taught by one or another of the school clergy. I must say I enjoyed it, as the his-tory of Christianity, the Church, the Saints, the monastic orders and the Reformation was basically the story of the post-Roman western world. In the Fourth Form I won the Sacred Studies prize for that year: *The Book of a Thousand Tongues*, published by the American Bible Society. In it appeared the first few verses of the Gospel According to Saint Mark translated into over 1,000 languages of the world, complete with a thumb-nail sketch of each tribe or people who spoke that lan-guage, and in the native orthography. It was my earliest introduction to the cross-cultural world of anthropology and writing systems.

My fall from religious grace into a state of skepticism actually began with Sacred Studies. Our Fifth Form teacher was Mr. Labigan, an ordained minister with a terrible handicap, as he had been born an achondroplastic dwarf. He was attempting to teach us the arguments advanced by Thomas Aquinas for the existence of God. The most important of these, he explained, was the "prime mover" argument, that the universe existed and was in motion, hence there had to have been some being who had created it and set it moving. I raised my hand. "But, sir, what if the universe is eternal, without a beginning or an end. What then?" There was a long silence, and tears came into Mr. Labigan's eyes. I had been sincere in my question, and I was sorry for him, and felt like a heel. But disbelief had taken hold in my mind.

The ruin of my religiosity was inevitable when I checked out from our library the abbreviated version of Sir James Fraser's multi-volume *Golden Bough*, an anthropological classic. The scales fell from my eyes, as Fraser argued that all of my cherished beliefs about Christmas, Easter, and even the death and resurrection of Christ could all be explained as cultural responses to universal concerns, that Christianity was not fundamentally different from any other religious system, such as those of Classical times and even of so-called primitive peoples. Taking Fraser in conjunction with the Darwinism that I had absorbed in biology, by the time I graduated from SPS, I had become a complete agnostic and skeptic, and have remained so throughout my life.

Yet even today, when I hear a Christmas carol, or the singing of a choir in an English church, I grow misty-eyed: such is the hold of the irrational over the mind.

𝔔

When I entered the school, my father had worked it out that I would be placed in an advanced science group, always one year ahead of most of my classmates. The first year of general science was a bore, but in the Third Form I took introductory biology, taught by Stanley McConnell, "Mr. Mac," one of the two best teachers at SPS (I'll come to the other one shortly). I truly loved it – the laboratory, peering through the microscope at live amoebas and paramecia; Mendel's wrinkled and smooth peas; even the dissections of everything from earthworms to triple-injected cats. Mr. Mac also encouraged us to read books on natural history, and I devoured those by William Beebe, above all his *Half Mile Down* describing his descent into the ocean depths in the newly invented bathysphere. Biology was the only subject in which I was getting more than mediocre grades.

The next year I took physics from the other great teacher who turned out, like Mrs. Benzaquin, to be a powerful influence on the course of my life. This was Frederick Arthur Philbrick, an upper-class Englishman who had left Great Britain in 1939 on the eve of the war, just as his idols Auden and Isherwood had done. Whether like them he was evading military service I never knew, but I suspect so. Philbrick had been a Balliol man, and knew Evelyn Waugh while at Oxford; Waugh seems to have disliked him, and it is hardly accidental that he used the name "Philbrick" for the ridiculous school butler in *Decline and Fall*. Mr. Philbrick was thin and slightly bald, with a toothbrush moustache; he was pretty clearly a homosexual (a "fairy" in unkind schoolboy parlance), but he never made any passes at me or my friends, or any of the other boys while school was in session.

I had heard from other boys that he had a studio on the second floor of the old school building, and that anyone was allowed to come there and try his hand at painting. I had always liked to draw, but I had never used oils, and I was itching to ask him after class if I could do this, but was too shy to make the request. Then as I was walking one day along one of the school's paths I ran into Mr. Philbrick, and screwed up my courage to ask. His answer was "of course," and within a few days I found myself in front of a blank canvas with brushes and all the tubes of paint I could wish. This was my Rubicon, for it led me into a totally different world than the one I was used to.

Although I had run into them before, it was through Philbrick that I got to know two classmates who also painted, Stuart Cary Welch and Joe Enders: these became lifelong friends. Mr. Philbrick's rooms in one of the residential houses (all boys not in the Lower School lived in these rather than dormitories) were a study in 1930s modern, and we were encouraged to read in his private library, which included wonderful books on art as well as first editions of writers of whom I had never heard in SPS's traditional English classes, such as Auden, Eliot, and Joyce. I also noted a paper edition of *Oscar Wilde et Moi* by Lord Alfred Douglas. This was indeed another world.

Cary had been schooled in Paris and could actually speak French. He was already an incredibly talented painter and graphic artist, and won the school's Greeley Art Prize that year (I won it the next, simply because they couldn't give it to Cary two years in a row). His musical tastes were far more sophisticated than mine, running to Bach and Stravinsky, rather than Louis Armstrong (who had been my youthful hero). Joe was the son of the great epidemiologist John Franklin Enders, and an interesting if offbeat painter; but his talents lay more in the literary line, to poetry and modernist fiction.

There was a fourth member of our "Renaissance" set, although he had one foot in the athletic camp. This was Rowland "Rollo" Cox, a nephew of Max Perkins, the legendary editor at Scribner's of Hemingway and Thomas Wolfe (the latter a Herculean task), and destined to become future rector of Groton School. I had also been writing short stories heavily influenced at first by the science-fiction yarns of H. G. Wells, and later by Saki's more sophisticated tales. I even wrote poetry, but Joe was much better at this than I. By my Sixth Form year, Rollo Cox and I were co-editors of the *Horae Scholasticae*, the school's venerable literary magazine. I had discovered that I liked to write, and I was better at it than I was at painting a picture.

As for Fred Philbrick, the rest is tragedy. Two years following my graduation from SPS, the parents of an adolescent boy in the school had engaged him as tutor and *cicerone* to their son for a summer to be spent in Great Britain. They must have been singularly uninformed in thinking that nothing would happen. While in the Cotswolds, Philbrick tried (unsuccessfully) to seduce the youth. On his return to SPS that fall, the boy told a friend of his, who in turn felt it *his* duty to inform the authorities. These had no recourse but to dismiss Philbrick on the spot, especially since the boy's father was a United States Senator. Cary and I ran into our old teacher and mentor once more in 1950, in the British Museum's Print Room. He was then living in Norway, and died a few years later of cancer.

♃

It will be remembered that I was in the advanced science curriculum. Consequently, I looked forward to taking a freshman level science course in my final, Sixth Form year, especially since was to be in biology, and taught by Mr. MacConnell. I was really thinking about a future in this field, or in biochemistry, and fully intended to apply to MIT, in spite of my involvement with the arts and writing. By this time, my grades were good enough that I think I could have gotten in.

Chance, however, struck once more, just as it had when I met Mr. Philbrick on that path. "Mr. Mac" was then dating a woman that he loved and intended to marry, and to give himself more time for this amorous pursuit he unexpectedly went on leave. In his place the worst teacher in school offered what he claimed was college-level physics. Mr. French was known by the boys, not very affectionately, as "Bernoulli" since he could go on at length about Bernoulli's theorem and why a ping pong ball could remain floating atop a jet of water; this nickname was finally abbreviated to "The Nool." His course was unbelievably boring, all fulcrums and levers and pulleys.

After a fortnight of The Nool, I dropped his course, forgot about going to MIT and getting the Nobel one day, and applied to Harvard to study creative writing. I was admitted, along with Cary Welch and Rollo Cox – and George Ortiz, too, for that matter (although he never lasted long there). Who knows, if things had worked out other than they did, it might have been I who discovered the double helix, and not Jim Watson. As the Victorian novelist Wilkie Collins says in *Hide and Seek*, "Our destinies shape the future for us out of strange materials."

CHAPTER 5

The Age of Enlightenment

The war ended in early September 1945, and I had missed it. Even though I was only 16, there is little doubt in my mind that had those two atomic bombs not been dropped, in time I would have been drafted, trained, sent over as part of the final invasion of the Japanese homeland, and most likely have been killed, along with hundreds of thousands of other Americans. But this did not happen.

My entering class at Harvard was the largest in its long history, for there was not only the usual contingent of callow prep school graduates like me and my friends, but an equal number of returned veterans, even a former captain in the United States Navy – and Henry Kissinger. The first order of business was that everyone had to take a written test so that the university could determine whether one was required to take the beginning course in English or not. The English Department was then obsessed with spot passages, and there were two on this exam; one had to write a short essay on each. By great good fortune I saw that one long quote had come from *Crime and Punishment* and the other from *The Way of All Flesh*; I had read these the past summer, and I "aced" the exam. No remedial English. Good, I thought, I'm on my way to being a writer.

Nothing could have been further from the truth, for there was then no course in creative writing. What the English major mainly offered was literary criticism (Dr. Johnson and the others), and then more of the same, on and on. Even a course in the history of English literature failed to stir me, and I found myself falling into sloth and boredom. It wasn't that I stopped reading – far from it – but I read avidly in everything that wasn't on the assignment. For instance, if we were told to read Fielding's *Joseph Andrews*, I would perversely read *Tom Jones* instead. This didn't help my grades. What I did get from this, though, was a lifelong love and admiration for the 18th-century English novel – Smollett, Fielding, Defoe, and Sterne.

Something totally different was on the horizon, though. That summer between SPS and Harvard I had been at the ranch in Wyoming (after his heart attack in 1942 my grandfather was not allowed by his doctors to go there because of the altitude), and there I found on a bookshelf the Museum of Modern Art catalogue of an exhibition called *Twenty Centuries of Mexican Art*. The Colonial period and modern paintings didn't excite me, but those strange Pre-Columbian masterpieces definitely did. When I visited MoMA later that summer, I bought a set of postcards with these objects, and arranged them on the mantelpiece in my Harvard rooms. Who had made these hauntingly beautiful sculptures, and why?

By my sophomore year, Cary and I were rooming together in Eliot, the most stylish and snobbish of the Harvard residential houses – in our entry, everyone without exception had been either to SPS or to Groton. We had a third roommate who was one of the most amazing people I have ever known. Jay – John Jay Chapman – was a direct descendant of John Jay, our first Chief Justice, and of John Jacob Astor; he was a namesake of his grandfather, the American man of letters; one of his great-uncles was the eccentric society painter Robert "Sheriff Bob" Chanler, who had decorated several of the rooms at Planting Fields. On his mother's side he could claim Henry and William James as great-great-uncles; during World War II, his grandfather Edward James had erected a shrine to Hitler in his Concord house, which meant that it was under constant FBI surveillance; his mother's sister was married to Alexander Calder, and we had a mobile by "Uncle Sandy" hanging in our living room.

Regardless of all of this pedigree, Jay went his own way. He was a proto-hippie, what Norman Mailer would call a "White Negro": Jay owned a kind of zoot suit, talked "jive," had a black girlfriend in Harlem named "Bones," listened to bebop jazz while chewing raw garlic at three in the morning, and occasionally smoked pot, otherwise then unknown on the campus. At times he would play the bongos, at other times his bagpipes, at which he was an expert. He did terribly in most of his courses, getting 40s in French, for instance. But he spoke fluent Romany (Gypsy) and Spanish (with a Puerto Rican accent), both learned on his own. The one course in which he excelled was introductory anthropology, taught then by the equally amazing Carleton Coon, before he went to teach at Penn. "Man, I really dig that crazy anthropology stuff!" Jay would say, and he told me the fascinating details. I began to think I was missing something by majoring in English.

Jay's stay at Harvard didn't extend beyond his sophomore year. Exhausting though it was, Cary and I missed his company.

᪐

The goal of relatively lazy "white-shoe" types like myself was to take as many easy, pleasant courses as possible, and avoid being put on probation for bad grades. Harvard had a generous share of such "gut" offerings, and these were listed, rated, and described in *The Confidential Guide* put out each year by *The Harvard Crimson*, the undergraduate paper. Topping everyone's list was the enormously enjoyable, two-semester course on music history and appreciation conducted by Archibald Davison, a wonderful teacher and compassionate human being; I shall never forget his lecture on Gustav Holst and Ralph Vaughan-Williams, his two close friends whose music brought him to tears.

But not all of *The Crimson*'s ratings could be relied upon. During my senior year, when I was working desperately for honors grades so that I could be admitted to graduate school, Professor James Roland Ware's "Chinese History from Prehistoric Times to the Han Dynasty" got the top accolade, not because it was a great course – the guide considered it the most boring in the university – but because you were guaranteed an "A" even if you didn't attend classes. Professor Ware invariably wore a dark blue suit, which became covered with chalk dust as his incredibly dry lectures droned on. He spent most of the class (which had all of about ten students) showing us ancient, black-and-white lantern slides of his youthful sojourn in Beijing, and pontificating about the Confucian ideal of the *chün-tzu*, the scholarly gentleman. Cary and I thought we had aced the final exam, and I had slipped a self-addressed postcard into the blue book so I could find out that he had given me an "A" for sure.

I never got the postcard back, and everyone in the course was given a miserable C! Obviously this old fuddy-duddy was furious about his *Crimson* rating, and was going to teach those undergraduates a lesson. Just as obviously, he had never even opened our blue books. We complained to a sympathetic dean, but nothing could be done.

For many years my parents had been taking their winter vacations in Cuba, which they loved. They had many Cuban friends, and my father was on the board of directors of the Cuban national railway. That year, they invited my brother, then a student at Hofstra College, and me to join them for Christmas in Havana, and so we did, but we also had other plans. We had decided to spend one of those weeks in Yucatan, and see the Maya ruins. I had taken out several books on Yucatan and the Maya from the Widener Library – all of them junk, as I later found out, but it didn't matter. We were actually going there. It was really only an hour-and-a-half flight by propeller plane from Havana's Rancho Boyeros Airport to Mérida. It was a very different, quite exotic world that we flew into, as neither of us spoke much Spanish, and we had never been to any part of Mexico.

Our destination was the fabled Chichen Itza, where we spent a week while staying at the Mayaland Lodge. This was a fairly luxurious hostel with Maya servants beautifully clad in snowy white huipils; I thought that they were the most beautiful people I had ever seen. To me it was a revelation to roam the Castillo, the great Toltec-Maya pyramid; the round Caracol, Chichen's observatory; the Sacred Cenote; the so-called Nunnery with its mysterious inscriptions; and all the other buildings and reliefs. I knew little or nothing about the ancient Maya, but I burned to find out about them. When I returned to Harvard, I would scrap English literature and major in Maya archaeology!

I had seen the blinding light on the road to Damascus, but then what? Back on campus, I asked around about how to major in this wonderful subject. After I found out that there was no such major, it was not long before I found my way to the red-brick Peabody Museum on Divinity Avenue, and the office of the Anthropology Department, presided over by the kindly Earnest Hooton's battleaxe of a secretary. She told me in no uncertain terms that I would have to switch my major to anthropology, and sent me down the hall past life-size casts of Maya stelae to meet Alfred Marston Tozzer, only recently retired but still the *éminence grise* of the department. He was also, as I later discovered, the world's greatest Mayanist.

Tozzer was a dapper little man in a grey, three-piece suit, complete with watch chain. He had china-blue eyes, short, grizzled hair, and a grey toothbrush mustache. To my surprise, he spoke in a high, almost mincing voice. "Fools rush in…," as they say, and like a fool I gushed out my enthusiasms, especially about Sylvanus Morley's *The Ancient Maya*, which I had just devoured. Tozzer turned red (from his usual pink) and "hit the roof." "How could you say that? It's the *worst* book I ever heard of! It doesn't have one reference or footnote in it!"

But he didn't discourage me from becoming what I had my heart set on. He let me know, again with good reason, that if I were serious about this, I would have to go on to a Ph.D. some day; and that to get into graduate school, in view of my spotty record as an English major, not only would I have to take mainly anthropology courses in my junior and senior years, but I would have to get mostly As in these courses. This was truly a wake-up call, as up to now I had been coasting at Harvard, with mostly what were cynically known as "gentleman's Cs." Now I would actually have to work.

༄

Summer vacation between my sophomore and junior years saw my brother and me again in Yucatan, exploring every visitable Maya site. The most remote was Tulum, perched on a cliff over the blue Caribbean. Unlike today when thousands upon thousands of visitors pack in from tourist ships or giant jets to see this tiny site, in 1948 one had to fly in a rickety plane (a converted, fabric-covered De Havilland bomber) to an airstrip on Cozumel Island, then engage a fishing boat to cross the channel to the mainland. According to the guest book in the hut of Tulum's Maya guardian, only five other people had thus far been at the site that year. This part of Quintana Roo, then a territory not a state, was still in the hands of independent Maya chiefs. In the top room of Tulum's diminutive Castillo was a "Talking Cross," a clothed crucifix on top of a crude altar; the floor was littered with broken bottles, the remains of the alcohol that had been offered by the local Maya to this important cult. Poor little Tulum – now far too close to Cancún (Mexico's answer to Miami Beach) – currently sees 8,000 tourists each day, few of whom have the slightest idea of what they are looking at.

Back once more on campus, I took up my new life as an anthropologist. Fair Harvard has never been known for the quality of its undergraduate teaching, and the Anthropology Department was no exception. The introductory course was a team-taught potpourri, in short a complete mess, and if that had been what anthropology was, I think that I would have given it up. What saved the day for me was Douglas Oliver's offering on the anthropology of Oceania. We started off learning about the Murngin tribe of Australia, based on Lloyd Warner's fieldwork. At first it seemed strange – and even shocking, for here I was in a mixed-sex class (i.e., with Radcliffe students) listening to the most intimate details of aboriginal ideas about procreation. But bit by bit it struck me that for the first time in my life I was learning about a complete society, in which every custom and belief, no matter how exotic, made functional sense. And then he took us in like manner from a hunting-and-gathering group right up the ladder of cultural evolution to end with the complex societies of the Philippines. I was transfixed.

But Tozzer saw to it that I also learned as much as possible about the Maya and Middle America (the term Mesoamerica had just been coined by Paul Kirchhoff, but Harvard ignored it). For this I was put into the hands of Alfred Kidder II, then an assistant professor, and of Joe Cason, an advanced graduate student and assistant to Tozzer; Cason was an ex-Marine who during the war in the Pacific had commanded a platoon of Navajos charged with ridding island caves of hidden Japanese troops.

ↄ

"Hello, boys, I've been expecting you. The Friends told me you'd be here some day."

The speaker was a scrawny, rather aged-looking white man, one-eyed, almost toothless, with sparse, scraggly strands of grey hair above a dirty bandanna tied to his head. He had nothing on but ragged shorts held up by a knotted rope; cradled in the stump of one arm was the blade of a machete held in his one remaining hand. He looked at us from bent, wire-rimmed glasses, with only one, hopelessly cracked lens (the one over his single eye). This was "Captain" Edward J. Moy, owner of Nohoch Ek, a tiny Maya site in western British Honduras.

By the winter of 1949, both my brother and I had decided we wanted to be professional archaeologists, to the immense (but temporary) displeasure of our grandfather. I had by that time met the great British Mayanist Eric Thompson, who worked for the Carnegie Institution of Washington (more of that later). Armed with letters of introduction from Eric, we arrived in the Colony during the following summer in hopes of digging into the Maya past. The District Commissioner for the El Cayo region, near the Guatemalan border, and the de facto archaeological commissioner, was Eric's old friend A. Hamilton Anderson, a dour Scot from Aberdeen, and it was Anderson who had told us about an eccentric Englishman who had some mounds on his property between the Maya village of Soccotz and El Cayo (now generally known as San Ignacio). El Cayo had been the jumping off place for the Carnegie Institution of Washington's fieldwork at the great Maya site of Uaxactun in the Petén jungles of northern Guatemala – all supplies brought up the Belize River were transferred here to mule caravans and taken overland to the west. It was at El Cayo that we obtained lodging, in the tin-roofed wooden house of Mrs. Bedran, a large and friendly lady of Lebanese origin.

So, who were these "Friends" who had told Mr. Moy about us? We soon found out, as he led us up the hill to his thatched-roof house, outside of which a wretchedly thin, tick-infested horse was grazing, with a kitchen at the back. Mr. Moy's dwelling had seen better times, but was now in a state of advanced decay and like its owner had a sour, moldy smell. In the middle of the grubby room was a four-poster double bed with a sagging mattress, covered with fresh blood. That morning, he told us, he had found a yellow-mouthed jumping tommygoff on it (this pit viper is short, fat, and highly poisonous, and is much feared as it can spring out on passersby from low bushes). He had dispatched it *in situ* with his machete.

On one side of the room was what he called his "office." The remains of a typewriter sat on a wooden table; since it had lost the return mechanism, to make it work Mr. Moy had tied a string to its carriage, weighted with a small rock. To one side of the typewriter and scattered in other places in the room were stacks of insect-chewed foolscap covered with blue typewritten text – hundreds, perhaps even thousands of pages. Was he writing a novel, we asked. "Oh no, those are all messages from the 'Friends.' They know all about you. They want you to dig in these mounds."

And so we did. The workmen were all Maya from Soccotz, and our foreman was Jacinto Cunil, Eric Thompson's friend, *compadre*, and main informant for his study of the modern Maya of western British Honduras. Our knowledge of excavation techniques was completely derived from reading archaeological reports, but Cunil had worked for Thompson, and was a quite professional digger. So deeply did Jacinto Cunil impress Eric that he devoted an entire chapter of his *The Rise and Fall of Maya Civilization* to this man, seeing him as a paragon of the "moderation in all things" ethic that he (Eric) claimed characterized the Maya throughout their history. But there may well have been another side to Cunil.

The site consisted of four long mounds arranged around a plaza, and over the next month or two we completely excavated one of these, revealing a rectangular, multi-roomed structure of white limestone that had once had a thatch roof. It was not a very big site, not in any way comparable to giants like Uaxactun or Chichen Itza, both of which had claimed the long-term attention of the Carnegie Institution of Washington. But there it was.

And why did Moy call it "Nohoch Ek," Maya for "great star"? To answer this, I must tell you something about Moy. Instead of taking Mrs. Bedran's sandwiches out on the mounds in the company of our workmen, Moy insisted we eat with him in his odorous hut. Although I believe he subsisted mainly on boiled lumps of maize dough, he insisted that we bring him canned fruit from a local store in El Cayo, and he ate these greedily; to this day I cannot stand the smell of canned peaches. Over the course of the first few weeks we learned about the weird saga of Edward J. Moy, who insisted that he be called "Skipper."

According to him (and his Cockney accent confirmed it), he had been born in London "within the sound of Bow Bells." As a boy he had lost his arm to a fireworks accident. When he reached manhood he had migrated to the United States, where he met and married a southern lady who he claimed was a granddaughter of General Robert E. Lee. The couple prospered, and he – now a naturalized citizen – became a stockbroker in New York City, joining all the right clubs. Then came the 1929 Wall Street Crash; taking what money they had salvaged, the couple bought a sailboat from a friend of theirs who was a professor at Yale, and sailed it down to Florida, where Skipper Moy moored what was now their only home. To confirm that this history was true, he opened up his trunk one day, and showed us its mildewed contents: his yachting costume and cap, his club memberships cards, his stockbroker license and the like.

Disaster struck them again in Florida, as an Atlantic hurricane destroyed their boat. But the Moys had been reading about British Honduras, and with the insurance money they took ship for Belize City. Learning there that there was a farm for sale in the Cayo District, they bought it and settled there, raising horses and cattle. Hiring Cunil as the farm/ranch foreman, they did quite well for a while. It seemed that their bad luck had turned a corner.

Now we come to Mrs. Moy, who had evolved into something of a clairvoyant. She began to communicate with the Maya gods and spirits: standing on one of the site's mounds at night, a strange wind would come up, ruffling her clothes, as the spirits – the "Friends" – sent their messages to her in the Maya tongue. She then relayed these to Jacinto, who verbally translated them into English so that Skipper could type them out. They were prophecies, the most important of being that at some time in the future the Great Star, Nohoch Ek in Maya, would crash down to earth on the very site we had been excavating. The two Moys would then become the god and goddess of a new universe.

But that is not how it turned out. One night, in the midst of a great thunderstorm, in a flash of lightning, Moy saw Cunil's face at the window, glaring at him malevolently. According to Skipper, Cunil had just put a Maya curse on him, lighting black candles on each of the four mounds. In short order, Moy's wife deserted him, most of his cattle and horses died, and his place fell to ruin.

Cunil told another version of this saga, however, one that was confirmed by Anderson and others in the district. It appears that Moy regularly tied up his wife to the bed and beat her with a horsewhip, driven mad with the jealous idea that Jacinto was carrying on with her (actually, this may well have been the case). Mrs. Moy had made friends with a Mrs. Carmichael, a Waika Indian snake-bite curer from Nicaragua's Mosquito Coast who had married a cousin of the songwriter Hoagy Carmichael. With the connivance and support of the authorities, both women made their escape from the Colony, away from a beserk Skipper who had threatened to kill them.

We finished those excavations just in time. One afternoon I was digging alone at the bottom of one of the site's chultuns, an underground chamber dug into the limestone and reached by a narrow vertical shaft, when Skipper appeared at the top of the shaft with his ever-present machete. "I know exactly what you're up to, you're trying to set a trap for my horse and cow to fall into." I was at the mercy of this madman, but I talked him out of whatever plans he might have had to chop me to pieces. It was time to leave Nohoch Ek, the Cayo District, and British Honduras.

My Senior year at Harvard was devoted to keeping my grades up to Tozzer's standards (which I did with the exception of Professor Ware's disastrous course), and to writing a senior thesis on Nohoch Ek. Alfie Kidder was an excellent advisor, and encouraged me to expand my dissertation into a wider exploration on just what lowland Maya civilization might have been like during the Classic period. Keep in mind that at that time, practically nothing of the ancient inscriptions could be read outside the dates, and that most Mayanists agreed with

Thompson and Morley that this had been a theocracy uninterested in such matters as warfare, conquest, and human sacrifice. Nothing at all was then known about the Classic political and social system. So I concentrated on the implications of the extensive system of agricultural terraces that I had seen that summer in the Cayo District, and what that might have meant for subsistence practices and population. None of this ever got published, but I kept it in the back of my mind.

One course taken in that year was truly inspiring, and was given by Robert J. Braidwood, on leave from the Oriental Institute of the University of Chicago. He had just returned from his initial season of excavations at Jarmo in Iran, where he had pioneered the archaeological search for the origins of agriculture and village life. A tall man with the appearance of a Turkish general, Braidwood taught his course on Near Eastern prehistory in a manner largely unfamiliar to Harvard. Piling up original reports in a variety of languages in a study room, he forced us to read them, not just sit there listening to him talk. We were treated as his colleagues, not as mere students. He was bristling with the excitement of his Jarmo research, and this excitement was communicated to us.

Then it came time for Braidwood's final examination. I put my hand up and asked him what kind of exam this would be. "Why an open book exam, of course." This may have been the rule at Chicago, but at Harvard it was unheard of. Only two students believed that he meant what he said. The exam was indeed tough and thorough, but Jim Deetz – in time, to become the 20th-century's most influential historical archaeologist – and I had brought detailed notes with us, and we sailed through it, both receiving an A. In those days, a C meant instant failure for a graduate student, and several of the ones taking Braidwood's course disappeared from Harvard as a result.

So, in the long run, the wake-up call that I had received from Tozzer two years before had done its intended job: I graduated with honors, and was accepted into Harvard's graduate school for the following autumn. My future as a Maya archaeologist seemed secure – or so I thought. But Joseph Stalin, Mao Tse-tung, and Kim Il Sung had other ideas.

CHAPTER 6

The Agency

⸙

Having gone out for honors, I didn't have to stay around for graduation. My parents with their usual generosity had offered me a summer vacation in Europe, and I left early for a continent that thus far I had only read about. On the S.S. *America* with me was a Harvard friend, Leo Martinuzzi, half Florentine and half Scottish, and anxious as I was to see the land of his ancestors (in his case, two lands). For much of the time I stayed in London, with several extensive visits to Anglesey Abbey near Cambridge, the home of my cousin Huttleston Broughton, Lord Fairhaven; but I also paid the usual American homage to Paris.

My Uncle Bob was then Chargé d'Affaires at the American Embassy in The Hague, and I stayed with him for two weeks, punctuated by the arrival in that city of Evelyn Waugh, a fellow member of White's Club in London. This was a writer for whom I had boundless admiration, and still do. Waugh was known to detest most Americans, but I must say that he was on his best behavior with us when the three of us (Waugh, my uncle, and myself) took a driving tour through southern Holland. The Dutch were somewhat astonished at the novelist's attire: a loudly checked suit, and a brown "hard hat" (derby) with a quarter-inch nap. Over those several days, we had some notable conversations. I remember one sardonic observation that he had of Dutch life: "The inside of their houses may be all scrubbed clean, but everything stills smells of shit." Just for the record, when we asked him what he thought was his best book, he unhesitatingly said "A *Handful of Dust*."

Right from the beginning of what would have been an idyllic summer in Arcadia, it was quite clear that there was something wrong with the world; in fact the international situation had been getting worse and worse ever since the Soviets began the blockade of Berlin in 1948. My age mates had missed World War II, all right, but we were definitely going to be swept up if World War III, or anything approaching it, ever started.

While crossing the Atlantic, Leo and I had made plans to tour the Western Highlands of Scotland and the Outer Hebrides, which I had been anxious to see ever since reading Boswell's delightful account of his journey there with a reluctant and skeptical Dr. Johnson. Reaching a rain-drenched Glasgow by rail, we went on from there by third-class bus, the passengers speaking less English and more Gaelic as we approached Fort William. We had no hotel reservations in Fort William, and the place was crammed with British tourists on holiday, so we shouldered our suitcases and went to the local police station, thinking they would put us up in the jail. Instead they directed us to a grey-haired lady who had a room for rent, and off we went. That night she told us some scary Gaelic ghost stories (in translation, of course). The next morning she refused to let us pay for the room, but we hid money anyway under our pillows.

Finally, we boarded a ferry for Stornoway, a small, strictly Presbyterian fishing port on the islands of Lewis with Harris. We were in the Outer Hebrides, and it was like being on the edge of the known world.

It was 25 June 1950, and we were sitting in a Stornoway pub quietly sipping our pints when the news came over the radio above the bar: the North Korean army had just invaded South Korea across the 38th Parallel. Stalin, Mao, and Kim Il Sung had gambled that the U.S. and its allies would do nothing about it. As I found out later from persons in a position to know, if President Truman had not committed American ground troops four days later, Stalin had fully intended to invade Western Europe. Mao already had all of China except Taiwan and some nondescript offshore islands in his hands.

Leo and I looked at each other over our pints: here we go.

My intended first year as a Harvard graduate student was pretty much a shambles, as the Korean War ground on. My friends were either being drafted or joining the Navy (which is what Cary did), and my father, still loyal to Annapolis, encouraged me to do the latter; I tried, but failed to pass the medical test due to a recurrent cyst at the base of my spine. So that was out. Jim Deetz signed up for the Air Force, and spent all his spare time digging prehistoric Eskimo sites in Greenland.

Clyde Kluckhohn was surely the most brilliant social anthropologist at Harvard, but certainly not the best teacher in the Department (he had a joint appointment with the Department of Social Relations) – that was Douglas Oliver, as far as I was concerned. Clyde's mind ran so fast ahead of everyone else's that he had difficulty communicating his ideas to his students. One day during that impossible year, Clyde took me to lunch at a local Cambridge restaurant, and put this question to me: "How would you like to work for the government in a really interesting capacity?" I grasped his meaning pretty quickly, as I knew that he had been instrumental in setting up an inter-university Russian studies program that was known to be linked to the Central Intelligence Agency.

And that was how I came to be a CIA case officer.

2

In those days, the Agency looked nothing like what one sees in Hollywood films and television thrillers. Created by Harry Truman in 1947, most of it was housed in so-called "temporary" buildings arranged along the mall between the Washington Monument and the Capitol, with the higher levels of its hierarchy in the old yellow Navy Department headquarters in Georgetown. After I had been cleared by the FBI and had come through an extremely unpleasant lie detector test, I found myself in what turned out to be the Far Eastern section, and was put into the hands of a young, blond, professorial type who informed me that I was going to be assigned to a project based in Taiwan. But first I had to be educated. In the first stage, which lasted about a month, he had me do research in the Library of Congress, finding out everything I could about the history of intelligence operations in China, from the beginning of World War II until now. This covered everybody: Nationalists, Communists, and foreigners.

When I had completed my report, my "master" seemed satisfied, and told me that after I had completed training, I was to be assigned as

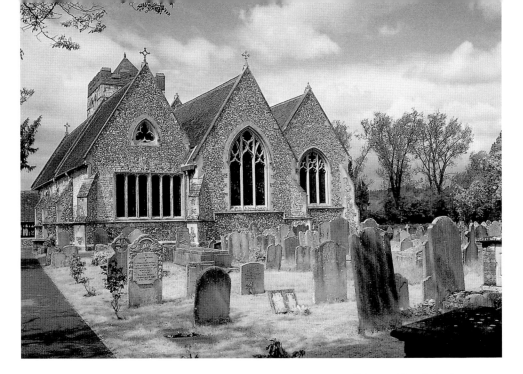

1. All Saints Church, Bisham, Berks. The two headstones in the right foreground belong to Robert Coe I and Robert Coe II, and their wives. The bank of the Thames lies on the other side of the church.

2. My great-grandparents Frederick Augustus Coe and Margaret Robertson Coe, on their 50th wedding anniversary. He was the Moses who brought the Coe family to America in 1883.

3. *Planting Fields in Oyster Bay, on Long Island's North Shore. The house, set in a 409-acre estate, was only one of the homes of my grandfather, William Robertson Coe. Planting Fields is now a New York State Park.*
4. *Henry Huttleston Rogers and his friend Mark Twain aboard the* Kanawha, *Rogers's fast steam yacht.*
5. *My father, William Rogers Coe, and myself age two or three.*

6. *I was a five-year-old at the Planting Fields wedding of my aunt Natalie Coe to the Italian diplomat Count Leonardo Vitetti in 1934. The Papal Nuncio officiated.*

7. *Cherokee Plantation in Yemassee, South Carolina. When I was a schoolboy I spent many spring vacations here.*

8. *Close-up of the Fay School group photo of 1937. I am the very small boy standing in front center, and had just turned eight when this picture was taken.*

9. *The Crow war bonnet that I'm wearing at age 10 in the first house at Irma Lake, Cody, Wyoming, was one of the finest known. It burned along with the lodge the following winter.*

10. My childhood hero was Bill Pawley, the foreman at Irma Lake. He is seen here riding a bucking horse at the Cody Stampede, the annual Fourth of July rodeo.

11. My grandfather William Robertson Coe looking out at his Wyoming domain.

12. *The second house at Irma Lake. The ranch, bought by my grandfather from Buffalo Bill Cody, was as close to paradise as I'll ever get.*
13. *Fall hunting at the Wyoming ranch. This was taken when I was a Harvard undergraduate.*

柯兄惠存

王調勳敬贈 一九五三、三、六、

白光攝影社
第一八號一號光山照相生製

14. *Lunch with W.E. colleagues in one of Taipei's fine restaurants, 1953. Counterclockwise from myself are George Olexo, Ben Collins, and Leo Pappas.*
15. *(Left) General Wang T'iao-hsun, commander of the NFACNSA forces on Paich'üan Island. My name in Chinese appears at the upper right.*
16. *The tiny harbor on the south side of Paich'üan, seen from our headquarters.*

17. View of Angkor Wat in 1954. Angkor was the most memorable stop on my journey home from Taiwan. I vowed I would return some day, but four decades passed before this could happen.

18. Myself in February 1954 at the air strip in Siem Reap, Cambodia, clad as a pukka sahib.

a case officer to an operational group newly formed by the Agency, with the cooperation of General Claire Chennault (the famed head of the wartime Flying Tigers and the husband of a fiercely pro-Nationalist Chinese lady), and Mme Chiang Kai-shek. Although the official attitude of the American government to the struggle between the Nationalists and Mao's Communists had heretofore been one of "hands off," this was to be a clandestine operation in support of anti-Mao guerrillas still fighting the enemy both within China and on the offshore islands. It would be decided later whether I was to be dropped into far western China to be with a large contingent of Muslim anti-Communists (gulp!), or whether I would be sent to Kinmen (Quemoy) or another island. Luckily for me it was the latter option.

The operation and the group were under the cover of an apparently legitimate import-export business known as Western Enterprises, Inc., with headquarters in Pittsburgh and an "office" in Taipei.

In the next phase of my education, I was sent to school to learn the "craft of intelligence." Parenthetically, I never heard the words "spy" or "spying" at any time when I was an Agency employee; these were in use only by journalists and other ignorant amateurs. In our world, "agents" were run by "case officers" for the purpose of "intelligence gathering." Classes were held in another group of temporary buildings near the Jefferson Memorial. I was supposedly under cover, and so went under a pseudonym. The first day, I found myself at a desk behind another student who seemed oddly familiar to me, with his reddish hair, somewhat rosy cheeks, and large blue eyes. My God, it was none other than Willie Stevenson, the boy who had been cut by flying glass when the hurricane blew in the window at Fay those many decades ago! It wasn't long before he recognized me, but he kept quiet and bemusedly addressed me by my phony name.

These classes were enormously interesting and instructive. In the early stages we were taught such subjects as map reading (very useful later on in my archaeological career), and above all, the preparation of reports – this was the writing course that Harvard had never offered when I was an English major, and I did well in it, even learning how to boil down long sentences into "telegraphese." Maybe I should have been a headline writer. Our group learned how to recruit agents, how to test them for reliability, how to elicit information without the subject knowing, and how to detect lying. There was amazingly good instruction in modern history, and particularly the history of Marxism-Leninism, and its philosophical roots in the French Revolution and in the philosophy of Hegel. We were never told the names of our teachers, but I'm positive they came to us from the best campuses in the land (much later, when I had just joined the Yale faculty, I would recognize one or two of these instructors in the Sterling Library elevator!).

I loved the field problems that we were given – they were as much fun as paper chases and treasure hunts had been in my kindergarten days. This is how we were instructed in the craft of "casing a location," dead drops, passing messages, and the ilk, all to be carried out on the busy streets of Washington. Occasionally one of us would get picked up by the municipal cops and hauled away to jail under suspicion, only to be released when someone from the Agency showed up.

My biggest triumph came during the "Union Station problem." The assignment was to find out the details of the security set-up in this very busy railway terminal, which boasted what was then the largest room in the world. Here I cheated a bit. I went straight to the station-master's office and produced my Pennsylvania Railroad pass as my bona fides for this story: my father was an executive of the Virginian Railway Company (true), and that in the interest of having me learn the railroad business from the ground up (untrue), would this gentleman please give me a full account of how security was maintained in the terminal? I was flabbergasted at how many kinds of police and other groups patrolled this place, with overlapping jurisdictions, and learned that most of the public announcements that came over the loudspeaker system were actually coded communications. I got an A on this one.

Georgetown, where I shared rooms with a fellow student, was crawling with CIA recruits day and night; each of these Ivy League types had some kind of a cover story to tell others why they were there, and not some other place. The lamest was that they were working for the Department of Agriculture. There was even a complete "spy" section for them in a local Georgetown bookstore.

෨

Landing at Taipei's Sungshan Airport at noon, after a very long and tiring flight by propeller plane from San Francisco was like dropping out of one universe into another. The airport was located in the midst of a sea of jade-green rice paddies dotted with red-roofed farmhouses, and I was instantly assailed with the eye-watering stench of "night soil" – human excrement. "Is *this* what I'm going to be breathing for the next two years?" I thought. It was, but I soon became so inured to it that when I was at last back on U.S. soil, the air seemed as flat as stale soda water.

Taipei in January 1952 was a completely traditional, walled Chinese city, with all the exotic sights, sounds, and smells of the Orient, not the sky-scrapered megalopolis that it has now become. I was pleasurably overwhelmed with culture shock. The Nationalist government had given W.E. (that is, Western Enterprises, Inc.) a Japanese-built headquarters near the T'an-shui River in northern Taipei, and here is where we were based, with Col. William R. "Ray" Peers as our Chief of Mission. During World War II, Ray – a born leader of men – had organized a highly successful commando group known as "101" against the Japanese in Burma, using local Karen tribesmen as troops; it was from this group that he had put together the core of the new operation, adding to it American marines, Montana "smoke jumpers," weapons experts, supply specialists, communications personnel, and even certified public accountants, among many others. About half of these were stationed on the offshore islands: Tach'en, on the Chechiang coast, Paich'üan off northern Fuchien Province, and Kinmen near Amoy. The rest were in Taipei and in a special training center to the north of the city, at the mouth of the T'an-shui River.

My first night at W.E. headquarters was an eye-opener. After dinner Ray called us all together for a lecture. "Gentlemen, I've just heard some very bad news from our medical staff. About one third of this group has contracted VD. Most of it's the clap, but there are two cases that are not. This has got to stop." There certainly were plenty of chances to sow one's wild oats in the vicinity. Very popular among W.E. personnel was a downtown Taipei brothel called the Tsui Pa Hsien, "Eight Drunken Immortals," so named from the first line of a famous poem by the T'ang Dynasty poet Li Po, who liked to get inebriated with his friends. This institution was brutally frank about what it had to offer; the English-language side of its calling card read:

PROSTITUTION
Finest whisky and cold beer,
beautifully decorated,
attractive girls, excellent
service, makes you comfortable
and satisfied.

Even more in favor was Peit'ou, a mountain north of Taipei that was dotted with hot spring "resorts" in Japanese style; the best of these was considered to be the "Literary Inn," not exactly a place to check out a book.

A few nights later, W.E. threw a cocktail party for Mme. Chiang, and I was introduced to this formidable but strikingly beautiful woman. Remember that I was only 22, and looked young for my not very advanced age. She smiled at me and said in the soft accent of an American southern belle, "I know exactly what's in your mind, you're thinking that you'd like to meet a lovely Chinese girl, and you're going to want to marry her. But just remember that that won't work out. You'd both be unhappy." For once in my life I didn't know what to say in reply. I certainly didn't then have marriage on my mind. That came much later.

The following week I was invited out to dinner by the Quartermaster General of the Nationalist army, to whom a letter in my behalf had been sent by Gen. Albert Wedemeyer, former commander of all U.S. forces in China and a friend of my parents. Hitherto, my imperfect knowledge of Chinese food had been limited to chop suey joints and to the dreadful Young Lee restaurant on Harvard Square. I didn't even know how to use chopsticks. I quickly learned how that evening, as my host came from Szechuan, and he had that province's finest chef in his employ. My mother was a fine cook, and I had eaten in some of Paris's best restaurants, but this was the greatest meal I had ever had. In fact, all of Taipei in those days was a gourmet's paradise, as chefs from every province on the mainland had fled there with much of their kitchen staff and set up shop.

*Taiwan and the Offshore Islands. I was
stationed first on Kinmen, then on
Paich'üan.*

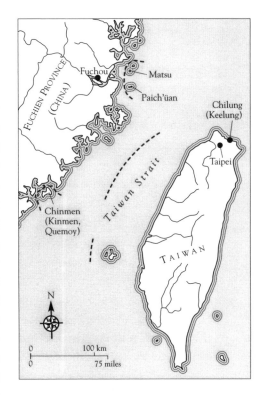

Kinmen (Chinmen in Mandarin, "Golden Gate") is a dumbbell-shaped island sitting smack in the middle of Amoy harbor, on the southern Fuchien coast. It was there that General Hu Lien had destroyed a major Communist invasion force a few years before, and it was to there that I was transported along with supplies in a Civil Air Transport DC-3. Our small contingent of six Americans lived in an ancient, two-story farmhouse, training a guerrilla force with the resounding name of the "South Fuchien Anti-Communist National Salvation Army," abbreviated to SFACNSA. They had just returned with a group of prisoners from a raid on the mainland coast near Amoy, and many wounded, groaning, SFACNSA soldiers covered with blood lay by the air strip waiting to be treated by medics. I had seen tableaux like this only in movies, but here it was real. Of the two SFACNSA generals with whom W.E. had planned this operation one was corpulent and the other very small; they were known to us as "Fat Wang" and "Little Wang," and they reminded me of Sidney Greenstreet and Peter Lorre in *The Maltese Falcon.*

In the two months that I was on Kinmen, my only job was to teach map reading to SFACNSA troops, and this I did with the help of an excellent U.S. Army manual, only to find that they mostly flunked my course since only a handful of them were literate, and numbers and maps meant nothing to them. So I was very happy to learn that I was going to be sent north, to another island, where at last I would be doing real intelligence.

77

❧

Jayne's Fighting Ships of the World would have been hard-pressed to find a classification for the 711. Before the Agency bought it, the 711, so the story went, had been a Philippine Coast Guard cutter, busy hunting down and catching the numerous smugglers and pirates that plied those tropical waters. Thanks to its gasoline-powered engines, it was extremely fast, but one misplaced spark could have sent it and every-body in it sky-high. Top heavy with a 40 mm gun, it rolled and pitched, even in the calmest seas. The bane of anyone even slightly prone to seasickness, this was the well-nigh useless craft that took me to Paich'üan, "White Dog," where I was to spend many happy and truly interesting months. Paich'üan was actually two islands, "West Dog" and "East Dog"; we were headed for "West Dog" or Hsich'üan, a precip-itous, rocky isle slightly more than two square kilometers in extent, and the headquarters of a Nationalist guerrilla army.

We left Chilung (Keelung) and its grim, industrial harbor late one afternoon. On board the 711 were a Chinese naval captain and his crew, along with W.E.'s own Stanley Barton. The British-born Stan was a white-haired veteran of decades of skippering cargo ships along the China coast, and he knew every part of it, far better than Capt. Chiang. The two passengers on this journey across the Taiwan Strait were myself and "Gentleman Jim" Creacy, a colorful communications officer. Jim was a 100-percent Texan who looked and talked rather like Slim Pickens in the film *Dr. Strangelove*. With his cowboy hat and boots, and with an ivory-handled six-shooter hanging from each hip, Jim was an object of wonder to the sailors hanging over the taff rail of a U.S. naval supply ship as we slowly moved past them, out of the river and into the harbor.

Jim and I had bunks below, but once we got out in the strait the ship started to roll, and never stopped until we reached our destination, so I decided to stay on deck for the entire trip, which was to take all night. Darkness fell as we proceeded on our northwesterly course towards the Chinese mainland. Fairly immune to motion sickness of any kind, and sitting aft in a wicker chair with my feet propped up on the rail, I enjoyed the magnificent phosphorescence of our wake and the bril-liant stars, while Jim and about half of the crew were violently seasick below. Suddenly, about midway, the 711 was held in the white blaze of a powerful searchlight: this was a destroyer of the United States Seventh Fleet, assigned to patrol the Taiwan Strait. Its guns were trained on us.

"Who are you? Identify yourself!" came over a bullhorn.

Stan, who had been sustaining himself with nips from a whiskey bottle, soon assured the destroyer's commander that we were friendly, and that our mission had been approved by higher authorities. So on we went.

As we grew nearer the Chinese mainland, at about 5 AM we entered a dense fog, in very tricky waters replete with hidden rocks. This became a true "white-out," with visibility no more than a few hundred yards. Here was where Barton's encyclopedic knowledge of the coast probably saved us from shipwreck. I must admit that I was pretty worried, given the explosive fuel we were carrying. Then, out of the mists came a plaintive bugle call on the right, answered by another one ahead on the left; back and forth they went, in a kind of stereo dialogue. We had arrived at Paich'üan – the signals had come from guard posts on two rocky promontories of the island.

Between these two points was a small harbor with a shingle-covered beach. Sampans took Jim and me ashore, along with our gear and other supplies, and we began the long, zigzag climb up through the fishing village to our quarters. I say "climb," because the stone-built houses were on land so steep that they had to be kept from falling downhill by stilts. Because of the frequent rains and high winds, not to mention typhoons, their tiled roofs were weighted down with stones and lashed with ropes. I had never seen anything like it – this was the China of past centuries – but this was to be my home for the next eight months.

The little island's commander was General Wang T'iao-hsün, once chief aide to General Tai Li, a man who had been Nationalist China's premier spymaster during World War II, and the fearsome head of Chiang Kai-shek's secret police until his death in a mysterious plane crash in 1945. General Wang and his two fellow commanders, both named General Lin (the most common family name in Fuchou) along with their force of several thousand irregulars were impressively designated the "North Fuchien National Salvation Army," with the acronym

NFACNSA. While the officer corps of this force could speak Mandarin, all of the others along with the island's native fishermen and farmers spoke only the Fuchou language, which sometimes created difficulties for our "Mandarin only" interpreters. Twelve miles to the north of Paich'üan was the much larger Matsu Island, a major outpost of the Nationalist government's navy and regular army, from which Wang maintained a kind of semi-independence.

The quarters for the "American friends" had been newly constructed adjacent to General Wang's headquarters, and were quite comfortable, with a magnificent view south across the shining South China Sea and west towards the mountainous coast of northern Fuchien, 20 miles away. With binoculars, one could spot fishing junks and other commercial traffic at the mouth of the Min River. While there was no running water, and lavatory arrangements were Chinese style (a local entrepreneur actually paid us for the privilege of carrying away the buckets containing our high-grade effluvia to the terraced fields of sweet potatoes!), life was hardly Spartan as we were assigned two orderlies to attend to our needs. Our weekly baths were taken in deep, barrel-like, wooden tubs with charcoal-burning immersion heaters.

The W.E. contingent on Paich'üan was headed by Philip Montgomery, a fascinating character in his own right. Phil, né *Philippe de Montgoméry*, was a member of a very wealthy French family that had the good fortune to own the Noilly Prat vermouth firm. Educated in France, he joined the Resistance when the German armies invaded his country. Perhaps due to his American-born mother, he was able to flee to the United States, where he joined the United States Naval Intelligence service. Instead of sending him to North Africa, where his absolute fluency in French would have served him well, his naval superiors assigned him to the Sino-American Cooperative Organization or SACO, a paramilitary enterprise engaged in highly successful guerrilla warfare and intelligence gathering in Japanese-occupied China.

Phil didn't talk much about this period in his life, other than his respect for SACO's joint commanders – Admiral Milton "Mary" Miles and Tai Li – but it appears that at some point he married a Chinese girl who was later killed by the Japanese. He never married again. After the war, he ran a wine and liquor retail business in the U.S., until the Agency recruited him for Ray Peers's offshore-island operation. Needless to say, our stock of alcoholic beverages on Paich'üan was nothing but the best that Hong Kong had to offer.

Phil was a delightful companion, full of stories delivered in a hybrid French and American upper-class accent, with ever-present pipe clenched in his mouth. He was fond of the good life and knew how to lead it, and was much liked by the Chinese. On the other hand, he was singularly uninterested in moving our NFACNSA colleagues into raiding actions against the Communists on the coast. I really didn't care as my job was intelligence, not paramilitary operations; it wasn't long before I learned that General Wang's people also had no ambitions along this line. Their goal seemed to have been the status quo – a really serious raid against a mainland target might just persuade the "Chicoms" to hit Paich'üan, and all of us, Chinese and American alike, knew that this little rock was basically indefensible, in spite of the wall that General Wang had built around it. If Paich'üan was ever in danger of falling, there were no plans at all to evacuate us, and we would probably have been shot or, more likely, ended up with life sentences in solitary confinement.

I had come to realize that Chiang Kai-shek's oft-repeated refrain, "strike back at the mainland," was largely hot air. Wang T'iao-hsün and his staff were perfectly happy with this situation and with our presence, as long as W.E. continued to be his main supplier of military equipment.

Every night we had to make radio contact with W.E. headquarters in Taipei, and for that we had a communications officer. For much of my stay on White Dog this was Don Wallace, a balding young man from Peabody, Massachusetts, with a Boston accent and a fine New England sense of humor. While Don was good at his job, the actual transmission of the coded message in Morse was in charge of the 16-year-old "Junior" Tsou, a Hakka Chinese from southern Fuchien, most of whose family had been murdered by the Communists in 1949. Escaping to Kinmen, he was one of a number of orphaned boys recruited by General Hu Lien and trained in "commo." All became masters at radio communication by Morse code. So the staccato sound of the Morse key and the squeak and crackle of our radio as the operator tried to find the right frequency were a regular evening feature.

On the floor below ours were our interpreters. Chief among them was Louis Wu, who was to become one of my closest friends during my stay on "the rocks" and on Taiwan. Like all the other W.E. faniguans, Louis had a university degree, but he was head-and-shoulders above the others in intelligence and general knowledge. His father was then a professor of Chinese literature in a Japanese university, and a friend of General Chiang Ching-kuo (of whom more below). Louis always had the ability to put away an enormous amount of food, above all Chinese noodles, while remaining remarkably skinny; I sometimes called him "Noodles Wu."

Speaking of food, for us Americans (except for the "meat-and-potatoes" types) Paich'üan was an eaters' paradise. Mistakenly considering that we would prefer American-style food to Chinese, Taipei headquarters had sent us a scrawny cook who could supposedly produce it, but by popular demand Phil soon had him recalled to Taiwan. Through Phil's efforts, "Cookie" was replaced by the wonderful Lao K'ung, a one-eyed descendant of Confucius and a specialist in Peking-style cuisine who had been master chef to "Tiger" Wang, the commander of the Nationalist air force. K'ung was a kind and humane person who loved animals; sadly, his pet Alsatian dog was eaten one day by the crew of one of the island's guard posts.

Before K'ung's arrival, we and our interpreters took most of our evening meals with Wang T'iao-hsün and his officers (the wives of the latter ate separately in another room, a traditional if somewhat sexist arrangement). Being the newest arrival on Paich'üan, and the youngest of the Americans, General Wang at first put me in the seat of honor, facing the door. What I had initially not realized was that I would be the object of innumerable toasts. These were made in small porcelain cups filled with warmed *hsiao hsing* rice wine (apparently smuggled in from the mainland) that at first seemed to me to be no stronger than weak sherry. Complying with numerous challenges to *kan pei* ("dry the cup" – i.e. "down the hatch!"), it would not be long before I became completely tipsy.

As befits such a successful warlord, when he evacuated the mainland for his island redoubt, Wang brought with him Fuchou's finest chef, and at Wang's table we ate like princes, if not kings, often on the finest fresh fish and other creatures that the surrounding waters could produce. One evening banquet featured a dish of baby lima beans mixed with what I took to be bean sprouts, but when I raised the porcelain spoon to my lips, each "bean sprout" turned out to have two small, black eyes. These were actually small marine worms that swarmed in the Taiwan Strait in this season, perhaps even the *Amphichaena* worm with a primitive notochord that I had learned in Mr. Mac's biology class to be a possible ancestor to all the vertebrates including ourselves! They were truly delicious.

The pecking order as far as these Chinese toasts were concerned was minutely choreographed. It was all an elaborate game, in which the winner was the one who ended up drinking less. For the Chinese, the usual game in its simplest form was for two "combatants" to throw out fingers, while shouting out their guess as to whether the total number would be odd or even; the loser then had to *kan pei*. Before long, I noted that General Wang almost never drank himself. Behind his chair stood his tall, heavily pockmarked, and quite sinister personal bodyguard, carrying a large Luger pistol on his hip. Wang would pass his cup to him, and it was he who had to "down the hatch" for his lord and master. The general assured us that if he told this man to jump out the window, he would instantly do it.

I immediately took to Wang T'iao-hsün. Probably then in his early 40s, with a gruff, straightforward way of speaking, he radiated both power and self-confidence without arrogance. Unfortunately, due to what some said was a health problem but others ascribed to trysts with a lady friend (not his wife), he was often away in Taiwan.

My initial task was to establish liaison with the NFACNSA intelligence on the island, with Louis Wu as my interpreter. This was far from easy, since it became clear that Paich'üan was overrun with mutually competing security entities. One had only to look at the rooftops below our quarters – they were bristling with radio antennas. My immediate contact was with a lieutenant who was not much older than I was, a man of considerable charm. He would pass me reports gathered by the mainland agent network of the Ministry of Defense, and I would analyze these and transmit anything new nightly to Taipei. On one wall of our quarters I had stapled up all of the 1:250,000 sheets of the northern Fuchien coast made by the U.S. Army Map Service, with grease pencil notations on the Chicom order of battle, continuously updated.

But there really was no way of checking the reliability of much of this information, nor did we know anything about their agents. It also turned out that we really didn't know who we were dealing with in the first place. On the "rocks" and back in Taiwan there was an intense rivalry between Tai Li's old organization, the Pao Mi Chu (PMC), and military intelligence, but it was not easy to tell who owed loyalty to whom. The Agency also wanted to know the real names, not pseudonyms, and CV's for the agents of the organization that we were supporting, that is, NFACNSA. At one point, the PMC in Taipei told us the true identity of one of the agents that we were jointly running, not at all the name given us on Paich'üan, and this was transmitted to us by radio. The next morning, I had an eyeball-to-eyeball confrontation with one of the two Generals Lin (Wang was off in Taiwan) and his intelligence chief; they were forced to admit that they had been giving us false CV's for a number of their agents, and promised to give us better cooperation in the future. I can't say I really believed this.

Early one morning I heard a confused shouting below our quarters, and saw a crowd of soldiers and civilians moving along the narrow, cobbled street. In their midst was a man in tatters. Stuck down the back of his collar was a white wooden placard with Chinese characters written in black on it. I rushed downstairs to ask Louis Wu what was going on, and he told me that the characters identified him as an enemy agent who had infiltrated the island, and was on his way to the execution ground; before 15 minutes had passed, he was dispatched with a bullet to the back of the head by a soldier who had lost his family to the Communists. The Chicoms themselves must have had many of their own agents on the island. It later turned out that the personable, English-speaking Colonel Huang who was aide-de-camp to Wang T'iao-hsün and his chief of intelligence as well as our genial dinner companion was also a Communist spy. He was taken on a one-way trip back to Taiwan, tried, and shot. In a way, Paich'üan was a House of Mirrors.

At last I was able to recruit a real, flesh-and-blood agent. This was a rather thin, plain-looking lady in her early 30s who was able to visit the island by fishing boat about once a month, crossing from the mainland at night. The agency code-named her "Argentina," and we successfully tested her against some verifiable data. In my reports, she was thus raised from an "F" (unknown reliability) to a "C" (fairly reliable). She lived not far from the Ihsu Airfield, south of Fuchou city, a facility often used by MIG fighters, and she gave us some pretty good data on air traffic.

On one of her last clandestine visits to Paich'üan while I was still there, Argentina complained of severe abdominal pains which seemed to be gynecological, and I radioed W.E. headquarters for medical help. Pat Hildreth, our young and highly competent doctor from Philadelphia, came in by PBY seaplane with a medical kit. The only trouble was that Argentina, like other traditional Chinese women, wouldn't take her clothes off for a strange man, even for a doctor. Luckily we found on the island an ivory figurine kept for just such a purpose, and the patient pointed out on it just where she hurt. Pat gave her the proper medicine, and she recovered.

I had been experiencing hurricanes ever since the great storm of 1938 that devastated New England, so typhoons were nothing new to me. During the late summer to fall season, they came up from the South China Sea at regular intervals. We would track them via short-wave reports from Sangley Point, the U.S. Naval weather station in the Philippines. When wind speeds reached Force 12 on the Beaufort scale, we knew that our island redoubt was in trouble, with seas that often reached the rating "phenomenal." In a way, we had grandstand seats, perched high above the harbor. One such storm was heartrendingly unforgettable. One fishing family had decided to ride it out on their junk, as tremendous waves roared in from the south. Watching with binoculars, we wondered how long they would survive. It seemed hours to us, but it was really within minutes that before our eyes and to our horror the junk was pounded to pieces on hidden rocks, and the people on board drowned before they could reach the beach.

The NFACNSA command may have had little inclination to raid the enemy, either on the mainland or on the islands controlled by the Communists, but coastal shipping was another kettle of fish. The

Chicoms had little ability to move materials by sea in support of their troops, other than by sailing junk and sampan. Before the start of the Korean War, most of the maritime trade along the China coast was in the hands of two great, British-owned companies: Jardine Matheson and Butterfield & Swire, both then based in Hong Kong. Supposedly, in accordance with the United Nations embargo on trading with the enemy, no British-registered ships were to have anything to do with the Chicoms, but it was general knowledge within intelligence circles that this was more honored in the breach than in the observance. The Nationalists on Taiwan and the offshore islands certainly believed in the perfidiousness of Albion in this matter. Hence, interdiction of such shipping was considered defensible.

If W.E. had any part in such (perhaps justifiable) piracy, it would have raised the most serious diplomatic questions, since the UK was our closest ally and with whom we shared much of our intelligence. An additional consideration was that British units were fighting in Korea next to our own troops.

The NFACNSA navy may have been pathetically small, with one small freighter converted into a gunboat, and several motorized and armed junks, but they took several prizes, including the *Helikon*, a 1200-ton British freighter that was plying between Shanghai and China's southern ports. It proved to be fully loaded with flour destined for the People's Liberation Army; for days, Wang's guerrilla troops unloaded the cargo, covered with white flour dust. Every cook on the island, including our own Lao K'ung, was kept busy making man-t'ou, the delicious steamed buns typical of the northern cuisine.

My job was to retrieve the ship's manifest, and to interrogate the British captain without letting my presence on the island be known. Louis Wu was then in Taiwan, so I sent a newer interpreter, Benedict Kuo, to do the ship, after briefing Benedict on what questions to ask, and how. This seemed to be satisfactory, since the skipper seemed cooperative. However, some time later a coded message came to us from W.E. headquarters in Taipei that this captain, on arrival in Hong Kong, had blown our cover with British intelligence, giving them all our correct names and our functions. The one exception was myself, probably because as pronounced, "Coe" makes a perfectly good surname in Chinese! The only way that the captain could have learned all this would have been from Benedict. Benedict was a somewhat fanatic convert to fundamentalist Christianity, and the captain may have used this fact to elicit intelligence from our gullible interpreter, rather than vice versa.

Unlikely though it may seem, Paich'üan was a wonderful place to read. Effectively isolated from the rest of world – none of my family or friends had any idea where I actually was, nor could they be told – there was plenty of time for this. When in Hong Kong, I bought not only books on Buddhism and on the Chinese language and the history of China, but also large numbers of general works on archaeology, principally as Penguin paperbacks. Whether I stayed in intelligence or not, I was determined not to lose touch with this particular intellectual world. Cary Welch had managed to send me the Sherlock Holmes stories collected in one volume. These books, and the many classics that I had on my shelf (all of Jane Austen, for instance), I am convinced kept my brain from atrophying. At one point, I read all of *Paradise Lost* aloud to myself (sotto voce, of course). Curiously, the worst fear that I had entertained in the event of a Communist takeover of the island was that my modestly sized library would be consigned to the flames by the invaders.

My most recondite book was one that I had brought from the U.S.: the first (1950) edition of Eric Thompson's *Maya Hieroglyphic Writing*. In those days, this was the vade mecum for any aspiring Mayanist, and I was awed by Thompson's vast erudition but puzzled – even then – by the great man's apparent failure to make much sense of any of the script beyond the calendrics. Yet I read all of it with awe, an admiration that became considerably tempered in later years. What would the Chicoms have thought of it if it had fallen into their hands? A secret code? It would have taken them at least a year to translate.

One November day, towards the close of my nine-month tour of duty on White Dog, the island received a visit from non-Communist China's second-most powerful individual. This was the formidable and much-feared General Chiang Ching-kuo, eldest son of Chiang Kai-shek by an earlier spouse. Educated in Soviet Russia, with a Russian wife, he was the head of the Peace Preservation Corps, responsible for the arrest of thousands of dissidents of many stripes, and sometimes their execution. These included leftist students, and workers for Tai-wan's independence. Chiang Ching-kuo held the Gimo's "chop" (personal seal), and was thus the *de facto* ruler of the island, its armed forces, and its intelligence organizations. He was known to detest his stepmother Mme. Chiang and her corrupt relatives, and he was held in suspicion by the Agency and the U.S. Government in general.

But my interpreter Louis Wu was a kind of godson to Chiang, and we invited him to visit our quarters, and so he did, accompanied by his "court jester" Jimmy Wei, publisher of the English-language *China News*. It was actually an amazing evening, in which we consumed at least a bottle each of brandy and scotch; as the night wore on, General Chiang became more and more fluent in English, which according to our faulty intelligence he couldn't speak, nor wanted to. I found him a tremendously appealing and intelligent personage, and reached the conclusion that the Agency had bet on completely the wrong horse when it decided to work mainly with the powerless Madame instead of with him. Ironically, it was some years later, as President Chiang Ching-kuo, that he introduced to Taiwan the first and only truly demo-cratic government that the Chinese people have ever known.

For all of 1953 I was stationed back in Taipei, which gave me the chance to immerse myself in Chinese culture. I took private lessons in spoken and written Mandarin in my spare time, traveled to many parts of that beautiful, mountainous island (the name "Formosa," "lovely," was given it by the Portuguese who once owned it), collected Chinese paintings and antiques, went to the Chinese opera as often as I could, and explored the local restaurant scene with like-minded W.E. colleagues.

One of these was an old acquaintance from Long Island days, R. Campbell "Zup" James, who was sent to White Dog after I had left the island. A graduate of Groton and Yale, Zup later became famed among correspondents in Laos during the Vietnam War for his guards' style mustache, tiger-claw watch fob, and love of good champagne, but he was less flamboyant in his days with W.E. He was a very effective intel-ligence officer in both wars. Another close friend was Leo Pappas, a

Greek-American whose father had once run a hotdog stand in Coney Island and whose mother had been a Ziegfield Follies showgirl. Leo was on Tach'en for almost a year, sending back intelligence reports in an all-but-illegible scrawl to headquarters at frequent intervals, but he returned to Taiwan when the Nationalists, under American pressure, evacuated the island as basically indefensible.

Before I had left home for Taiwan, Earnest Hooton had given me a letter of introduction to the grand old man of Chinese archaeology, Li Chi, who had received his doctorate in anthropology at Harvard. This great scholar had been the excavator of Anyang, capital of the Shang Dynasty, and he had escaped from the mainland to Taiwan with fellow members of the Academia Sinica and all of the Anyang collections. Dr. Li received me cordially at his Chinese home in his traditional blue gown, and it was he who led me back into the world of anthropology and archaeology.

One of the key figures in the Anthropology Department at Taiwan National University was a young Taiwanese named Chen Chi-lu, who was already an outstanding authority on the Formosan aborigines, the Malayo-Polynesian-speaking native peoples of the island's mountainous interior. He and I were to travel together to the Ami tribe on the east coast, and eventually to publish a joint paper on their religious practices. I went over to the Department as often as I could, and it was there that I met the very young Chang Kwang-chih, Dr. Li's favorite pupil and the number one student in the entire university – keeping in mind that the student body consisted entirely of hard-working Chinese, this was a mind-staggering achievement. Kwang-chih's lady-love was the departmental librarian, and he and Li Hwei were to marry when both eventually moved to the United States. Once he had entered Harvard, this brilliant scholar metamorphed into K. C. Chang, and in a decade or two had become recognized as one of the greatest archaeologists ever produced by China. Later, when both of us were studying at Harvard and then teaching at Yale, he became one of my closest friends.

Li Chi persuaded me into giving a talk on the Maya, which I did one day, illustrating it from my copy of Thompson's *Maya Hieroglyphic Writing*, viewed with the Department's overhead projector. I don't know what I said, but years later, Kwang-chih assured me it was a good lecture even though his English was then so bad he could only understand every third word! Regardless, Li Chi and all these Chinese friends and colleagues had reintroduced me to an intellectual world that I had almost forgotten.

PRESIDENT CHIANG KAI-SHEK
Request the pleasure of your company
to a dinner party on Wednesday at
seven thirty in the evening,
January the Seventh, 1953. at
SHIH-LIN RESIDENCE

Shih-lin was the Generalissimo's hideaway in the hills above Taipei. Like the Ministry of National Defense, it looked very much like a leftover from the days of Japanese imperial administration. Why was I, a not very high-ranking personage in W.E.'s table of organization, receiving such a prestigious invitation? The answer must have been that I had recently been put in charge of the "T-Area," our agent training camp on the other side of the T'an-shui River from the capital.

Along with W.E.'s "wheels," which of course included Bob Delaney, the current Chief of Mission, our group rode up at dusk in several jeeps, eventually passing into a wooded area with various checkpoints. Then we lined up in the entrance hall, and the great man entered, attired in the long silk gown of a Chinese scholar. The Gimo was a small man (even compared to myself), with a shaven and very shiny pate. I am afraid that I was reminded of the irreverent nickname that his old enemy General Stillwell had once given him, "Peanut." As he passed along and greeted each of us with a smile and a handshake, he repeatedly muttered *hao, hao*, "good, good."

Then we sat down to dinner at a long table, at which of course he occupied the center seat. I had expected to enjoy an incredibly good Chinese meal, prepared for the supreme head of non-Communist China by one of the world's great chefs. Instead, we got mediocre American-style food reminiscent of what I had been forced to eat all those years in boarding school. The Gimo, like Adolf Hitler, was a teetotalling Puritan in private life.

And speaking of his private life, why wasn't Mme. Chiang at his side? In fact, this was a married couple only for official, ceremonial purposes. It was common knowledge in the Far East that the Madame had been so disgusted with the Gimo's unworthy behavior during his 1936 captivity in Sian by Chang Hsüeh-liang, the "Young Marshal," that she swore never to sleep with him again, and she had stuck to her promise. This didn't stop her from having many affairs with handsome young aides, and it was rumored that her current lover was a good-looking and personable colonel who occupied an office on the ground floor of our headquarters, and who acted as our principal military liaison with the Nationalist government. This astonishing woman eventually settled in Long Island and in New York City, where she recently died at age 106!

As usual, there were the usual toasts to and from the "American friends," but the rice wine was scanty compared to what I had become used to on Paich'üan; the abstemious Gimo was probably drinking ice water. The real entertainment of the evening began after dinner, when we were all ushered into the Gimo's private film theater.

I have always been fascinated by the fact that so many dictators and autocrats of the past hundred years have had their own movie theater, and by their taste in films. A great book could be written on this subject, and maybe it has been. Hitler loved *Gone With the Wind*, and Himmler was fond of *Bambi*, while Stalin was reported to have laughed so hard at Laurel and Hardy shorts that he was left breathless. Our fare this evening was *Duel at Silver Creek*, a shoot-'em-up Western with Audie Murphy, the most-decorated GI of World War II. Watching the action with us were the Gimo's two small, half-Russian grandsons (by his son Chiang Ching-kuo). Outfitted from head-to-toe with Hopalong Cassidy cowboy costumes – probably straight from the F.A.O. Schwarz store in Manhattan – these noisy brats kept up a sporadic gunfire with their cap pistols, blazing away at the screen as soon as there was any action.

In a way, it was touching of the Gimo to have provided us with the food and entertainment that he thought we would best enjoy, and I'm sure that these were what a few of my fellow guests felt at home with, but for my part I would have preferred Peking duck, followed by a Chinese opera recital or perhaps by one of the brilliant Japanese samurai films that were beginning to be shown in Taipei theaters.

Once the film ended, we descended in the darkness to Taipei with the smoke from the capguns still stinging our nostrils.

♌

In late 1952 the Korean War began winding down, and finally came to a halt with the signing of an armistice in July 1953. Eisenhower, newly elected President in November 1952, had made a campaign commitment to seek an end to the conflict, and he kept his word by visiting Korea the next month, but on a stop-off in Hawaii he was to receive a briefing on the entire Pacific and East Asian situation. My job was to prepare a report for him on all the supposed anti-Communist guerrilla forces then operating on the mainland. After sifting all the intelligence we had, and discarding Nationalist propaganda, it was obvious that they were pitifully few to non-existent – the People's Liberation Army and Mao's security service had wiped out almost all resistance, other than the troops on the offshore islands.

So, had W.E. been a failure, a very expensive, bloated waste of resources that preyed on itself as more and more personnel were added? Yes, as far as its original charter went. As far as I could see, the infrequent raids against the Chinese mainland had been little more than minor annoyances to Mao, but they did bring one plus to the United States: they tied down along the southern Chinese coast several hundred thousand Communist troops that otherwise would have gone to Korea to fight the United Nations forces. The truce line that was drawn at the 38th parallel might then have been far to the south; perhaps *all* of the peninsula would have ended up in the hands of "Great Leader" Kim Il-sung.

The Korean War was over. Stalin was dead. My two years of overseas service with the Agency were up in early 1954, and I was due to return to Washington for reassignment, almost certainly at a desk job. I did not look forward to being one more government bureaucrat. I had already settled in my mind that I would resign when I got home, and go back to Harvard to complete my Ph.D.

Strangely enough, as the end of my stay in Taiwan approached, I began to be homesick, something that had not hit me since my earliest days away at boarding school. In short, I missed my parents – my tolerant, equitable, generous father, and my mercurial but loving mother.

Mention "CIA" to the average academic, and he or she would recoil in horror, yet the three years I spent with the Agency were wonderful ones, and I have no regrets whatsoever. I received an important part of my education from "the company," and at a young age I was given some immense responsibilities. I learned how to work with all kinds of people, Americans and Chinese alike, and among them I made some friends for life. In short, I grew up, and could plan my future with some degree of confidence, without playing second fiddle to anyone. I was also getting tired of bachelor life.

So, in many important ways, China made me.

In early February 1954 I left Taiwan, never to return.

CHAPTER 7

The Long Voyage Home

Columns of smoke rose high from the land below as the Bangkok-bound Cathay Pacific plane passed over Vietnam's coast at Hué, the ancient capital: this was not the burning of rice fields, but a visible sign that a major battle was in process between the French army and the Viet Minh insurgents. The debacle of Dien Bien Phu, which ended the French role in their former colony, was only a few months away. After it, more than a few of my W.E. colleagues were going to be reassigned to Saigon, as the United States became increasingly involved in what was going to be a conflict with disastrous results for us and for Southeast Asia.

I would like to say that all this was on my mind as I sat reading on the plane, but I was actually laughing helplessly at Stephen Potter's *Gamesmanship*, which I had just picked up in a Hong Kong bookstore.

Typical of my improvident ways, I had made no hotel reservation in Bangkok. This was in the days before jet travel and mass tourism, and hotels were in very short supply in Thailand. When I arrived at the time-hallowed Oriental Hotel, I was told that I could stay only one night; they meant this, and I was ejected the next morning. In desperation, I repaired to the U.S. Embassy, told them my predicament, and was transferred to a new hotel owned by the Thai government, where I had almost the entire top floor to myself.

Bangkok was then a reasonably small city, rather like an Oriental Venice, and its many canals had not yet been filled in in the interests of progress (i.e. money). It was a magical place, almost a fairy-tale city, especially along the Chao Praya River at sundown, when the sun's rays would burnish the gold of the city's many pagodas and stupas, and light up the wonderful Royal Palace and its temples. I totally fell in love with it, and with Southeast Asia. While on "the Rocks" I had read many books on Buddhism, the only religion that has really attracted me –

perhaps because it was more a philosophy or way of life and thought than a religion, and basically agnostic in outlook. Some of the absolutely most evil people I have ever known have been practicing Christians, at least in their definition; I suppose there are some bad people who are Buddhists (Burma's current military rulers come to mind), but the Buddhists I have known over many decades seem somehow to be better human beings.

The owner of my Bangkok hotel was a devout Buddhist. If I would rent a car, he said, we (including his small son) could travel north to Saraburi for the annual festival of the Buddha's Footprint, and he would act as guide and translator. I jumped at the opportunity. On the hot, dusty plain around the shrine were encamped thousands of Buddhist monks in their saffron and yellow robes, and temporary markets had been set up by pilgrims from all over Thailand and even Laos to sell their local wares. Long processions of the faithful affixed squares of gold leaf to the images of Buddha and the Bodhisattvas, while temple bells were struck and small gamelan groups played music. It seemed that I was the only foreigner there, and I was transfixed. Incidentally, the Footprint itself was a huge depression in a natural rock but believed by everyone to be a place where the Founder had once trod.

My ultimate goal in Southeast Asia was mysterious Angkor, which I had read about in Osbert Sitwell's delightful travel book, *Escape with Me!* Cambodia had only recently been granted its independence from France under pressure from its young king, Norodom Sihanouk, so I picked up a Cambodian visa from his embassy in Bangkok, and took an Air Vietnam flight to Phnom Penh, the capital.

Phnom Penh was then a lovely city, laid out by the French on the confluence of the Mekong and Siem Reap Rivers. Its fine villas and tree-lined streets reminded one of a French provincial town; and it was the French who had designed the magnificent Royal Palace (in native Cambodian style, of course). What really struck me was the absolute beauty of the Khmer statuary in the National Museum, to my mind the finest structure ever built for the display of an art collection. Phnom

Penh was crowded with French officers in their white uniforms and kepis, along with their elegant wives dressed in the latest Paris mode; Cambodia was also at war, this time with a native Communist insurgency.

With luck, I managed get a seat on a plane northwest to Siem Reap, the little town that had sprung up on the southern margins of Angkor. Once there I talked the manager of the Grand Hotel d'Angkor to let me have a room, which I had to share with two other travelers. Only the week before the rebels had stormed through Siem Reap, and tossed hand grenades into the hotel's lobby and bar, so that large holes still showed in its walls. At that very moment, the king was ten miles outside of Angkor, fighting the Communists with his war elephants (and beating them, by the way).

Angkor was a revelation, and has remained in my mind throughout all of my archaeological career. The world's largest ancient city, its monsoon-forest surroundings, its ruined temple complexes and their architectural sculptures all reminded me forcefully of the Classic Maya sites that I both knew firsthand and those that I had only read about in books, but on a far grander scale. The brick-built Baksei Chamkrong temple-pyramid looked to me identical to the great temples of Tikal which I had seen pictured in Tozzer's Peabody Museum monograph. The hauntingly beautiful structures of Ta Prohm were caught up in the roots of the same strangler fig trees and ceibas that grew over the Yucatan ruins. It was all very strange and exciting.

In 1950, for the International Congress of Americanists (ICA) meetings in New York, Robert von Heine-Geldern, the Austrian dean of Southeast Asian archaeology, and Gordon Ekholm of the American Museum of Natural History had organized an exhibit that purported to show that much of pre-Spanish New World civilization had been imported from the Hindu-Buddhist world of Southeast Asia – and that the Maya pyramids imitated those of the Khmer in Cambodia. This was a novel and challenging and even infuriating show, but unfortunately they had gotten their dates wrong: the Maya were putting up these structures centuries before the Khmer had erected theirs. If there had been trans-Pacific diffusion, at least some of it went from east to west, and not the other way around!

There was nothing particularly Maya-looking about the huge Angkor Wat, the world's largest religious structure. I virtually had this place to myself, entranced by the more than one thousand reliefs of *apsaras*, divine nymphs created by the god Vishnu, to whom the temple was dedicated; their enigmatic Khmer smiles and lovingly depicted costume made one realize that these were probably portraits of the women in the ruler's palace harem eight centuries ago.

In a Phnom Penh bookstore I had picked up two excellent books, which I had with me in Angkor. One was Maurice Glaize's French-language guide to Angkor, in many ways still the best ever written, with its excellent maps. The other was a paperback by the epigrapher George Coedès, *Pour mieux entendre Angkor*, a wonderful synthesis in which he demonstrated that the Angkor temples, including the great Angkor Wat, were funerary structures erected to house the remains of dead kings. This made me wonder if that wasn't also true of the Maya pyramids, a subject on which I later wrote and published a paper in the *Southwestern Journal of Anthropology*.

My guess is that there weren't over 50 tourists in Angkor that week – today there might be as many as 5,000 or more. Among these was a nice little old American lady in a pink dress, carrying a parasol. In 1954, the guides spoke only French, and hers was trying to explain to her exactly what a linga was, while they were standing in front of the Phimeanakas temple. According to the 12th-century Chinese traveler Chou Ta-kuan, it was to this structure that the king repaired every night to sleep with a snake-woman. I couldn't help but overhear the explanation:

"*Mais madame, c'est une sorte de phallus.*"

"A what?"

"*Un phallus, madame, le membre viril du dieu!*"

I'm not sure that she ever accepted this.

The École Française d'Extrême-Orient – the counterpart of the Maya area's Carnegie Institution of Washington – had been in charge of excavating and reconstructing Angkor's glories ever since the late 19th century. They had done an outstanding job, but the ultimate origins of Khmer civilization had not concerned them much. I began to wonder about this, and this was the start of my lifelong concern with cultural beginnings. During World War II, French Indo-China was under Vichy rule, and the French archaeologist Louis Malleret was allowed to explore and excavate a fascinating site in the Mekong Delta known as Oc-Eo; this was a walled town dating to the early centuries of our era that had been a trading emporium with artifacts from all over the ancient world, including India and even Rome. I had read about it in an *Illustrated London News* bought in Hong Kong.

That was interesting enough, but what about even earlier time levels? Was there a Khmer Neolithic? This turned my thoughts to the Tonle Sap, the Great Lake just south of Angkor. Would there have been Neolithic villages all around it, on the order of the Lake Dwellings of Switzerland? Perhaps this would make a great dissertation subject when I returned to Harvard. I thank my stars that I didn't stay with this for long, as during the following three decades Cambodia fell apart in a way that nobody then could have predicted.

ℒ

My introduction to India consisted of about two hours of hostile interrogation in a hot, stuffy office by customs and immigration men. I had landed at the Calcutta airport that late February afternoon on a flight from Bangkok via Rangoon, and I was apparently the first American to arrive following the signing of a military cooperation pact between the U.S. and India's arch enemy, Pakistan. I was fair game for bureaucratic harassment, but the major accusation centered on the Thai and Cambodian textiles that I was carrying as gifts for my family back home. Was I intending to sell them in India without a permit? This line got nowhere, and the officer in charge set me free after admonishing me not to drink so much (he had noted my nose, red from sunburn, *not* alcohol).

Actually, for me Calcutta was but a way station on my route to Ceylon, that fabled tropical paradise that I had long hoped to see with my own eyes. In those days, the only way to get to Colombo from Calcutta was via a kind of airborne "milk run" across the Indian subcontinent, hopping south from city to city on propeller planes. After my nasty experience with the Indian authorities, I was not sorry to leave Calcutta at dawn the following morning. At this hour, there was no traffic whatsoever, but the taxi had to proceed slowly as it wound its way to the Dum Dum airport among white-shrouded bodies – tens, perhaps hundreds, of thousands of the city's poorest citizens slept at night in the streets. I have never seen such hopeless destitution anywhere, either then or since; skeletal arms extending to me in supplication from these wretches made it obvious that they were close to starvation.

If Calcutta had been a nightmare, Ceylon was a dream. Shaped like an enormous pear diamond, this was obviously the real jewel in the British Empire's crown. The Raj had only recently left, and the island's infrastructure was in perfect shape; the ethnic civil strife between Tamil Hindus and the Sinhalese Buddhist majority that has torn Sri Lanka apart in recent decades was not even on the horizon. Its magnificent beaches were crowded with colorful outrigger fishing boats, not European tourists. Every village in the lowlands was shaded with coconut palms and surrounded by green rice fields. I had never seen such a beautiful place, or such happy, healthy people. The great archaeological cities of the island – Anaradhapura and Polonnaruwa – were impressive, even if a bit of a letdown after Angkor (what place wouldn't be?), but I was particularly struck with Sigiriya. This site is a brick palace complex built in the 6th century AD on top of a huge red formation reminiscent of Australia's Ayers Rock. It is reached by a broad, balustraded staircase; the visitor ascending to the upper level is periodically confronted by natural niches in the rock containing polychrome paintings of well-endowed heavenly nymphs, the Technicolor counterparts of those *apsaras* on the walls of Angkor Wat.

The old Sinhalese capital of Kandy lies in the exact center of the island, at the pleasant elevation of 1,640 feet, and is the site of one of Buddhism's holiest shrines, the Temple of the Tooth or Dalada Maligava. To pious Buddhists, the tooth is one of the Founder's molars; some skeptical Westerners who claim to have seen it claim it is a fossil elephant tooth. The temple itself is a large building complex on an artificial lake created in the early 19th century by Sri Vikrama Raja, the last king of Kandy; he named the lake the "Sea of Milk," the cosmic ocean of the Hindu creation legend. One of the buildings adjoining the temple was built by Vikrama to hold the world's largest collection of

99

palm-leaf manuscripts in Pali, the sacred language of Theravada Buddhism.

I intended to spend several days in this beautiful town, but I had typically neglected to make a reservation in the Queen's Hotel, a grand colonial-era structure that was Kandy's only decent hostelry, located not far from the lake. After pleading with the front desk people, they gave me a relatively airless room located upstairs and at the back. What I had not counted on was that the hotel was jammed to capacity with a Hollywood film crew. They had just completed shooting *Elephant Walk*, starring Elizabeth Taylor, Peter Finch and Dana Andrews. When it appeared, this turkey of a movie was thoroughly savaged by the reviewers as a second-rate soap opera; its denouement was the destruction of a plantation by a herd of rampaging wild elephants, but this climactic moment was stupidly shot in a studio rather than in Ceylon.

Sadly, the stars had departed for their various homes. But I had already seen Miss Taylor in person, back in the summer of 1948, on Long Island's North Shore. An immensely fortunate acquaintance of mine had successfully invited the 16-year-old beauty to the Piping Rock Horse Show in Oyster Bay. And there she was, certainly the loveliest person I have ever laid my eyes upon. It was hard to look at the horses after this vision.

My first night in the hotel was the crew's last night before their return to Tinseltown, and they raucously and drunkenly celebrated until about 4 AM. The music and general racket weren't the only problems keeping me from my sleep. It turned out that there was a large, very live rat trying to get out of the toilet bowl in my bathroom. Flush though I did, the rat kept its head above the waters, until about my sixth or seventh try, when down it went to who knows where.

After breakfast, still a bit bleary from a very disturbed night, I decided to take a walk around the lake, in what turned out to be a delightfully wooded tropical park. About halfway around the four-kilometer circuit I encountered a British couple, an older, grey-haired man and a much younger woman. They introduced themselves as Frank Kingdon-Ward and his wife Jean, and we spent the next hour or so pleasantly chatting. I immediately warmed to these people, while trying to recall the name "Kingdon-Ward." Then I remembered. This was the world's most renowned plant explorer. Along with his many other adventures, in 1950, in the mountains of Assam, he and his wife had experienced the greatest earthquake ever recorded and had survived against tremendous odds. When I returned home, my father, an avid collector of rhododendrons including some of the ones discovered by Kingdon-Ward, was far more impressed by my acquaintance with the great explorer than by my having met the Chiang Kai-sheks.

It was almost noon, so the Kingdon-Wards, who were also staying in the Queen's Hotel, suggested that we repair to the hotel's lounge and have a drink with their friend Jack Ritchie, the Scots owner of a tea estate in the hills above Kandy. The beverage of the day was pink gin, a relic of Britain's tropical Empire. Now the lounge area faced onto the exit corridor of the hotel's ground floor. A young, mustached, olive-skinned man – clearly not a Sinhalese – walked by us on his way to the front door, a thermos flask tucked under his elbow. Jean suddenly stood up, saying excitedly, "That man has my flask!" What could I do? I was by far the youngest of our little group, and here was a lady in distress. Accordingly, and emboldened by what can only be called Dutch courage, I sprang up and ran after the alleged culprit, just in time to see him hop on a small bus parked outside the front entrance.

Like the fool I was, I entered the bus and tapped him on the shoulder.

"A lady in the hotel says that you have taken her thermos flask."

He spun around. The next thing I knew all the passengers in the bus leapt up menacingly; my heart sank as I realized that every one of them looked exactly like the supposed thief – young, swarthy, and with the same mustache. The shout went up:

"You have insulted the Royal Egyptian Navy!"

With that, I was manhandled out of the bus by a number of these naval officers (for that is what they turned out to be), who systematically started to beat me up, until two Sinhalese policemen rushed up and stopped the mayhem. Ushering me inside the hotel entrance, they told me I was lucky, since the Egyptian contingent (officers of a frigate that was paying a visit to Trincomalee) was in their cups, the result of drinking toddy – the local palm wine – for most of that morning.

Somewhat tattered and a bit bruised, I returned to our group, only to see Jean holding the identical flask, a tan affair marked with the royal monogram, "ER II."

"I found my thermos. I thought that man had stolen it."

It seems that both Jean and the Egyptian had been in London during the Coronation ceremonies of the previous year, and both of them had bought the flasks as souvenirs. As for myself, I felt like an idiot, but by others I was considered the chivalrous hero of the hour, and treated to much generous hospitality for the remainder of my stay on the island, including a visit to Jack's tea estate in Hewaheta.

The high point, however, took place in Kandy, where I was invited to the judging of the famous Kandyan dancers, to decide which group was to have the honor of performing before the Queen and Prince Philip on their imminent state visit to Ceylon. On the appointed day, I was allowed to sit in the front row with the very distinguished Sinhalese judges, all experts on this subject. This was by no means ballet in the western sense. Since this was still a caste society, in spite of the fact that most Sinhalese were Theravada Buddhists, the dancers and drummers were quite low caste. In fact, each troupe belonged to a distinct temple in the Kandyan uplands, including the Temple of the Tooth; in the days before the coming of the Raj, some of them were owned by the King of Kandy. Each year, on a specified day in July or August, they spectacularly dance and drum in the splendid Esala Perahera procession, along with numbers of gloriously arrayed temple elephants – the greatest of Asian ceremonies or celebrations, which my wife and I were fortunate to experience 24 years later.

The Kingdon-Wards and I traded Christmas cards for many years. There was an odd coda to the tale of the dust-up outside the Queen's Hotel. Early in our marriage, Sophie and I subscribed to the *Illustrated London News*, that wonderful but now defunct weekly journal that almost always had articles of archaeological interest. The ill-fated Suez crisis had started in late October 1956, when Britain, France, and Israel foolishly invaded Nasser's Egypt, and our magazine gave it complete coverage. This included a photograph of some Egyptian naval officers lying face down on the Suez sands, with a tough-looking Israeli soldier pointing a submachine gun in their direction. The caption noted that they were a contingent from a captured frigate. Were these my friends from Kandy? How many frigates could there have been in the Egyptian navy of those days? I kept this photo for many years.

𝒬

It took forever for my BOAC propeller-driven plane to get to Rome, where I was to spend a week with my Italian uncle and aunt. It broke down in Karachi, where the passengers had to spend a wretched, hot night courtesy of the airline; then subsequently landed at Bahrain without operational wing flaps, in a combination dust storm and fog, stopping just before it dropped over the runway's end into the Persian Gulf. I was more than a day late when I arrived at Rome's old Ciampino airport at 2:30 AM.

Aunt Natalie and her husband Count Leonardo Vitetti then occupied the middle part of the Palazzo Orsini, which in Renaissance times had been built into what remained of the classical Theatre of Marcellus. When I woke later on that morning, I looked out from my window across to the Capitoline Hill and the Campidoglio; just below the window were the columns of Roman ruins. Then the butler drew my bath, and I sank up to my chin into blue waters that had come straight from some old Roman aqueduct. Small wonder that the ancient Romans were so devoted to their baths.

You may well ask how my Italian relatives had survived the war. As Director-General of European Affairs, my uncle had become one of Count Galeazzo Ciano's right-hand men. But both had been marked by the Gestapo and SS as anti-German and perhaps even pro-Allied. There are SS documents describing Uncle Leonardo muttering "Schwein!" as he walked by a portrait of the Führer. The Nazis had apparently planned to arrest my aunt, whom they labeled "an American Jewess" on the basis of her maiden name, which they confused with "Cohen," and send her to a German concentration camp.

In all events, under German orders Mussolini signed his son-in-law Ciano's death warrant, and my uncle's also, in January 1944. Ciano was shot the next morning, but my uncle escaped and was hidden by the Vatican in Rome's Catacombs; my aunt and her small boy Tino were secreted in a series of convents. When Uncle Leonardo emerged from hiding with the liberation of Rome next July, he was pasty-white and had a long beard. He returned to the Italian Foreign Office, and over the next few decades became, successively, ambassador to France and ambassador to the United Nations.

I had never been in Italy before, and I fell head over heels in love with it and with Rome, already beautiful in early spring, as I was taken around it by my somewhat wild young cousin Tino, now an adolescent. All the world seems divided between Francophiles and Italophiles, and I must admit to being one of the latter. So were my parents, and my future wife and parents-in-law.

The last stage of my journey was a flight to Denmark, where my Uncle Bob was ambassador; this was another country new to me, and he took time off from official duties to drive me to see sights like Elsinore Castle.

Four days later, I was back in New York. My *wanderjahr* away from academia had taken me three years instead of one, but in the long run it had been worth it.

CHAPTER 8

Return of the Native

When I returned home, I found that my old friend Cary Welch was living in Cambridge, studying art history, and had become engaged to a Radcliffe student named Edith Gilbert. Edith, with her charming Khmer smile, told me about her best friend at Radcliffe, Sophie Dobzhansky, an anthropology major who among other singularities spoke Russian and Portuguese, and kept a tarantula spider in a bottle in her room. I would *have* to meet her, she said. Now "Dobzhansky" was a name that I knew well: Theodosius Dobzhansky, her father, was a near-icon to anthropologists, a great evolutionary biologist who had addressed the problems of human and racial origins from the perspective of population genetics.

That summer I spent at the ranch in Wyoming, where the foreman and caretaker was now Henry Westerman, a humorous, balding, old-time Westerner, and the best hunting guide in the state. The fall semester at Harvard was due to start in mid-September, and that is when I was supposed to register in the Graduate School. But I delayed it as long as I could for the trout fishing in Irma Lake, and above all for the hunting season; Henry and I stalked deer, pronghorn antelope, and elk, and he taught me how to butcher my kill. The first snows had already fallen at this altitude, and we could hear bull elk bugling across the valley as we approached tree line and looked down on the herd with binoculars. It was an experience not to be missed.

Not surprisingly the Anthropology Department's secretary was not pleased when I showed up late. Professor Howells's graduate course in physical anthropology was obligatory for all students. Known as "Bones" to us, it was supposed to do two things: 1) teach us all about the human skeleton and 2) teach us elementary statistics. All of Part 1 took place in an ancient lab room on an upper floor of the Peabody, and the class assignment for each budding anthropologist was to determine the cranial capacity of an Indian skull that had been excavated years ago in the ruins of Pecos Pueblo, New Mexico. As instructed, I inverted "my" skull, and was pouring mustard seed through the *foramen magnum* – this was to later be poured into a graduated cylinder – when I glanced across the table at a blonde, blue-eyed Radcliffe student who was also holding "her" skull in one hand. After a while we began to chat, and of all things got on to our mutual interest in Byzantine history (I had just read Robert Graves's *Count Belisarius*). Then I found out who she was: Edith's friend Sophie Dobzhansky. The minute I laid eyes on her, I knew that we would marry. And this we did the following June.

By late fall, we had decided to get engaged. Nothing would stop us, but there were a few obstacles that would have to be overcome, one of these being that I would have to tell my parents. This took place one evening on a weekend trip to their home (and mine) in Glen Cove, Long Island. My father was typically standing behind the bar with a scotch and soda in his hand, my mother was in the kitchen cooking dinner.

"Pop, I think there's something you ought to know. I'm going to be married."

The glass fell from his hand and landed on the floor. Neither he nor my mother had an inkling of this, and they neither knew nor had even heard of Sophie. But they took it wonderfully well, perhaps remembering their own elopement that had so angered my grandparents, and we broke out a bottle of wine to celebrate.

The next big step was for me to ask Sophie's father for her hand. I knew her parents well, as I had already been invited a number of times to dinner and to parties at their apartment on Claremont Avenue, near Columbia University where her father taught. Natalie Dobzhansky – Natasha – my future mother-in-law, was one of the finest human beings I have ever known, and I was sure that she was in favor of this marriage. Even though Sophie's advisor Clyde Kluckhohn had put in a good word for me with his friend Dobzhansky, I was still a little worried when I showed up by appointment one morning at his office and lab in Schermerhorn Hall. The entire place smelled strongly of Indian pudding (an American dessert of corn meal and molasses), since that was the food on which his many generations of *Drosophila* (fruit flies) were nourished for his genetic research. I need not have worried: in his rich Russian accent – much imitated by his many students – he gave his approval.

♃

Alfie Kidder had been denied tenure by Harvard in 1950 and was now at the University Museum in Philadelphia. A search then went out for a replacement for Tozzer and the chair he had occupied, the prestigious Bowditch Professorship, which carried not only a large salary, but publication money for final reports, half-time off for research, and financial support for field work. As usual, Tozzer, the kingmaker in the Department, had the final say. One would have expected him to find another Mayanist, but instead of this, and on his strong recommendation, Harvard hired an archaeologist who had never been in the Maya area, and who admittedly knew little about it.

This was Gordon Randolph Willey, a young archaeologist at the Smithsonian whose main achievements were his work on the prehistory of Florida's Gulf Coast and, more significantly, his pioneer study of the settlement pattern of one Peruvian coastal valley, done under the direction of James Ford (who thought the project up) and Julian Steward. Other New World specialists had been concerned about where ancient populations actually lived, and how, but Willey was the one who put this subject on the map, and this was enough to get him a Harvard appointment.

It was a fine appointment, for Gordon turned out to be a great teacher – not of undergraduates, for he was abysmal at this, but of graduate students such as ourselves. When I say "ourselves," I mean the unusual group of doctoral candidates who were in his orbit within the Peabody. Among these were the charismatic Don Lathrap, soon to become a pioneer archaeologist in South America's Montaña jungles; Don Thompson, Eric's son but more of an Andeanist than Mesoamericanist; Lee Parsons, another Mesoamericanist; Bill Bullard, a Southwesternist but destined to conduct the first broad settlement pattern survey in the Maya area; and Henry Nicholson, already an Aztec expert and deep in his study of Quetzalcoatl, the Aztec god and culture hero.

A bit on the periphery of this cluster of hard-core Americanist archaeologists was Morton Levine, who became a close and dear friend to Sophie and me. Mort was much older than we were, a Californian "with a face like an unmade bed," who had come to anthropology late after a varied career in radio and cultural affairs. He was entranced with Hallam Movius and his course on the European Paleolithic, and had planned (but never completed) a thesis for him on cave art. Mort was a great lover of art, and knew personally all of the main figures in the New York School of "Action Painting"; in a way, he was a kind of Boswell, or at least a Greek chorus, to these amazing people and the new world they had made. He was especially close to Mark Rothko, and it was that friendship that led to his sad downfall. When Rothko committed suicide in 1970, Mort was one of the three executors of his estate, and got inextricably tangled in the financial mess and civil suits that resulted from a controversial sale of the dead artist's canvases. He never recovered from this, and I'm sad to say died an unhappy man.

It was Willey's extraordinary seminars that made one appreciate his genius. He took Socratic teaching one step further – he wasn't the one to ask the questions, we were, and we had to answer them. He had a way of making you want to work as hard as you could so as not to let him down, and he treated us as colleagues with original ideas to be discussed, not as inferiors to be talked down to. It was an extraordinary time. In several of his seminars I found myself being drawn more and more into the origins of the earliest New World civilizations, such as the Chavín culture of Peru, and the much-fought-over Olmec civilization of Mexico. And in one seminar, Willey assigned me the job of trying to make sense out of Mesoamerica's Formative or Preclassic period, using published work.

This was no easy task, for very little that was reliable was then known about it. The very first radiocarbon dates were just coming out, but they weren't much help. Tulane University's Robert Wauchope had published a survey of the period, and concluded that there was a Neolithic-like "Village Formative" followed by a more complex "Temple Formative." Most authorities agreed that the very oldest village culture consisted of the simple pottery and figurines excavated years before in the Valley of Mexico by George Vaillant, which he called El Arbolillo and Zacatenco. For "Temple Formative," Wauchope pointed to the Late Formative massive temple mounds at Kaminaljuyú, on the outskirts of Guatemala City, that had been explored by Carnegie archaeologists.

Most contentious and puzzling of all was what to do with the Olmec civilization of Veracruz and Tabasco, claimed by George Vaillant, Matthew Williams Stirling (of whom more later), Mexican archaeologist Alfonso Caso, and the artist Miguel Covarrubias to be earlier than the Classic Maya; in opposition to this idea were virtually all of the Mayanists, especially Eric Thompson and Sylvanus Morley. Willey set me to sort this one out, too, and I quickly became convinced that the Mayanists were dead wrong. But at that point in time, neither I nor any other brash young graduate student would have dreamt that the Olmec culture – colossal heads and all – was not only earlier than the earliest Maya, but that it began centuries before El Arbolillo or Zacatenco or anything like it existed (so much for the "Village Formative" and the "Temple Formative").

I suspect that we who were in Willey's orbit let some of the other courses offered by the Department slide a bit – there simply wasn't enough time to do more than a perfunctory job in them. For example there was Hugh Hencken's offering – European prehistory from the Neolithic until the beginning of Rome, sarcastically known to the bored students as "Safety Pins" (Hencken was enamored with minute changes in bronze *fibulae*, garment pins). We did, however, work hard for Hal Movius, who put the students to assembling each year a massive bibliography on the Paleolithic, rewarding them at the end with ice cream bars.

Sophie's parents used to insist that they didn't know many Russians. Nothing could have been further from the truth. Their Claremont Avenue apartment was a virtual recreation of the apartment that they had occupied on Leningrad's Bolshoi Prospekt prior to their leaving the U.S.S.R. once and for all in 1927. It always seemed to have had émigré Russians in it, especially for Russian Easter, when Natasha – a great cook, like Sophie – produced *pascha* (a cholesterol-rich pyramid of farmer's cheese, heavy cream, hardboiled egg yolks, sugar, and vanilla) and *kulich*, a yeast-raised cylindrical cake. Everyone, including Sophie, would be babbling in Russian, and Sophie would have to translate for me.

There one would also meet many of her father's closest colleagues in evolutionary biology, such as L. C. Dunn, George Gaylord Simpson, and Ledyard Stebbins. During the latter part of the war, Dobzhansky had taken Natasha and Sophie to Brazil, and there over the course of two years he had set up a pan-Brazilian genetics program, so that Brazilian biologists would drop by, too. In his native Russia, though, he was considered an enemy – "a child of darkness," as the Communist propagandists put it – since he had not only refused to return to Stalin's Soviet Union, but he had attacked in print the infamous Trofim Lysenko, Stalin's pet scientist.

Occasionally, though, a visiting Soviet scientist or group of them (always attended by a political nursemaid) would drop by his lab. Dobzhansky had been to England for the centennial of the publication of Darwin's *The Origin of Species*, and he took an impish pleasure in telling these visitors that during the celebrations at Down House, he was allowed to look at the copy of *Das Kapital* that Marx had dedicated and sent to Darwin, and that he had found the pages – uncut!

My parents and Sophie's immediately took to each other, and remained friends until the ends of their lives. I don't know what the reason was. They inhabited totally different worlds; perhaps it was the unity of opposites. Politically, mine were rock-ribbed Republicans, and Sophie's had consistently voted for FDR once they became citizens, but it didn't seem to matter.

❧

Sophie had been raised in the Russian Orthodox church. Although both of her parents were evolutionary scientists, they were basically religious people, and her father wrote several books trying to reconcile

Darwinian evolution with a belief in some sort of mystic force (like Richard Dawkins in *The Blind Watchmaker*, I don't believe it can be done). However, he was by no means a Creationist, and would certainly have scorned the "Intelligent Design" notion that today grips a very small minority of biologists. Being anthropologists with a strong conviction that rites of passage were important, we both agreed that we should have an Orthodox wedding, which we did on 5 June 1955, in a now-disappeared Russian church on upper Madison Avenue. I had spent the morning in Bob and Betty Motherwell's brownstone on East 94th Street, with Mort Levine trying to calm my nerves by telling me funny stories.

The service itself, as a concession to all those American guests (largely my parents and their friends, fellow graduate students, and old colleagues from W.E.), had been shortened from the usual three hours to just one. As crowns were held above our heads, we had to circle the altar three times with the priest – whom Natasha said was another Varlam, right out of *Boris Gudonov* – as he enjoined us to have many children "who would wind up our legs like grapevines" (this turned out to be prophetic!). As the groom, I had paid for the many hundreds of candles, and for the choir. Don Thompson and Don Lathrap assured me later that it was the greatest singing they had ever heard, but I was so overwhelmed I don't remember any of it.

After the reception at Columbia's Faculty Club, we left right afterwards by train for our new apartment in Cambridge. The next morning Sophie took a final exam in the Byzantine history that had been a factor in bringing us together in the first place.

We honeymooned that summer at the ranch. Sophie, like her father, was a natural rider, and we had a fine time exploring on horseback all the trails on Carter Mountain. I bought a quite decrepit, second-hand Chevrolet in Cody, and we took a long camping trip down through the Rockies to the American Southwest, with only sleeping bags for equipment.

When in New Mexico, we stayed for a few days at the Ramah ranch of Nan and Evon Vogt. "Vogtie" was one of our Harvard teachers from whom I had learned most of what I was to know about the anthropology of religion, and he much later became Sophie's dissertation advisor after the premature death of Clyde Kluckhohn. The high point of the visit was the afternoon he drove us to the nearby Zuni Pueblo; with his two small boys, we sat on a roof above a plaza and watched in awe as one of the six rain societies performed a Kachina dance. It was electrifying: as the long line of masked dancers chanted in deep unison, a Turquoise Kachina ran up and down the line shouting in a high voice and shaking a turquoise-covered wand held in each hand. Shivers ran down my back.

Afterwards, Vogtie took us to meet a Zuni lady who had been one of his principal informants. She was the number one jeweler in the pueblo, and was proud of a complex eagle pendant of shell and turquoise that she was going to enter in the forthcoming competition in Gallup. As Vogtie and Sophie talked to her, I touched the pendant, which rested on a vinyl-covered table. It immediately separated into its constituents, since she hadn't yet fastened these together. Horrified at what I had done, I tried to push the pieces back without having anyone notice. I think she knew well what I was doing, and was amused.

The following summer, when Sophie was already a first-year graduate student, we went to Italy, bought a little Fiat 1100 sedan, and traveled all over that infinitely pleasing country. In 1956, it was grindingly poor, few people had cars (but lots of noisy Vespas), and one could still see farmers plowing with teams of white oxen. In Sicily, the main vehicle on the roads was a donkey-drawn, brilliantly painted cart, and threshing was carried out by horses. It was all very wonderful. We then drove the Fiat through France and crossed the English Channel to Dover, where we were detained for hours because I didn't have the right papers for the car.

After several weeks we had the car loaded on a small American freighter to carry us from the Port of London to Boston. Half way across, we ran smack into a North Atlantic hurricane, and spent several days facing into fifty-foot waves which could have broken the ship in two if the captain hadn't decided to just keep the propellers turning over. Neither of us got seasick, but the same couldn't be said of the other passengers, a miserable group of Yemenis on their way to jobs in Akron's tire factories. The only reading books I had with me all had terrifying shipwrecks in them, and this included *The Odyssey*.

Our first child, Nicholas, arrived that February, and when I brought him and Sophie back from the Mt. Auburn hospital in Cambridge, I don't think either of us knew what to do as he cried lustily and nonstop day and night. After two weeks we were exhausted from sleeplessness and anxiety. Rescue came in the form of the Dobzhanskys' close friends Dr. Ernst Mayr and his wife Greta: "Give us the baby, and you two go off to a good restaurant and don't come back till evening." We did so, and things went smoothly from then on as we learned how to take parenthood in our stride.

As I write this, only yesterday I learned from a Rome paper that Ernst Mayr had died at the age of 100; their correspondent hailed him as "the Darwin of the 20th century," and in many ways that was no exaggeration. Mayr, along with George Gaylord Simpson and Dobzhansky, had put together the "evolutionary synthesis" that was to dominate biology for over a half century.

In our married life in Cambridge, the Mayrs were very much like godparents to Sophie and me, and we saw much of them. They had bought a farm in southern New Hampshire, and spent every weekend there with their two good-looking daughters, often inviting us to bring small Nicholas along for the day or for a longer stay. One Saturday, just before lunch, a red MG came bouncing up the dirt road leading to the farmhouse, and a slim, curly-headed young man with a superior smile on his face alighted; I was told that this fellow was then dating the Mayr's daughter Christa. I instantly disliked him. But then I found out what the superior smile was all about: this was Jim Watson, fresh from the Cavendish laboratory where he and Frances Crick had just discovered the secret of life: the double helix of the DNA molecule.

Years later I have gotten to know and like a much mellower Jim Watson. Both of us were brash, arrogant young men then – but he had more of a right to be arrogant than I had!

10 Frisbie Place, the Cambridge location of Carnegie's Division of Historical Research, did not look much like Mt. Olympus, but to me it was exactly that. An old, three-story frame building with drably painted clapboards, it must have once been some Harvard professor's house back in the Victorian era. Anyone looking for it now would never find it: it was demolished many years back to make way for the enormous biochemistry labs of a more modern Harvard. The ghosts of its Maya archaeologists – all gone now – must wander like disconsolate wraiths among the glassware and computer screens.

In fact, 10 Frisbie Place was right next to the Peabody Museum, an arrangement that must have been simultaneously an advantage and a disadvantage to both sets of archaeologists, for relationships between the two had historically been somewhat uneasy. Tozzer had taken a dim view of Sylvanus Morley's *The Ancient Maya* for its glaring lack of scholarly apparatus, i.e. footnotes, and was not on the best of terms with Alfie Kidder, then the head of Carnegie's Maya operation. In fact, it was Tozzer and his close departmental ally Clyde Kluckhohn who were the faculty sponsors of Walter Taylor's *A Study of Archaeology*, the Harvard Ph.D. thesis which gave the Carnegie archaeologists a severe critical drubbing, and effectively finished Carnegie as an archaeological institution.

I began dropping in on the Carnegie archaeologists when still an undergraduate and neophyte Mayanist, a practice I resumed on my return to Harvard as a graduate student. They were like Olympian gods to me, seemingly always returning from the field and writing up their magical reports. Without exception, they were all about as kind and helpful as a newcomer to the subject could hope. Of course, not all of them were always there. Eric Thompson, for example, did most of his writing and research in his home at Harvard, in the rolling, apple-orchard country west of Boston, and only seldom came to Cambridge. The legendary Gus Stromsvik, the Norwegian excavator and restorer of Copan, was on hand for only a week or two each year (I suspect that some Carnegie people were not sorry to see the hard-drinking, party-loving "Don Gustavo" a long way from staid Cambridge).

"Doc" Kidder looked more like an archaeologist than anybody I have ever known. Not so long ago I saw a youthful photo of him, taken in his beloved Southwest (possibly at Pecos); with stubbly beard and a slouch hat, he was the spitting image of Indiana Jones. When I knew him, he had silver hair, a white mustache, blue eyes, and the kind of high color that often goes with pure English genes. He was on the best of terms with the students in Peabody; most of these were also Southwestern specialists, and for them he had the status of Founding Father. Every inch the gentleman, he was supportive of all of us, especially when grant-getting time rolled around.

From the intellectual standpoint, Tatiana "Tania" Proskouriakoff was clearly the Carnegie archaeologist with most direct influence on my generation of Harvard students. As I have said, I had become convinced that Thompson was dead wrong about the dating of stone monuments in the Olmec and somewhat later Izapan style. I went over to Carnegie and brought my ideas to Tania in her office. After exacting a promise not to tell Eric about her interest in this, she went on to give me a great deal of surreptitious support, even working out for me all possible calendar positions for the inscription on a stela from El Baúl on Guatemala's Pacific coast; Eric had claimed this to be Postclassic, that is, later than AD 900, when it actually dated to AD 36.

While a very cautious and conservative person herself, I think that she got vicarious enjoyment when brash young students were willing to go out on a limb; she made sure, though, that the limb was sturdy.

Another memorable person at 10 Frisbie Place was Karl Ruppert. Shy and retiring by nature, he had a delightful sense of humor. To me he was another Olympian, one who had worked closely with Sylvanus Morley (whom I never knew) and with Earl and Ann Morris at Chichen Itza – the first Maya site I had ever seen. More of an engineer than an anthropologist, Karl was a seasoned explorer of the old school. He was a good friend of Lydia Weare, the lady who ran the Cambridge Center for Adult Education, where he and Ledyard Smith – also a Carnegie great – had taken a course in, of all things, upholstering! She had asked Karl to give a course in Maya archaeology to the local bluestockings; Karl was not the teaching type, so he declined, but offered my place in place of his. This became my first teaching experience and the basis for all my subsequent courses (and, I must admit, for my book, The Maya).

One day, on the eve of Karl's retirement from Carnegie, I dropped in for a chat with him at 10 Frisbie Place. After describing to me his new house in Santa Fe, where he was going to move in the next few months, he asked me if there were any books I wanted in his office, as he had very little bookshelf space in Santa Fe. I looked around me in wonder. There were all of the Carnegie publications in their green cloth covers (including the classic, five-volume *Inscriptions of the Peten*), the Tozzer festschrift, a complete run of *American Antiquity*, and so on. In a small voice, I asked which ones I could take. Karl's reply was, "They're all yours!". This man, a great pioneer of Maya archaeology, had enough confidence in a mere graduate student to give him his entire working library. The thought still humbles. Many years later, I dedicated *The Maya Scribe and His World* to his memory.

Let me not leave the idea that Eric Thompson was some kind of curmudgeon. He could also display considerable kindness to young students, and always answered their questions with long, thoughtful letters. Walter Taylor was certainly right in singling him out among the Carnegie archaeologists as the one most concerned with important cultural problems. Eric was often right, but when he was wrong, he was very, very wrong, as became only too clear in the next decade or two over the question of the nature of the ancient Maya script.

CHAPTER 9

Into the Past on the Soconusco Coast

In the cohort of graduate students that orbited around Gordon Willey and his seminars, our Bible was a Penguin paperback called *Archaeology from the Earth*, written by Sir Mortimer Wheeler. Long out of print, I still think it is the best "how-to" introduction to field archaeology. It made one want to grab a trowel and go out and dig something old. But wait a minute! This is not what Sir Mortimer wanted you to do, far from it. He had utter contempt for what he called "shooting into the brown," digging a site just because it's there. Translating his military terminology into lay terms (he was a brigadier in World War II), you first had to formulate a problem, and then devise a campaign to achieve your goal. Controlled stratigraphy and recording of same were everything, and following his example you laid out a grid over the site and excavated it in squares, leaving vertical balks between squares, thus giving you three-dimensional control. From this you could read the story that the site had to tell (look at the plates of my published final report on the site that I used for my Ph.D. dissertation, and you will rightly guess that I took Wheeler's paperback with me into the field).

Here is how I laid out the problem of the origin of settled life in southeastern Mesoamerica:

1. A few years back, Richard "Scotty" MacNeish had discovered a preceramic (pre-pottery) Archaic stage in the relatively dry regions of central Mexico and Tamaulipas, but this seemed more closely allied with the Desert Culture of the arid American West. It was unlikely that this is what the earliest village cultures would have looked like in the Maya area and elsewhere.

2. In contrast, for this period in the southeastern United States, there were extensive shell-midden villages along the river systems and

near the coast, indicating a stable way of life based on fishing, gathering of shellfish, and hunting. Especially along parts of the Florida coast and in Louisiana these were often found on lagoon-estuary systems near the sea. In the latest levels in these middens, primitive pottery made its appearance.

3. Ergo, if I made an intensive survey along the Pacific coast of Guatemala, where there was a whole series of lagoons and estuaries from the Chiapas (Mexican) border in the northwest to the frontier with El Salvador in the southeast, there was a good chance that I would not only find Archaic shell mounds but also the beginnings of Formative village culture. On the Chiapas Coast, Philip Drucker had found just such a shell mound at a site called Islona de Chantuto, and although his publication on it didn't tell us very much, it did seem like the sort of site I was hoping to find.

The only archaeologist who had ever bothered himself very much with Guatemala's hot, flat Pacific coastal plain was Carnegie's Ed Shook, who proved that this region was extraordinarily rich in sites of all periods. But Ed, while in my mind the person who knew more about Guatemala than anybody else, had a very poor track record when it came to publishing his data. However, I knew that everyone who worked for Carnegie had to keep a field diary, and was obliged to send back its duplicate pages to 10 Frisbie Place at regular intervals. With the dismantling of Carnegie's archaeological program, these were now in the Peabody archives, and I got out Ed's detailed and informative notes on a survey that he had done all along the Guatemalan border with Chiapas, from the highlands down to the seashore at the little fishing village of Ocós.

Lo and behold, just north of Ocós, a dirt road had sliced through a mound on a small *finca* called La Victoria, and Ed had seen quantities of marine shells scattered in the dusty track, along with potsherds that he said looked like those of Las Charcas, then the oldest Formative culture known in the Guatemalan highlands. *This* would be my target site.

The next step would be to get some money to go there and dig La Victoria. Under Willey's advice, I applied to two possible sources, Philadelphia's American Philosophical Society and the American Council of Learned Societies (ACLS), foolishly splitting my budget

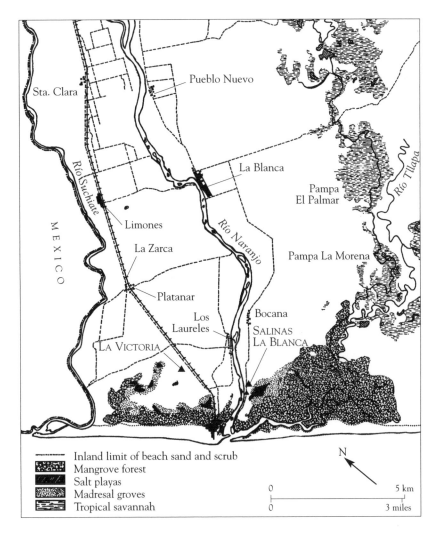

Map of the Pacific coast of Guatemala near the Mexican border, an area rich in Formative sites. I excavated La Victoria in 1958, then returned four years later with Kent Flannery to work at Salinas La Blanca.

between the two. Only the people in Philadelphia came through, so I was left with only half the money I needed, so I had to dig into my not-all-that-large savings account to make up the rest.

Now, one can't just go off to a country like Guatemala and dig away where one pleased. I had no permit, nor did Gordon Willey, who wanted to dig at the Classic Maya site of Altar de Sacrificios, nor did

Bill Bullard, who had plans for a foot survey of the northeastern part of the country. So, I became point man for all three permits, and flew down to that lovely country to make contact with the authorities.

In 1955, there was no huge archaeological bureaucracy of the type that already existed in Mexico. The country's Instituto de Arqueología, Etnología e Historia (IDAEH) consisted of a handful of very nice scholars and artists, housed in offices of an old museum that had been built decades before for an international exposition, and was headed not by an archaeologist but by a charming, gentlemanly intellectual named Carlos Samayoa Chinchilla. Carlos, whom I came to know as a friend, had been private secretary to Don Jorge Ubico, longtime president, and had written a wry, humorous account of his experiences in a book called *El Dictador y Yo* ("The Dictator and I"). His wife Claudia Lars was one of Central America's best known poets, and a powerful personality.

As Director of IDAEH, Carlos had been given an antique black Packard sedan that had once been the official car of former President Juan Arévalo; a real gas-guzzler, Carlos had baptized his temperamental vehicle as *El Dinosauro*. Months later we were driving together to visit the site of Mixco Viejo, and Carlos was in the front passenger seat, and Sophie, and Claudia, and I in the back. Claudia turned to me and, pointing to her husband, said in a strong voice, "Look at him! He is all water, I am all fire!"

An archaeological permit had ultimately to be signed by the President of the Republic himself. Carlos may have been "all water," but in five days he had guided me through all levels of bureaucracy, and I flew back to Cambridge with all three permits signed by *El Presidente* himself. Those were wonderful days!

Sophie and little Nicholas came with me to Guatemala, and we lived for a year in a rented house with a garden, in the upscale Zona 10. All this had been arranged for us by Barbara Aldana, Doc Kidder's daughter who was married to the best doctor in the country. Among the other amenities, we had hired what everyone agreed was the capital's finest cook; at first María Teresa Hernández apologized to us that she couldn't cook American food, but we assured her that we wanted to eat Guatemalan style, and so we did. I had had enough American food in all those boarding schools. The capital was then a small, clean, colonial-style city, not the polluted, crowded megalopolis it later became.

Next I bought a used – as I found out later, much used – Land Rover, and drove down to the Pacific coastal plain. It was like descending from a New England spring into a raging furnace. The nearer I drew to Ocós the hotter it got: this is a part of the world where it doesn't even cool off by night. Small wonder it had been studiously avoided by other archaeologists. Ocós itself was almost on the beach, a small, thatched-roof fishing community with one combined store (*tienda*) and bar. Sophie was going to join me there as soon as Natasha arrived in the capital to baby-sit Nicholas, but where were we going to live? There was a palm-thatched dance hall just above the lovely, white-sand beach, and this I rented, and there is where we slung our hammocks.

La Victoria consisted of about ten low, very unprepossessing mounds about a mile north of Ocós. After I had gotten permission from Don Oscar Méndes, its owner, I began work there with 14 local laborers, laying out a grid of squares just like Sir Mortimer had recommended. At the same time, I began mapping it. In graduate school, even though Harvard offered a fairly useless course in field archaeology, I learned nothing about how to make a map, so I had taken on my own a semester course in the subject given by the Dean of the Engineering School; his mantra, constantly reiterated in a Kansas twang, had been "if it is not right, it is wrong." Between that and what I had learned with the Agency, I knew what to do.

Before I had gone down to this part of the coast, a member of one of the five or six elite families who pretty much ran the country warned me that these people – all Ladinos (mixed race), not Maya Indians – were mostly dangerous Communists, and to watch out. One day Alberto, my foreman asked me this:

"*Jefe* ('boss'), we've been having an argument while you were eating your lunch. Tell us, which of these two countries is Communist, Russia or the United States?"

So much for the Red Menace.

While we would be out at the site during the day, and since the dance hall had no real walls, I had hired Augusto, a reliable, middle-aged local to watch it for us. One day we sat together on the edge of the platform watching the sun go down as a golden ball into the Pacific. Augusto turned to me and remarked, "Some people here say that there is no end to the ocean, it just keeps going on and on." I assured him that wasn't the case, since I had been on the other side, in a country called China. He was astonished; I'm not sure he believed me.

This was actually the finest beach in Guatemala, consisting of white sand rather than the usual black, foot-burning black sand, the gift of the chain of volcanoes. We once witnessed it used in an astonishing way, one not recorded in any anthropology book. One afternoon we came back from La Victoria, and saw that there were many hundreds of Mayas walking about, all the women in the yellow embroidered *huipils* (blouses) typical of the Mam people of San Marcos. We found out that they had come down from the highlands on a pilgrimage, stopping at the border town of Ayutla to pay homage to the *Señor de Las Tres Caídas*, Christ of the Three Stumbles (on his way to Calvary). One elderly lady was squatting in our doorway, obviously relieving herself. When we protested, she insisted, "*pero solo aguita,*" "only a little water"!

The following day was a Sunday, and we weren't working. By now there were thousands of Mam Mayas on the beach. They had brought their shamans, who had constructed sand altars. All were praying, we learned, "to the God of the Sea," and everyone was taking ritual dips in the ocean. We did nothing about this astonishing ritual, as we had assumed that some smart social anthropologist had already written all about it. Later we found that nothing could have been further from the truth. I learned my lesson: archaeologists should do their own ethnographic observation, even if it only means asking one's workmen about their lives and the environment in which they and their families make a living.

Sophie eventually stayed in Guatemala City, for as we dug down into the site, more and more materials – especially broken pottery – had to be taken up to the capital in white cloth bags, washed, and labeled. It wasn't until then that I really could see what we were uncov-

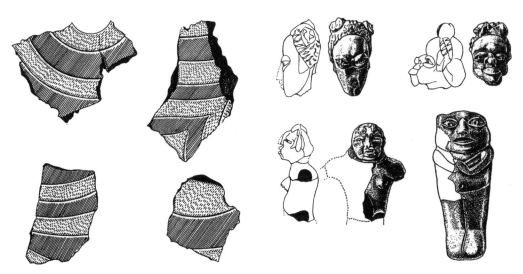

Pottery and figurines of the Early Formative Ocós culture at La Victoria.
The potsherds have zoned iridescent bands applied over a specular red slip.

ering, so I drove to the city with a fully-loaded Land Rover every two
weeks or so. Here is what we were finding:

The top meter of the site was full of a locally made pottery called
San Juan Plumbate, a lustrous, probably glazed ware that Eric Thompson had previously proved belonged to the end of the Late Classic – a
date of about AD 800–900 wouldn't be so far off. The next couple of
meters below that proved to represent the main occupation of the site,
a cultural phase which I christened "Conchas"; it had white-slipped
pottery as hard as concrete, and quantities of hand-made, clay figurines
with big punched holes for pupils. Several of the sherds were trade
items from Ed Shook's Las Charcas phase, so if he was right I had
already hit a really early occupation in the Formative (I now know that
Conchas and Las Charcas both belong in the Middle Formative).

But cultural remains kept on going below this, along with lots of
marine shells, especially mussels. I had thought that I would find the
elusive preceramic Archaic that I had hypothesized would be here, but
it never did show up. This new phase, which I called Ocós, was like
nothing I, or anyone else, had ever seen. Back at our house in the city,
Sophie had laid out the pottery and figurines on trestle tables in our
garage. I've examined and handled Mesoamerican ceramics from every

period and area, including the spectacular painted and carved vases and bowls of the Classic Maya, but I still think that Ocós (and related) pottery is the most perfect and beautiful ever produced in the Pre-Columbian New World. The typical form was the *tecomate*, a thin-walled, neckless, globular jar, but there were also flat-botttomed clay dishes. Many of these had been decorated with all sorts of weird techniques, such as rocker-stamping – where the edge of a cockle-shell has been "walked" in zigzags over the surface of the wet clay; and impressing with textile- or cord-wrapped paddles. But the strangest of all was painting in zones or stripes, or just on the rims, with a lustrous, iridescent, reflective slip with a generally pinkish cast. It reminded me of what women sometimes use to paint their fingernails.

We never did find a whole vessel, but one could reconstruct these on paper from fragments. Consider one kind of *tecomate*: this was completely slipped in deep red, specular hematite, so that the surface gave off glints of light as you turned the jar. Over it some ancient potter had applied an iridescent slip in bands contained between lightly incised lines. Spectacular! Ocós clay figurines were very strange, running to what reminded me of grotesque caricatures by Leonardo da Vinci.

What I had uncovered, not at all on my original agenda, was the first Early Formative material ever discovered in southeastern Mesoamerica and the Maya area. By the radiocarbon method, it had to date no later than 1000 BC, and probably a lot earlier.

I may have been *jefe* to my workmen, but my own *jefe*, Gordon Willey, came to visit me near the end of the season, accompanied by Ledyard Smith; Ledyard, one of Carnegie's finest archaeologists and the main digger of Uaxactun, became Gordon's right-hand man at Altar de Sacrificios. This was now the height of the dry season, and it was broiling hot even by Ocós standards. The only way I had to cope with this was by jumping into the surf at the end of each day's work. The Petén jungle where the big Maya sites were located was the Arctic compared to this, and I don't think either of my visitors liked it. I took them out to the site, where Gordon gave me a great piece of advice: "Mike, you've dug more than enough for your thesis. Stop here, or you'll never get it finished."

After a sweaty night in our hammocks, I was to drive them up the next day to a coffee *finca* owned by friends of Ledyard. The dust on the road, which passed through banana plantations, was almost two feet thick, and choking clouds of it swirled up into the Land Rover's interior. The vehicle came to a sudden stop, as we had hit and snagged a tree root hidden in the dust. Gordon, who was sitting in the front passenger seat, was hurled forward, slamming his forehead against a bolt sticking out from the windshield. Blood steamed down from the wound. "My God," I thought, "I've done it now. There goes my Ph.D." I'd come close to giving my thesis director a frontal lobotomy. But we staunched the wound, and Gordon emerged none the worse for wear. Ever since they had joined me, I had been trying to convince them that Harvard should give up the Petén for the Pacific coast, where there were untouched sites everywhere, but it was now clear to me that this was not to happen.

Once back in the city, Gordon came to see what I had. He was genuinely impressed with our Ocós ceramics and especially with iridescent painting, for he had seen almost identical pottery from the excavations by Betty Meggers and Cliff Evans (of the Smithsonian) in early sites on the coast of Ecuador. They were going to be at the forthcoming ICA meeting in San José, Costa Rica, and he encouraged me to go and bring a sample of my pottery with me for a "show-and-tell" session.

I spent the rest of the year in Guatemala in the basement of the National Museum, analyzing my collections. Doc Kidder and several Carnegie archaeologists had made a remarkable research laboratory here, with type collections from every phase of every site ever surveyed or excavated in Guatemala, so I could really make valid comparisons with what I had dug up. Unfortunately, this basement was also where the walrus-mustached, cantankerous janitor of the museum, old Don Aparicio, had established his home, along with his even more surly, fat wife and a few of their noisy grandchildren. The mere smell of his wife's cooking – she liked old, rancid grease – was enough to turn one's stomach, but I persisted.

One morning Carlos Samayoa came downstairs with an elderly British couple, to show them what I was doing. It wasn't long before I realized who these distinguished-looking people were: Professor

Arnold Toynbee and his wife. They stayed on after Carlos returned to his office, asking highly intelligent questions about my archaeological work. I tentatively asked them if they had any plans for lunch. No, they said, so I invited them home. They went back to their hotel, and I called up Sophie. Unflappable as always, she and our cook María Teresa were quite ready when the Toynbees arrived. The entrée was a fresh fish just bought in the market, with a sauce of tiny, fiery *chiltepes*, the very hottest of all the chile peppers that Guatemala had to offer. I was horrified whether this might be more than our guests could take. Quite the opposite – the world's most renowned historian asked for more of the same, and then even more after that!

꩜

In looking to solve a problem, I had found another problem. Most archaeologists from the 19th century on have believed in a progressive cultural evolution: that human cultures have evolved from the simpler to the more complex, and that is probably mostly what has happened. But, we now realize, not necessarily so. For example, some of the most advanced art ever made by our ancestors is also the earliest – the 30,000-year-old paintings of Chauvet Cave in France show advanced anatomical knowledge, scenography, and a degree of three-dimensionality that was not to be seen again until the days of Classical Greece and Rome. Ocós pottery and its strange clay figurines were vastly more sophisticated than the Conchas culture that followed. When I showed my results to Román Piña Chan in Mexico, this dour supposed expert in the Mesoamerican Formative dismissively informed me that I had a case of reversed stratigraphy, that is, somehow the bottom of the site had ended on top.

Doc Kidder came to my rescue. He urged me to pay a visit that summer to the New World Archaeological Foundation (NWAF) in Tuxtla Gutiérrez, the capital of the state of Chiapas, where their archaeologists had uncovered a very long sequence of Formative cultures at the site of Chiapa de Corzo. Kidder had a secondary motive in making his recommendation, though: he was on the NWAF board of directors, and wanted to find out if this really was a scientifically legitimate program. The reason for his disquiet was that the NWAF had been set up by his lawyer friend Thomas Stuart Ferguson, a retired FBI operative and a believing Mormon, and was totally funded by the Church of Jesus Christ of the Latter Day Saints. Ferguson and others had convinced the Church authorities that Zarahemla, the Promised Land of the Book of Mormon, was in Chiapas, and that extensive digging in Formative period remains there would provide proof of the truth of the Book of Mormon.

What I actually found when I arrived at their headquarters was not a group of naïve fanatics (these sometimes showed up from Salt Lake City) but some of the finest archaeologists I have ever known. At their head was Gareth Lowe, an absolutely serious and dedicated scholar who then and until his recent death was, as far as I am concerned, "Mr. Formative Mesoamerica." I was taken through all of the Chiapa de Corzo materials, and Gareth showed me that what I had found was no anomaly: their oldest culture, Chiapa I, also had lots of *tecomates* and rocker stamping, and was stratigraphically underneath something that looked like Conchas, but still probably not as old as Ocós. This is why I wasn't at all worried later when Piña Chan pulled his long face.

And Doc Kidder need not have worried about the NWAF: this was a first-class operation.

So, I *did* go down to Costa Rica that July for the Americanists' meeting. The hostess for the whole event was Doris Zemurray Stone, probably the richest person in all Central America; her father had been Samuel Zemurray, a fruit peddler on the New Orleans waterfront until he figured how to take over the banana business by bringing this product into the United States by refrigerated ship. Eventually he became Chairman of the United Fruit Company.

She had organized the ICA event with two close friends and associates. One was the respected archaeologist Samuel Kirkland Lothrop, an old Grotonian and Harvard graduate who had written the standard work on the pottery of Costa Rica and Nicaragua. The other was considerably more dubious, one Charles (Carlos) Balser, a San José *hotelier* and the kingpin of a ring of *huaqueros*, the semi-underworld looters of ancient Costa Rican burial grounds. Doris was used to having her way in everything; the Spanish-born archaeologist Pedro Armillas once described her to me as "a *Guardia Civil* type," not exactly a compliment.

Doris had worked out the room assignments for those attending the conference. The really big shots like Gordon Willey were put into San José's best hotel. I, a mere graduate student, found myself in a hot, windowless room in what I soon discovered was a whorehouse. Through the thin, pasteboard walls that night I could hear everything that transpired in the adjacent rooms. The next day I moved quarters to a very pleasant motel on the outskirts of the city.

Well, Cliff and Betty did show up with their Ecuadorian material, and so did several Ecuadorian archaeologists, so we had an exciting time comparing my iridescent pottery with theirs. I wrote this all up in a later article for the *American Anthropologist*, suggesting that there had been extensive sea traffic at a very early date between the two areas along the Pacific coast, via sailing rafts. I still think so.

The *Guardia Civil* lady and Lothrop gave a general lecture on Costa Rican prehistory which was notable in that they had concluded there was *no* history here: that everything on view in the museum could be assigned to one or the other tribal-linguistic group, such as Chorotega or Boruca or Nicarao, and that none of it was very old. But I had seen in a number of cases some pottery whistles from the Nicoya Peninsula in the northwestern part of the country that had been decorated with zoned rocker-stamping much like what could be seen in very early cultures in both Mesoamerica and in Peru. At the end of their presentation, I rashly popped up to point out this fact, and that I was willing to bet that excavation would prove that there was a long sequence of cultures here. What I didn't dare say was that their kind of pre-stratigraphic archaeology was based on pot-hunting, not on science. It didn't take long for both of them to stand up and say that I didn't know what I was talking about. In other words, "Pipe down, pipsqueak."

"All right," I thought, "I'm going to come back some day and prove you guys wrong." And so I did, the next year. But that is another story.

CHAPTER 10

Tennessee

The job market for anthropologists during the late 1950s was not good. A few years earlier it seemed that anyone, no matter how incompetent, could land a teaching post in a university, and many did. Nevertheless, Willey found me one, at the University of Tennessee's main campus in Knoxville, and I took it gratefully. But I hadn't finished analyzing all my materials from La Victoria in Don Aparicio's basement, and I needed to do this for my dissertation, and that hadn't been written yet, either. So Sophie and I and our first-born didn't move to Tennessee until after Christmas 1958.

It must have been a wrenching move for Sophie. I know it was for me. The UT Department of Anthropology back then consisted of just two people, with office and laboratory in the basement of the Biology building. This, like other academic structures at the university, was arranged around the gigantic UT football stadium, as though ancient Rome had been arranged around the Colosseum, which it was not. The two anthropologists were both well-known archaeologists, Madeleine Kneberg and T. M. N. "Tom" Lewis. Madeleine was blonde, in her middle age, and very bright; she had been a graduate student in physical anthropology at the University of Chicago, but never took her degree. Rumor had it that while there she was the mistress of a visiting professor from Great Britain, the famed A. R. Radcliffe-Brown, which would not surprise me as "A.R." was a notorious womanizer, and she must once have been very good looking. Tom had only a Princeton undergraduate degree, but had gravitated into Southeastern archaeology.

I had no real office, nothing but an empty space between storage shelves, where I placed the wonderful Mesoamerican library that had been given me by Karl Ruppert; this was my lifeline to another world. Right outside my window was a large, open garbage can where they placed the discarded sacrificed animals from the biology labs upstairs.

Madeleine and Tom were a real team, and had collaborated on the widely admired final report on their excavations along the Tennessee River, *Hiwassee Island*, with Madeleine responsible for the watercolors reconstructing Mississippian cultural life on the river before the arrival of the Europeans. They were a team in another sense, since they had been lovers for decades, but couldn't marry as Tom's wife refused to give him a divorce. So when I arrived in the Department it became a *ménage à trois*, if only in the academic sense. The first thing they did was to have themselves declared research professors, and leave all the teaching to me.

This was no small matter. Although there was only one course given by the Department, an undergraduate "Introduction to Anthropology," when Madeleine taught it, it had about 800 registered students, with exactly one instructor (soon to be me) and no assistants. Because of its sheer size, the course had to be given in three sections, with identical content and even the same jokes to be repeated each day, three times over. It wasn't long before I learned that this was the most notorious "gut" course at UT, almost a guarantee of an easy pass, which made it a favorite with the university's athletic coaches.

Much has changed at UT since I was there, but in my time anyone who was white, and whose daddy had paid his taxes, was assured of admission (blacks had a "separate but equal" institution, Knox College, but it was far from that). Curiously, although UT was theoretically segregated, native Cherokees were OK, so there were quite a lot of these in the university. What this meant was that it was up to the instructor to get rid of obviously hopeless students, but these had to fail a course three times to be in real academic trouble.

Since UT was on the quarter system, the course had three segments (so Madeleine instructed me). The first was physical anthropology, *not* human evolution – I was told that if I wanted to bring in evolution, I would have to teach it only as a possible theory. This got my back up; I assured her I would teach it as a fact, even though I was quite aware I was breaking Tennessee law. The next segment was to be world archaeology and culture history, most of it, she told me, to be devoted to Tennessee, with their book *Tribes that Slumber* as the text (somewhat obstinately, I never mentioned the name of the state at all in my classes).

Last was to be social anthropology, and here is what I did with it. I took three cultures or peoples that existed on increasing levels of complexity, and told the students about them in turn. We began with the Central Australian aborigines as described in the classic ethnography by Spencer and Gillen, and I took a perverse delight in describing in gory detail the practice of initiation by sub-incision: splitting the penis "just like you'd do to a hotdog." This got their attention! Having dealt with a hunting-gathering group, we next moved to an agricultural village culture, that of the Hopi, and this was a big success. As a finale, I told them, we would be studying a great, complex civilization. I'm sure that most were thinking of Greece or Rome, instead of which they got – the Ashanti kingdom of West Africa. There were gasps and groans of disappointment. The lady professor who taught a popular course on "Dixie History" tried to have the administration censure me, but they backed me up.

In actuality, some of these young men and women were as good as any that I have seen anywhere, and I felt sorry for them in the midst of such mediocrity. As you might have guessed, among the students were the complete football, baseball, and basketball teams, but there were salvageable candidates even among these. One particular football player (whom I'll call Leon) intrigued me, since he looked and talked just like Andy Griffith and was really a charming guy. He had a bunged-up eye that I assumed had come about on the gridiron, but others told me that he had been injured as a boy when his daddy's illegal still blew up. I really wanted to pass Leon, and learned that he came from a place up in the hills called Soddy-Daisy, where his family made moonshine and raised roosters for cockfights (also illegal). So, I gave him an assignment to write a paper on chicken-fighting, about which I knew almost nothing. He passed.

This was about the only essay-based grade I gave in my one-and-a-half years at UT. With 800 students, one could only give multiple-choice exams, and I could only correct all of these with Sophie's help. I was near despair, as I had a dissertation to write, but I completed it, in spite of everything.

If I've made it sound as though Madeleine and Tom weren't making it easy to write my thesis on La Victoria, that would be a large mistake on my part. Tom had almost single-handedly created the Tennessee Archaeological Society, the most active such organization in the country, and he edited their journal, *The Tennessee Archaeologist*. He and Madeleine had first-hand knowledge of how to write and illustrate an archaeological report, and they taught me these skills, which I never would have learned had I hung around Harvard hoping for an appointment some day. This was the first time I had written anything like a book, and I desperately needed their advice. We had our differences, to be honest, but for this I'm eternally grateful.

❧

We had rented a very small house in a development in Maryville, a town to the south of Knoxville and very close to the beautiful Great Smoky Mountain National Park. It wasn't much of a house – like all the others in the development it was a jerry-built affair put up to house the family of an officer attached to the nearby air base. Maryville was still a very Southern place – if you didn't belong to one of the local fundamentalist churches, you basically didn't exist. Like Knoxville, it was totally "dry," although you could buy liquor from one of the parsons. The KKK (Ku Klux Klan) was in the Yellow Pages, with headquarters over the Sherwin-Williams paint store. But one could easily escape up into the Park, a truly breathtaking experience.

I would drive north to Knoxville every morning, leaving Sophie behind to cope with whatever such a place could offer. It was a very lonely life for her, but she never complained. Our second son Andy was born in our first year there, so she had her hands full with two small boys. Her greatest worry was also mine – that we would be stuck here forever, and Nick and Andy would grow up with East Tennessee accents, talking through their noses like former Republican senator Howard Baker.

In spite of our isolation, friends among the UT faculty did their best to make us feel at home. Our particular friend was J. Ives "Tack" Townsend, who had been one of my father-in-law's Ph.D.s from Columbia. Tack was a real Southerner from South Carolina; his UT students once complained that they couldn't understand his Southern accent! Through Tack we got to know practically the entire Biology Department; they had a strong genetics program, thanks to money from the nearby Oak Ridge atomic facility, and had no compunction about teaching Darwinian evolution, either.

As usually happens when there is Prohibition, everyone drank more than they normally would have. To buy alcohol, one had to drive all the way to Nashville, and then bring the bottles back home hidden in the car's trunk. For this reason, I and my friends more often had the higher proof hard liquor in our homes rather than the less economical (in space) wine. It was therefore like manna from Heaven when my parents appeared in Maryville one day, on a drive through the Blue Ridge and Smokies. My father had kindly brought for us a case of Möet & Chandon pink champagne, along with a jar of beluga caviar, and we made a feast of the latter with Sophie providing Russian *blini* pancakes.

That June, I showed up in Cambridge to get my Harvard Ph.D. Doctoral candidates didn't receive their parchment during the commencement ceremony itself; instead we repaired in our crimson gowns to University Hall. Clyde took me over, inveighing against President Pusey for his hypocrisy and psalm-singing (he was right about that). The coveted documents were handed out by the Dean, McGeorge Bundy, soon to become famous as one of John Kennedy's best and brightest. Here is approximately what "Mac" Bundy told us:

"Men (!), soon you will go out all over America and you will be marching in academic processions like the one today. I can assure you now that the quality of the institution in which you are teaching will be judged by how many crimson gowns like yours can be seen in that procession."

And this from a Yale graduate!

During these celebrations I managed to slip away for a meeting with Tania Proskouriakoff in the basement smoking room of Peabody. Nervously puffing at her ubiquitous cigarette, she told me that she had found "something interesting" while working out the dates on the stelae of Piedras Negras, the Maya site where she had worked as a staff artist in the 1930s for the University of Pennsylvania. "Something interesting"! – what this supremely modest woman had found out was that these dates marked not astronomical events or anything like that, but important points in the lives of the Maya dynasts who had ruled this Classic city. I immediately realized that she had made one of the greatest archaeological discoveries of all time: the texts on Maya monuments recorded real history, not mumbo-jumbo. She published her data the next year in *American Antiquity*, and a new era began in Maya studies.

But how to actually *read* these texts in the Maya language? How this aspect of the Maya "code" was broken is another story that I'll touch upon later.

ℒ

Dear Mr. Coe,

We recieved your letter of May 22nd making enquiry
about getting rooms are are a motel accommodation
from June28 1959 to Agust 12, 1959, at this time
I don't of any rooms that you might get, but there is
three nice Motels in and near the city, Cherr's Motel
here in the city Joe Earhart about ½ miles out of the
city and the Spring Grill which is about 2 miles out
of the city, all three of the places are very nice, if
there is any way that we can help you, please feel free
to call on us at any time that you wish to.

Yours very truly,

Dover Chamber of Commerce

My heart sank as I read this kind but semi-literate letter. My two colleagues, Madeleine Kneberg and Tom Lewis, had virtually decreed that I was to spend most of the summer of 1959 doing salvage archaeology in the northwestern part of the state, like it or not, and I was looking for a decent place to stay for Sophie and our two boys (one still an infant). As it transpired, I found a tiny cabin on Kentucky Lake for my family, and gave the honor of staying in Dover to my field assistant Bill Fischer, a UT undergraduate, and two Knoxville high school students – Hiram Tipton and Jeff Chapman, the latter now Director of UT's McClung Museum and a renowned expert in Southeastern U.S. archaeology.

In those days, Dover was one of three small towns famous, or infamous, for a kind of unofficial competition. The other two were Linton and Golden Pond, just over the state line in Kentucky. In brief, the competition was focused on which town could do more killing (of humans, not animals) in a given year. The preferred method of dispatching one's enemy, I was told, was by a shotgun blast as the victim stepped out on the front porch. I can't remember who was the winner in 1959, but happily it wasn't Dover. Golden Pond, incidentally, then had some renown as "the moonshine capital of the world," but more about moonshine later. In the same vein of lightly repressed violence, the star attraction in the shabby museum of the local historical society was then a decommissioned electric chair.

Why were we here? During the Great Depression and the New Deal era, much of this part of the south had been transformed by the Tennessee Valley Authority, a gigantic hydroelectric project that had flooded the entire Tennessee River, creating huge impoundments such as Kentucky Lake. Hundreds of small communities and tens of thousands of dirt-poor farmers found themselves with cheap and abundant electricity for the first time in their lives. In the process, however, many thousands of prehistoric Indian sites went underwater, sites that only sporadically reappeared as the artificial lakes were drawn down in wintertime. As a consequence, archaeological salvage was carried out by the Works Progress Administration (WPA) to save what it could before the dams were completed. The scale of this effort was huge; commanded by the formidable Major James Webb were dozens of archaeologists – among whom was Tom Lewis – and a virtual army of hillbilly laborers.

Until the late 1950s the Cumberland River, which flowed into the Ohio River as did the Tennessee, had been spared this onslaught. But this was all to change with the authorization of the Barkley Dam in Kentucky. A brief survey by John Goggin of the National Park Service (NPS) showed that the Cumberland Basin was peppered with important sites, ranging from the Paleo-Indian through the Mississippian periods, and all were to be drowned and irrevocably lost. So, Tom and Madeleine had selected me, an ignoramus in the field of Southeastern archaeology, to do the job, with NPS funding.

135

They already knew me as a square peg in a round hole, a Yankee maverick, and worried that I would have a problem communicating with the Cumberland locals, in fact, would be treated with downright suspicion. Accordingly, I would be accompanied by a "real" southerner, who turned out be an employee of the real estate office of the Army Corps of Engineers in Nashville. This gentleman, a thin, middle-aged purveyor of racist jokes, was none other than the official who had put what were considered to be ridiculously low values on the farms and houses that the Corps had condemned to a watery death. I didn't spend very long in the field before I realized that my colleagues could not have made a worst choice for a *cicerone* – he was hated by everyone that I had to deal with.

The diplomatic problem was that although the entire lower Cumberland Basin had been condemned, most of the inhabitants had not yet been moved, and they continued to farm and make moonshine and otherwise carry on with their old way of life. Although, as state employees, we could have dug wherever we wanted, it was still politic to get at least their informal permission before we moved in with surveying instruments and picks and shovels and trowels. Once I had persuaded my colleagues in Knoxville to get the detested real estate man sent back to Nashville, I found that our very best ambassador, one who had the confidence of everyone from hillbilly farmer to "quality" gentry, was E. J. "Bill" Pratt, the Superintendent of Fort Donelson, a National Military Park on the site of General Grant's first great victory over Confederate forces.

I have mentioned moonshine, bootleg whiskey. This was a kind of cottage industry and a major source of income in the region, and was produced from corn mash in illegal stills. As we drove around in our station wagon looking for the sites previously identified by Goggin, often on mere tracks winding through the forest, from time to time one would see wisps of smoke drifting through the trees. I was more than worried, as we had official Tennessee plates on the car, and could easily be mistaken for "revenooers," that is, tax authorities on the trail of moonshiners. It was pretty well known that shotguns hooked up to tripwires were sometimes used to blow the heads off nosey drivers of official vehicles.

Then I made a lucky move. On John Goggin's recommendation, I recruited Dumas Melton as my foreman. Dumas was part Cherokee, and looked it; since he had been raised in a family of dedicated moonshiners, he was able to put out the word that we were *not* Federal Government men. His father was currently locked up in the Kentucky State Penitentiary. When I asked him "what for?," Dumas answered "they caught my daddy double-shooting it through two automobile radiators." From his father Dumas had learned how to find and dig archaeological sites, since his "daddy" had once worked as a local pothunter for Clarence Moore, a pioneer archaeologist of the Southeast who traveled up and down the region's then-undammed waterways in his houseboat, collecting as many ancient pots and stone artifacts as he could.

Dumas even had his father's probe fashioned out of a length of steel. When we ran across a "stone box" cemetery of the late Mississippian culture (the civilization that De Soto had seen when he crossed the area), Dumas showed how easy it was to use this tool to find these burial cysts. Such burials were easy to excavate, but it was somewhat unnerving to clear off the dirt from the grinning skulls and gaze upon tree roots entwined in the eye sockets. There were only a few offerings with these skeletons (I had hoped to discover at least one of the incised shell gorgets for which the culture is renowned), but one corpse had been adorned with a necklace containing a few bear teeth. Dumas exclaimed, "Just look at them b'ar tushes!", an archaic usage that dates back to Shakespearean times. Dumas also had the opinion that you could always tell apart Indian bones from those of whites, since the former were red, and the latter white.

Apart from Dumas and my two students from Knoxville, I can't say much for our labor force. Perhaps because I am a thoroughgoing Yankee, Bill Fisher and I had hoped to use black workmen, but my colleagues and, of course, the real estate man from Nashville, absolutely vetoed this idea. In fact, there were very few blacks in the region – according to Dumas, it was because the "night riders" (the KKK) had "run them out" at some earlier date. Instead, we ended up with about a dozen white louts from the local high school, along with an out-of-work janitor. Admittedly, the work was not easy, since it was carried out either in broiling sun or, more commonly, in the rain. They were constantly telling each other how much they needed a Falstaff beer, right then and there. I ruefully compared them to the wonderful workmen who had dug for me in British Honduras (Belize) and Guatemala. On one particularly hot day, the fattest and laziest of the bunch, Irl (that was his first name, "rhymes with girl," his father told me), leaning on his shovel and stripped to the waist to expose his flabby, bright red torso, asked me "Are you a doctor?" I replied that I was a kind of doctor, but not a medical one. "But ah need help," he gasped, "ah caint sweat!" I was sorely tempted to tell him "That's because you aint workin'."

There were so many sites to be excavated before the inundation that it was impossible to do more than make a small sample of the riches. This was a fairly depressing thought. Almost every farmer that we spoke to had a shoebox or cigar box collection of stone projectile points, many of them Cumberland points from the Paleo-Indian period, recognizable by their fluting and by their general fishtail shape, picked up after rains had fallen on newly plowed fields. But the area was rich in remains of all the later periods: Archaic, Woodland, and Mississippian. In the midst of our excavations of a site in which a Woodland village had been covered up by a small Mississippian temple complex, we had an unexpected visitor from the other side of the world. Our visitor was Sung Wen-hsun, a young prehistorian from Taiwan who was touring excavations in the United States to catch up on the newer archaeological techniques. I had met him in Taipei five years earlier.

Sung couldn't have come at a worse time for me. The weather was terrible, and with all the rain and given the impervious clay hardpan underlying occupation layers, the site itself was wet and muddy. Time was pressing, and the site was slated for destruction anyway. So, to speed things up I decided to get rid of most of one mound by having it carefully bulldozed, so that we could get to the Woodland period post-hole pattern. Sung, who had never seen bulldozers used on archaeological sites, was horrified at such crudity, and I admit to being a bit embarrassed. Nonetheless, he diplomatically took careful notes, and was actually helping find post-holes with a trowel when I noticed that various unshaven strangers in dirty bib overalls were watching him with great interest. After finding out that some had even come from beyond the state line, and remembering the famous three-town competition, I was considerably shaken to overhear this conversation:

"Look at him. They say he comes all the way from China!"

"He must be really rich, then. Whar do you suppose he keeps his money?"

Luckily my friend Sung, who was staying in a local motel, moved on to another state and someone else's excavations before these hillbillies could take any action.

Years later I saw that terrifying film *Deliverance*, and realized that the killer hillbillies in the movie were not all that different from the visitors who had been staring at Sung. The plot of the James Dickey novel on which it was based even included the flooding of a river and the transformation of the backward people who lived on and near it.

But not all of the people who lived on the land where the sites were situated were underclass, stubble-chinned, and relatively unwashed farmers, living in unpainted houses with washing machines on the front porch and hound dogs under the bed. There was "quality" here, too, in the Cumberland Valley, but these gentlefolk would also have to go one day as the waters inexorably rose. One such family was situated on what may have been the richest Archaic-period site in the state. Archaic settlements in the lower Cumberland region generally were situated on knolls overlooking the river where a tributary stream led into the main current. This particular one was on an abandoned farm and was covered with high grass; while we were surveying it, we killed an enormous copperhead, one large enough to have produced death if it had bitten anyone.

When it came time to actually dig the site, we first had to ask the usual (but sham) permission from the owners. These were three middle-aged spinster sisters who lived in a beautiful antebellum house with French windows and an adjacent rose garden. They were indeed "quality," and I needed an introduction. So one sunny afternoon Bill Fischer and I went there accompanied by Bill Pratt from the fort, who did know these ladies. As we walked through the gate, I noted with satisfaction one of the sisters, with a floppy but elegant straw hat, clipping roses from the garden. What I had failed to see was the nasty dog that tried to bite the seat of my pants, apparently unrestrained in any way by its owner.

In all events, we were invited into a large, sunny room lined with bookcases – these ladies were literate and university-educated. Pratt introduced us, and I began to explain why this particular site was so important to Tennessee prehistory, and why and how we wanted to dig it. It soon struck me that this conversation was getting nowhere, as the sisters were constantly detouring into irrelevant matters and not answering my question (the impatient Yankee once more). After what seemed an hour of this shilly-shallying I told them that we had to leave soon, and they realized that they would have to make some kind of response.

In her best "moonlight and magnolias" accent, the dominant sister announced that they were going to retire upstairs, and ask their father, who was the real authority here. Up they went, and we waited anxiously. After about a quarter of an hour they returned, only to announce, "Father doesn't approve of what you suggest." This truly made me furious – the whole business was a charade, as all of the land had been condemned and we had the perfect right to dig when and where we pleased. Who did that father think he was, anyway? But I restrained myself, reminding them only that they had received a virtually free education from the University of Tennessee, and I was disappointed that they had not seen fit to pay back to the university some of what they had taken out.

As we passed through the gate once more, but in the opposite direction, Pratt turned to me and asked "Do you know about their father?"

I said "No, tell me."

"He shot himself to death ten years ago."

We never did excavate that site.

Now this little world is all gone. The Barkley Dam, over the Kentucky line, was completed by 1966, and the 134-mile-long Lake Barkley was created. All the sites that so concerned me are now underwater – ten millennia of prehistory forever lost. Power boats towing water-skiers roar over what had once been dog-trot cabins, illegal stills, and hardscrabble farms. Dover is now a waterfront recreation community, and Golden Pond is the tourist center for vacationers exploring the Land Between the Lakes, a kind of hilly, wooded peninsula contained between Lakes Barkley and Kentucky.

And what happened to all those people uprooted by the artificial lake? It's difficult to believe that those simple, isolated, poor, occasionally violent hillbillies could have found much of a niche in the late-20th-century South. I've often wondered about this, but don't know the answer, perhaps because I've never once gone back to this part of the world. I don't really want to.

You may remember that UT was on the quarter system, and I had an idea for the second quarter of the 1959–60 school year. This was to start an archaeological program in Costa Rica that would prove Doris Stone and Sam Lothrop wrong: that there really was a long culture history there, and that those rocker-stamped whistles were as early as I said they were. Not the most high-minded justification for digging, I will admit, but Betty Meggers and Cliff Evans thought it was worth doing, and located funds for the project at the Institute for Andean Research. Since I had sacrificed a good part of the previous summer's vacation in the wilds of northwest Tennessee, Tom and Madeleine couldn't very well keep me from going.

I sweetened my petition for research leave by agreeing to take with me two advanced UT undergraduates: Bill Fischer and his friend Bennett Graham (son of one of the key members of the Tennessee Archaeological Society). Both were to prove wonderful assistants, even though between them they had no more than a dozen words of Spanish.

That January all of us – Bill, Bennett, and Sophie and the two small boys – found ourselves in the hot, dry, northwest region known as the Guanacaste Peninsula. This was a region that was largely known through extensive and intensive pot-hunting. Our base was Liberia, a dusty cattle town on the Pan American highway not very far from the Nicaraguan border. Our initial survey found dozens of occupation sites along the Guanacaste coast, and we excavated a representative sample. These had been untouched by the local *huaqueros*, who had concentrated their efforts on the burial sites on ridges above the plains where we dug. It didn't take very long to see that there was a long stratigraphic sequence of cultures here, with the earliest one including bichrome ceramics resembling those of the Late Formative in Guatemala, as well as (you guessed it) whistles with zoned rocker-stamping.

We found a number of sites along the edge of Papagayo Bay, well south of Liberia, and my two Tennessee students and I established temporary headquarters at a run-down resort owned by three charming but shady Italians from Naples and Palermo. They had a side business marketing "Italian cashmeres" to the natives, sweaters that shrank to miniature size on first washing. Each afternoon after work I would take my spinning rod and catch fish for our supper, which the Italians did a magnificent job in preparing. At sundown one day, while I was ankle deep in water casting from the beach, I glanced back at the low hills behind me. Just above the crest of the hills, something the size and appearance of a full moon was slowly moving from north to south. I watched it for some time until it disappeared. I still don't know what it was (a weather balloon?), but the next day the San José tabloids had headline news about a *disco volador*, "flying saucer."

The most productive site, Chahuite Escondido, was a large complex of shell mounds on a ranch belonging to an absentee Alabaman landlord. This was on the Santa Elena Peninsula, a region largely owned by the corrupt Somoza family of Nicaragua. According to the workmen, to cow the local people, the Alabaman had imported two Texas gunslingers, one of whom had recently been shot to death in a local bar when he challenged a better gunman to "draw." To work at this site I had to pay a bribe in U.S. dollars to the surviving Texan, who was definitely *not* a friendly person. Nonetheless, every cent of the *mordida* was worth it as this site covered the entire cultural sequence from our "Zoned Bichrome" period right through what was probably historic Chorotega or even Nicarao occupation on the eve of the Spanish Conquest.

It so happened that while I was concentrating on coastal sites, a young French archaeologist named Claude Baudez was excavating far inland in Guanacaste, under the auspices of the French Embassy. He also had run afoul of "Doña Doris" and her pal Balser, and they had charged Claude with looting sites for gold. The only trouble with this accusation was that there had never been much Pre-Columbian gold to speak of in any Guanacaste site, as Balser, the king of *huaqueros*, should have known. An investigation by the embassy disclosed that "Don Carlos" had a record, and had served time in Devil's Island. The false charges were dropped.

Eventually, Claude and I got together and compared our results, drawing up a grand scheme of cultural changes for this part of Central America that we planned on presenting the following summer at the ICA meetings in Vienna. In the meantime, Doris and Sam came down to Liberia, at my invitation, to look over the pottery that Sophie and I had laid out for their inspection. Doris didn't stay long, but Sam did, joining us at lunch and warmly congratulating us on what we had done. He proved himself to be both a gentleman and a scholar.

"I'm sorry," said Madeleine not long after my return from Costa Rica, "but you can't go to Vienna next summer. We have you back in Dover to finish up on the Cumberland River survey." My heart sank. So desperate was I to get away from all this that I was ready to resign.

A few days later, though, a letter was awaiting me in the Anthropology office. I immediately saw from the envelope that it was from the Anthropology Department at Yale, and I was pretty sure I knew what it was going to say. First, a little background is in order. In 1953, Wendell Bennett, an outstanding Andeanist at Yale, had drowned while swimming at Martha's Vineyard, and Yale began looking for a successor who could teach the high civilizations of the New World (what was then called "Nuclear America," to the bewilderment of some). In my second year of graduate work, about ten students and recent Ph.D.s in several universities were brought to New Haven for interviews for this one job, which was then at a junior level.

Why I was brought down from Cambridge I don't know, since I hadn't even done my fieldwork. Most likely it was because Floyd Lounsbury wanted to pick my brain about Yuri Knorosov and his work on the Maya glyphs (see Chapter 13). Near the end of my day in New Haven, I was told that I had an appointment to be interviewed by

Cornelius Osgood, Yale's expert on the Athapaskans, in his Peabody Museum office. Nobody warned me about what to expect. When I was ushered into his presence (ironically, I later occupied this same office), there was Osgood, a white-haired, thin-faced man with blue eyes behind steel-rimmed glasses. Seated at his desk, he stared at me without saying anything for a full minute. Then his question came:

"Are you a Christian?"

All sorts of wheels turned in my head. These were the possibilities:

1. He was an anti-Semite, and thought I had changed my name from Cohen to Coe.

2. He was some sort of a Christian fanatic, and only wanted true believers at Yale.

3. He was an atheist.

After I mumbled something about having been raised a Christian, but really didn't feel I was now, Osgood slammed his fist down on the desk, and let me know that hypothesis number 3 had been the correct one.

Needless to say, I didn't get the job. Don Lathrap or Bill Bullard should have been their pick, but that didn't happen either. Instead, they hired a rather strange graduate student from the University of California; he had clammy hands like Uriah Heep and the hangdog look of a loser. I had a presentiment that he wouldn't finish his dissertation for Berkeley in the time allotted. He didn't, and Yale let him go.

That letter, on Yale's characteristically yellowish stationery, covered three, single-spaced typewritten pages, offered me that same job, and was signed by Irving "Ben" Rouse, the chairman of the Department. Within five minutes of opening it I called Sophie in Maryville; all I said, since Tom and Madeleine were sitting nearby, was "New Haven." She understood. But Yale was demoting me to the rank of Instructor, and I had been an Assistant Professor at UT. When I spoke by phone to Sophie's father later that afternoon, his advice was "take it!," so I did.

That June, as we crossed the Mason-Dixon Line in our VW van, with our two boys inside plus all our worldly goods (except for my library which I had crated up and sent separately along with our Danish-modern furniture), Sophie and I looked at each other and let out a large sigh of relief. We never looked back.

CHAPTER 11

Mesoamerican Genesis: the Olmecs and their Predecessors

Having resigned from UT, and with a house in the New Haven area already rented, we did go to Europe that summer. Before the meetings in Vienna, we spent time in England, then went to Greece to stay with Leo Pappas – now working for the Agency in Athens – and his wife Mildred. This included my unforgettable journey with Leo to the holy Mount Athos in northeastern Greece, with its myriad Orthodox monasteries perched on cliffs far above the blue Aegean.

While in London, we had traveled up to Cambridge to spend several days with Geoffrey Bushnell, an archaeologist who had done pioneering excavations in coastal Ecuador, and whose book *Peru* in the wonderful "Ancient Peoples and Places" series I greatly admired. The totally bald, snuff-taking Geoffrey always reminded me of the Phiz depictions of Mr. Micawber; on his pate would sit his beloved budgeree that he had named "Junius Bird" in honor of our mutual friend, Junius Bird of the American Museum of Natural History. I mentioned to Geoffrey that I would love to do a similar book on non-Maya Mexico in the same series, and then another companion volume just on the Maya. "Why not?" he said, "let's get together with Glyn Daniel right away!" This was the editor of the series and the man who had thought it up; his wife Ruth often supplied it with hand-drawn maps and plans that in my opinion have never been surpassed for their beauty and accuracy.

I was to meet Daniel the next afternoon in Miller's Wine Shop. Here is where my Agency training once more proved to be handy, for I knew beforehand that Glyn was a noted expert on food and wine, and had coined the delightful word "gastroarchaeology" to apply to the science of looking at ruins and caves in a place noted for its wines and cuisine (such as the Dordogne). "Of course, you'd like a martini?" he asked. "Oh no, I'd prefer wine," I replied. The bow-tied Glyn then handed me an enormous wine list. "Oh, no, you choose the wine, please," said I. He was clearly satisfied with this, and ordered two glasses of the best white. When I had outlined what I had in mind for a book to be called simply "Mexico," he said, "Go right ahead and do it."

Glyn had taken a very large gamble on a virtually unknown young archaeologist, a fairly recent Ph.D. who had never before written a so-called "popular" book for the general public. I owe him and Geoffrey a huge debt: I had always wanted to write, ever since adolescence, but now I could do that and be an archaeologist, too.

꒰

Before we moved to New Haven and I joined the Yale faculty, its Department of Anthropology had been split down the middle by a rancorous feud between the prickly Cornelius Osgood and the renowned social anthropologist George Peter Murdock. New recruits to the faculty as well as graduate students were forced to ally themselves with one or another antagonist. Since neither would allow his enemy to be Chairman, this office had gone by default to Ben Rouse, a paragon of good sense and responsibility. Luckily for my peace of mind, by the fall of 1960, when my term began, Murdock had left Yale for the University of Pittsburgh.

My 35 years at Yale have essentially been like a happy marriage: "nothing to report." To paraphrase, "All happy departments are alike, but all unhappy ones are different in their own way." Thanks to Ben, Yale had definitely become a happy one, especially with Murdock gone. Unlike the situation at UT, I could basically teach what I wanted; I did, however, change the title of my two-semester offering on Mesoamerica and the Andes from "Nuclear America" to something a little less alarming. I had wonderful colleagues, in particular the linguist Floyd Lounsbury, the closest approximation to a pure genius I have ever known. Floyd was deeply involved with writing systems, as I was, and taught a seminar on Maya hieroglyphic writing, using the Dresden Codex as a textbook; fascinated by it, and by his incisive mind, I sat in on it twice as an auditor. This was indeed a learning experience.

Another course that I joined, more as a spectator than a teacher, was a seminar on the Pleistocene (Ice Age) jointly conducted by geologist Richard Foster Flint, Ben Rouse as archaeologist, and the ecological biologists Edward Deevey and Paul Sears. This was the very first time I had participated in an effort to solve important problems in human prehistory from the perspective of different sciences; in other words it was truly interdisciplinary. Dick Flint, an impressively tall, somewhat bald figure, was thought by some to be a martinet, but to me he was the perfection of what a scientist should be: a person of immense intellectual integrity.

For the first time I was teaching graduate as well as undergraduate classes, and it was initially a daunting experience. But one afternoon Paul Sears sat me down in his lab and gave me a great piece of advice: "Just remember, Mike, you don't have to tell them everything that you know." I soon found out that I had as much to learn from my students as they from me. My very first Ph.D. student, whom I shared with my Egyptological colleague Kelly Simpson, was a brilliant young man who came to us from the University of Toronto – Bruce Trigger, now a towering figure in the philosophy of human prehistory. By the time my second doctoral candidate came along, Barbara Voorhies, I had a real Mesoamericanist to supervise.

In only one quarter did I have problems in my early career at Yale. George Kubler of the History of Art Department had taught a course in Precolumbian art for many years, and I think he greatly resented my arrival, since my take on what had happened in ancient Mesoamerica was very, very different from his. A part of Kubler's approach was based on a book by the French art historian Henri Focillon, *La vie des formes*, which he had translated and edited, and another part was derived from a theory put forward by another art pundit, Erwin Panovsky. Focillon's notion was that artistic productions have a life of their own, that there is no need to consider the social and historical (i.e. anthropological context) in which they occur. Panovsky's was that forms and symbols endure through all sorts of cultural stages and changes, but that their *meaning* usually changes drastically with each stage; this is the so-called

"Principle of Disjunction" which I basically think is nonsense, at least as applied to Mesoamerican art and especially when clothed in George's impenetrably Germanic, convoluted prose. I thought "Do these people really mean that a figure of a man hanging nailed to a cross doesn't have at all the same meaning to us that it had to a medieval onlooker?" I had seen all sorts of striking continuities in the meaning of Mesoamerican religious symbols, from the Olmec right through colonial and even into modern times.

In a way, George was a kind of early prophet of post-modern deconstructionism – a school that holds that it doesn't really matter what an artist like Michelangelo said or thought he was doing in creating the *Pietà*, or an author like Hemingway in writing *The Sun Also Rises*. It's what I, the critic, can say about the product – the "text" – that is all that counts, at least among academics.

Kubler had clearly stated in print his credo that archaeologists were incompetent to discuss art: they should stick to describing the "pots and pans" that were their stock in trade, and keep their noses out of "Art" (with a capital A). Presumably my predecessor Wendy Bennett had done just that, since he and George had been friends. I refused to put on these intellectual blinders, since I thought then and still believe that archaeologists should be anthropologists, and that nothing in human culture, including what we westerners label as "art," was outside the purview of anthropological analysis.

Some years later Kubler and I were participants in a symposium at the Metropolitan Museum of Art on Precolumbian sculpture. At breakfast with Eric Thompson the next morning, an exasperated Eric exclaimed to me, "My God, George talks such rot!"

As time went on, I came to realize more and more that I had not gotten the whole story at La Victoria: firstly, that there must have been an intervening cultural phase between Ocós and Conchas, and secondly, that I had failed to record the ecological information that my workmen there had been telling me orally, that would have clarified how and why settled life had sprung up there in the first place. I had a semester's leave coming to me for the dry season of 1962, and began planning a field trip back to Guatemala.

But I needed a graduate student assistant who was both an experienced digger and knowledgeable in paleo-ecology. Bob Adams of the University of Chicago and the Oriental Institute came to my rescue. He had just the person: Kent Flannery, who had been a field assistant at Bob Braidwood's project at Jarmo in Iran, and had helped the archaeozoologist Charles Reed analyze the animal bones from the excavations. On this recommendation, I hired Kent on the spot.

Sophie and the children, now three with the birth of daughter Sarah, were to join me in Guatemala City, where we had rented the house of our friend the dentist and enthusiastic archaeologist Guillermo Mata Amado. I drove down with four-year-old Nick as my co-pilot, meeting Kent in Mexico City. Then all three of us proceeded to Guatemala, stopping off in Tehuacán, Puebla, to visit Scotty MacNeish and his pioneering cave excavations. While there, I persuaded Scotty to take on Kent as his faunal expert after we had finished our project.

Once I got to Ocós, we found that the old dance floor was no more, so I rented a tin-roofed house in the village, and a local to guard it. The first job I gave this individual was to dig a pit for a latrine out in the back yard, and to make sure that there was plenty of white lime to throw in afterwards. He looked bewildered, and I soon saw why. The village pigs were the sanitation officers, efficiently making off with human waste as soon as it dropped to the ground. My old friend the widow Doña Luz, who had cooked for Sophie and me in her simple house near our beach home, was still available, so we ate all our meals with her. She had loved Sophie, but she hated Kent with a passion. One morning when I was up in the capital and Kent was eating alone in her hut, one of the other widows called out to Doña Luz if she had anyone with her. "No" answered our cook, "solo un gringuito" – "only a little gringo."

It didn't take long to find a suitable site. This lay in a place called Salinas La Blanca, on the other side of the Río Naranjo, east of Ocós, on the land of a dignified, rather elderly fisherman named Don Vicente Cuadros. His thatched home was situated on a large, low mound that was partly cut by the river and strewn with obviously early sherds from very large *tecomates*. This is where Kent and I and our workmen spent the entire field season, digging down through many occupation layers in two deep cuts that Kent later referred to as "telephone booths." We had discovered an entirely new phase – or perhaps two phases – of Early Formative culture that fitted, according to our radiocarbon dates, in the 1100–900 BC interval between Ocós and the Middle Formative Conchas. We called it the Cuadros phase in honor of Don Vicente.

The preservation of mammal and fish bones in this site was remarkably good. Here is where Kent's know-how gained in Iran came into play. To properly identify the faunal remains, Kent needed a study collection, so he drew up an announcement that we posted in the local *cantina*, offering modest rewards to hunters for bringing us live specimens of a whole hierarchy of animals, dead or alive. This had almost immediate results: our quarters became a part-time zoo and part-time abattoir. Off to one side were a couple of 50-gallon drums where Kent's animals were boiled up with strong laundry soap to free the bones from their flesh. The smell was pretty disgusting. Most disconcerting of all was a nasty, vicious black iguana tethered by a string to a table leg; at night it would try to bite anyone going outside on a call of nature.

And not only animal remains were in mint condition, but carbonates from midden layers of shells in the site had also preserved some plant remains, too. At first we began discovering casts of corn cobs, but eventually even "fossil" cobs – the carbonates had replaced the organic tissues. I later submitted them for identification to Paul Mangelsdorf of Harvard's Botanic Museum, the world authority on the prehistory of maize. They were small and primitive, and much like an existing, low-yield race of corn known as Nal-Tel. These people had agriculture, all right, but it never replaced a reliance on the collecting of fish, shellfish, and other resources of the lagoon-estuary system.

I won't say anything more about this project except that a couple of the potsherds that we found with Cuadros were very different and not made locally. They were from polished brown-ware bowls that had exterior designs made by gouging out or carving broad lines. In fact, the bowls that they came from would have looked just like the Olmec pottery that had been found in many of the burials of Tlatilco, a Formative site in the Valley of Mexico. Supposed experts like Piña Chan had pronounced these to be late in the Valley of Mexico sequence, that is, later than El Arbolillo and Zacatenco, which were supposed to be extremely early. But here we had them at 1100–900 BC. I would keep this in my mind when I really got to work on the so-called "Olmec problem."

Now, the entire area from the mid-Chiapas coast southeast to about 25 miles beyond Ocós is known as "Soconusco"; this was the Aztec province of Xoconochco, conquered by them to gain control of its rich cacao (chocolate) plantations. Sophie and I and Kent may have been the first to discover its Early Formative occupation, but it is now one of the best-known archaeological areas of the New World, thanks to intensive work by the NWAF, led by John Clark and his associates. From about 1600 to 1100 BC, this is where the Mesoamerican "Neolithic" revolution took place, where intensive village life began, and the making of fine pottery early on reached a high degree of sophistication. As John has shown, this is where some people began to be better and richer and more powerful than others, in a kind of unequal society that had not existed before.

This was the overture to the great Olmec symphony, to the origins of Mesoamerican civilization.

ॐ

It is no mean feat to discover a previously unknown major civilization. It just doesn't happen very often – in the last century, it happened just once. To the *savants* who accompanied Napoleon belongs the honor of having brought ancient Egypt to the western world's attention; to John Lloyd Stephens and Frederick Catherwood goes the credit for having done the same for the ancient Maya, and likewise to the French naturalist Henri Mouhot for his exploration of Angkor and the Classic Khmer culture. But the very last scholar to have done this was Matthew Williams Stirling, who uncovered the Olmec in a series of excavations for the Smithsonian and the National Geographic Society beginning in 1939 and ending in 1946.

Matt was one of that now-disappeared species, the complete, all-round, general anthropologist. A champion raconteur, he could tell wonderful stories of his three years in the untouched wilds of New Guinea, and his sojourn among the head-shrinking Jívaro of Ecuador. But he was only truly at home in backcountry, lowland Veracruz, for he unreservedly admired the rough-and-ready farmers and ranchers of Mexico's Gulf Coast, and he had a long-standing love affair with the art of the Olmec, a passion that was shared by his good friend, the talented artist-archaeologist Miguel Covarrubias.

I came to know Matt and his wife Marion well, for I also had fallen under the spell of the Olmec when a graduate student at Harvard, and devoured Matt's popular *National Geographic* articles on his Gulf Coast explorations. At that time, very few of Matt's archaeological colleagues, least of all the Mayanists, believed him or Covarrubias that the mysterious Olmec could have preceded the Classic Maya in time. Stirling's most persistent critic was the formidable Eric Thompson, the doyen of Mayanists, who insisted that this culture was actually *post*-Classic, that is, was later than AD 900; in retrospect he was only about 2,100 years in error, for the true starting date of Olmec civilization proved to be 1200 BC. Looking back on that period, it strikes me that Thompson had absolutely no intuitive feeling about art and its evolution, which Covarrubias had in spades; encyclopedic though his knowledge was, Eric just could not see that it was as impossible for Olmec culture to have followed that of the Maya as it would be for Michelangelo's Sistine ceiling to have been later than Picasso's *Les Demoiselles d'Avignon*. On the subject of the Olmec, he was just as guilty of talking rot as Kubler had been with his "Principle of Disjunction."

In my formative, graduate student days, I was as much a follower of Covarrubias as of Matt. One of the great regrets of my life was that I never knew this pioneer of Olmec culture, who died prematurely and needlessly in a Mexico City clinic in 1957. Many years ago, I was told by a Guatemalan friend who had been lucky enough to have heard him lecture on the Olmec in Mexico City in the late 1940s, that those present almost wept when this great man erased the blackboard at the end of his talk, for he had a way of capturing the feeling of that strange art style as none others have possessed. Covarrubias was not just a studio artist, but also a caricaturist, ethnologist, archaeologist, collector, and

19. Sophie and I leaving our wedding reception, June 1955. The young man throwing good luck wheat is Don Thompson, son of Eric Thompson and a fellow graduate student.

20. Professor Theodosius Dobzhansky in his genetics laboratory at Columbia University.

21. We spent our honeymoon at the Wyoming ranch. Sophie was an excellent horsewoman.
22. Sophie with Nicholas, our first child, during a summer in Wyoming.

23. View of La Victoria, the site on Guatemala's Pacific coast where I discovered the Early Formative in 1958. The excavation squares show the influence of Sir Mortimer Wheeler's Archaeology from the Earth.

24. The dig at La Victoria was low-budget. Our only wheelbarrow was rented from a local ice-cream vendor.

25. Don Vicente Cuadros mending a fishnet.
His house sat on a 3,000-year-old Early Formative mound at Salinas La Blanca, Guatemala.

26. (Opposite) One of San Lorenzo's Colossal Heads (Monument 17) after we set it upright. This is a portrait of an Olmec ruler. Kneeling to one side is Agustín Camaño, my foreman.

27. (Opposite below) The archaeological team at San Lorenzo Tenochtitlan in 1966, during the first season. From the left, Paco Beverido, MDC, Ray Krotser, Paula Krotser, and Dick Diehl.

28. Monument 34, San Lorenzo, just after I had completed its excavation in 1967. This half-kneeling figure once had movable arms, now missing.

29. Transporting Monument 34 to the village schoolhouse for safekeeping. The workmen's distant Olmec ancestors probably moved monuments the same way.

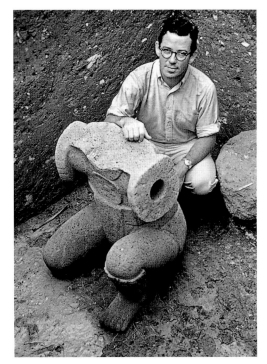

30. *Yuri Valentinovich Knorosov and Sophie in Leningrad, May 1989. It was Knorosov who had "broken the Maya code" in the early 1950s.*
31. *Matthew Stirling, the discoverer of the Olmec civilization, came with his wife Marion to visit us in the second season. He is looking at a buried San Lorenzo monument.*

32. The entrance to Juxtlahuaca Cave. Standing with me are the guide Andrés Ortega and Reinhold Ruge, a German aficionado of Mexican archaeology.

33. One mile deep into Juxtlahuaca Cave is this polychrome painting of a sinister Olmec lord threatening a captive.

34. *Fly fishing is my passion. This sailfish was caught on a fly rod off the Pacific coast of Guatemala in March 2005, not very far from where I carried out my Ph.D. research almost a half century ago.*
35. *Our house in Heath, Massachusetts. Here is where I first discovered the Primary Standard Sequence texts on Maya ceramics.*

ballet impresario. His book *Mexico South* and his articles on Olmec art convinced me that Thompson and his Mayanist followers were profoundly wrong about what Stirling had been finding in his digs.

Matt's great discoveries began in 1939, when he and his wife Marion uncovered the famous Stela C at Tres Zapotes, a huge site with a colossal head and dozens of mounds, located near the volcanic Tuxtla Mountains in southern Veracruz. This was a fragmentary basalt monument with a date in the bar-and-dot Long Count system on one side, and the relief mask of a very Olmec-looking god on the other. If it were read in the Maya manner – and Matt did so, first having to restore a missing coefficient at the top – it would correspond to a date in the year 31 BC, centuries before the first known Maya dated monument. This was the particular target of Thompson's attack, but time has totally vindicated Stirling, not least by the chance discovery decades later of the top half of Stela C with the missing coefficient.

The trouble with Matt's work at Tres Zapotes and later at another major Olmec site, La Venta in neighboring Tabasco, was that archaeological stratigraphy was not his strong point. He was unparalleled at discovering monuments, but basically he dug them up like potatoes. There was a baseless rumor that Matt's idea of field supplies centered on a case of whisky and a good supply of cigars; untrue, but you get the point. The fine details of ceramic chronology, in that pre-radiocarbon epoch the principal basis for dating, were left in not very competent hands. At Tres Zapotes, this was C. W. Weiant, a medical man from upstate New York. At La Venta and later at San Lorenzo, it was Philip Drucker, a fine field ethnographer with a degree from the University of California and a specialist in Northwest Coast culture; as my colleague Dick Diehl once put it to me, "Phil Drucker knows about as much about stratigraphic digging as I know how to fly a 747." The one really good digger that Matt had working with him was Waldo Wedel, who did a splendid job with the strange offerings of Olmec jade and other rare items at La Venta.

What all this meant was that the Mayanists led by Thompson stubbornly refused to believe in the great antiquity of the Olmec, even with the publication of Matt's reports by the Smithsonian's Bureau of American Ethnology – and I think that many of them still feel that way.

Nothing could be older than their beloved Maya. It was not until Robert Heizer and Phil Drucker published the radiocarbon dates on their massive 1955 excavations at La Venta that it became impossible to avoid the fact that the Olmec belonged to the Formative period of Mesoamerican culture history.

Gordon Willey had given me the job of writing the Olmec articles in an early volume of *The Handbook of Middle American Indians*, from which I found out that there was much still to be learned about the Olmec. One evening at a party at Matt and Marion's house in Washington, I couldn't help but hear Matt's remark to another guest: "I think Mike Coe's going to carry the ball for the Olmec." He was the archaeologist whom I admired above all others. I'd been given my marching orders.

Some time during 1945, Matt had been told by one of his Veracruz friends about a cattle ranch called San Lorenzo, on the middle reaches of the Río Coatzacoalcos (or, more accurately, on a side branch of it known as the Río Chiquito). There the local *campesinos* had seen a large stone eye looking up from the middle of a trail, and Matt immediately guessed that this must belong to a Colossal Head, for which the Olmec are famed. Along with Marion and the *National Geographic* photographer Richard Stewart, Matt went there and discovered what has turned out to be the oldest and greatest of all Olmec sites. He returned there the following year with Phil Drucker as his archaeologist (a mistake); by the end of that season he had discovered many more heads and major monuments. But how old was all this? Given the circumstances, there was no way to know.

During the fall semester of 1963, I studied the map of the Olmec area and made detailed notes on all known Olmec sites, and I pored over copies of the sketchy field notes that Matt had sent me. Now the Olmec heartland, where almost all of its stone monuments have been found, is a crescent-shaped area along the Gulf Coast, mostly in Veracruz but just lapping over into Tabasco (where La Venta is located). San Lorenzo is right in the middle of the heartland, and I was willing to bet that Olmec civilization had begun there, in the midst of rich levee lands of the Coatzacoalcos drainage. This, in spite of George Kubler's claim, "based on the principles of art history," that the San Lorenzo

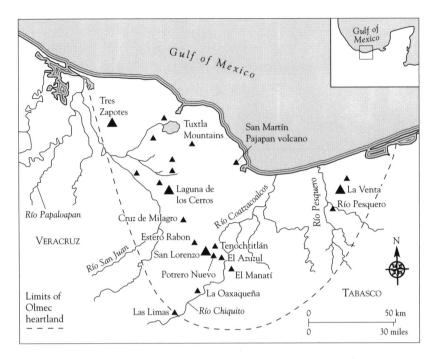

The Olmec heartland. San Lorenzo is the oldest Olmec site, and lies at its center.

heads were later than those of La Venta and Tres Zapotes – more rot, I decided.

If I were to start a large program at San Lorenzo, I should actually reconnoiter the place, which I did at the start of Yale's Christmas break. Until recently, there were no roads at all to the riverside village of Tenochtitlán, just to the north of the low mesa on which the site was said to be, so I hired a *lancha rápida* to negotiate the winding waterways. After two hours I was at the village, but a rude surprise awaited me there in the person of a most unpleasant Mexican army sergeant, who announced that he and his soldiers forbade me to go out to San Lorenzo. It seems that within the previous year the villagers had risen up and tried to lynch the well-known Veracruz archaeologist Alfonso Medellín Zénil, and that they were there to keep order.

I later found the reason why. Medellín had come to San Lorenzo Tenochtitlán to cart off one of the heads discovered by the Stirlings to an Olmec show mounted at Houston's Museum of Fine Arts by its then director, James Johnson Sweeney. When the locals protested, Medellín had mollified them by promising that the government would build them a school. Of course, they never got it, and when he returned some time later they were waiting for him with guns and machetes. The army came in and saved his life. From this, I learned that one must *always* keep one's promises with the local population: they may be poor and uneducated, but they're not stupid.

Well, I didn't get to see my target site, but I did make useful contacts in the village, and this was where any future project of mine was going to be based, anyway. But the trip back to New Haven was a trip from hell that is painful to recall. Because of foggy conditions all over the eastern U.S., the Air France plane out of Mexico City that was supposed to land in New York on Christmas Eve dumped everybody at Dulles, far outside Washington, with no further transportation provided. The train out of Washington was filled to capacity, and chose to be six hours late in getting to New Haven, which it finally did at dawn on Christmas morning. By this time I knew that I had a bad case of malaria, and I tumbled into bed with a high fever and a racking headache. "Daddy, Daddy, get up! We want to open our presents!" cried my children. I pulled the covers over my head and shivered.

What the general public never finds out in reading media accounts of archaeological discoveries is that the actual digging is only a small part of a field project (they also don't hear that excavation is a long, slow, tedious process – this is why making a film of archaeological discoveries is so difficult). To begin with, money has to be raised, usually from a large public or private foundation. At the same time, and if you are working in a foreign country, as most archaeologists dealing with the origins of a civilization are, you have to get official permission to do this research – no easy matter in a country like Mexico that has had long-standing problems with, and antagonisms towards, the United States, "*el coloso del norte.*" And lastly, if you have any scholarly standards at all – and some archaeologists don't – all of the data (maps, stratigraphic profiles, artifacts, and so forth) must be worked up and published as a final report, a task that usually takes several years or more to complete. The actual dig, then, is just the tip of the iceberg, or should be.

In brief, I submitted a three-year plan of research at San Lorenzo Tenochtitlán to the National Science Foundation (NSF), and got my financing; somewhat later I got a second NSF grant to undertake a program of ecological and ethnological research in the same area. And, most critical of all, I was given a three-year permit by Mexico's Instituto Nacional de Antropología e Historia (INAH). The INAH permit never would have happened if it had not been for the strong support of Alfonso Caso and Ignacio Bernal, both specialists in the archaeology of Oaxaca and long advocates of the Olmec as the *cultura madre*, "mother culture," of Mesoamerica.

Caso was among the most impressive figures I have ever met. He was one of those rare people who seem to radiate intellect and the easy confidence of power. It was he who had created INAH during the 1930s. I spent one wonderful afternoon with him in the library of his home, while he told me of his immense respect for the late George Vaillant, and his utter disdain for my colleague in Yale's History of Art Department. His disciple Ignacio Bernal, then the director of the Museo Nacional de Antropología, was a tall, saturnine man of great charm, a real aristocrat (he and his family were regularly listed in the *Libro de Oro*, Mexico's version of *Debrett's Peerage*), and he spoke many languages with complete fluency, including English. With his charming wife Sofía, he lived not far from his museum in a beautiful home along with what was surely the finest Mesoamerican library in the world.

Not so many years ago, in speaking of INAH as it was in the days of Caso, Bernal, and other archaeologists like Jorge Acosta, a respected Mexican scholar and friend remarked to me, "There were giants in those days. Now there are only pygmies."

I had my money and my permit. It was now time to put a team together. For Assistant Director, my old friend from undergraduate days Bill Sanders, who taught for many years at Penn State, put me in touch with his student and brother-in-law Dick Diehl; both of them had married sisters from Huimanguillo, Tabasco. I'm by nature an impulse buyer, and the minute Dick came to our house on Saint Ronan Street in New Haven for an interview, I knew I had my man. Dick and I planned out the next steps. Mexican law rightly decreed that we should also have Mexican assistants on our staff, and Medellín Zénil – who was really a very nice guy in spite of his dust-up with the villagers – warmly recommended his student at the University of Veracruz, Francisco Beverido Pereau. "Paco" Beverido, who was proud of his close resemblance to Captain Haddock in the *Tin-Tin* books, had sold out his automobile dealership in Córdoba to become a full-time archaeologist. He was hired, too, as was another Medellín student, Ramón Arellanos.

But we needed an expert who could handle the complex infrastructure to support our project in the field, and we needed someone who could map the San Lorenzo site. Out of the blue I received a telephone call from Paula Krotser, a middle-aged graduate student at the University of Arizona, offering her services as a digger. Her husband Ray was a retired civil engineer from the California highway department, and knew all about how to make buildings and map terrain.

Now I had my team, and we could start, which we did in January 1965. This project was to be a good part of my life until Dick and I published the two-volume final report 15 years later.

꧁

We set up our camp on a ridge just south of Tenochtitlán village; about one kilometer south, the San Lorenzo mesa with its mounds and Olmec stone monuments rose 50 meters above the swampy jungle that lay between us and it. At first we lived in very leaky tents, and it seemed to rain incessantly, due to the cold, wet *nortes* (northers) that plague lowland Veracruz well into the so-called dry season. But Ray began to work right away on building a permanent camp, real thatch-roofed houses with concrete floors, to a design given us by Ledyard Smith. Everything had to be brought upriver from the port of Coatzacoalcos or from the grimy oil town of Minatitlán by slow riverboat – chug-chugging vessels much like the one in *The African Queen*.

Just because I had a permit from the Federal authorities in Mexico City didn't mean that I could start work right away at San Lorenzo. In a process that took some weeks, I had first to get cleared by the Veracruz state government (Alfonso Medellín with his usual generosity helped here), then with the local military commander, next with the *jefe municipal* (political chief) of the closest town, and after that with the political boss of Tenochtitlán village, a man whom we got to know well during our three field seasons. But that wasn't all. San Lorenzo was an *ejido*, a kind of communal land-holding corporation that had been established during the Mexican revolution, and I had to stand before an assembly of the *ejido* members to explain exactly what we were doing, how we were going to hire labor, and what we were going to pay them. Warned by the hornet's nest that Medellín had stepped into, I promised them that we would move no monuments without their permission. Although one or two hotheads were against us, the assembly voted in our favor, and they stuck to the agreement.

In an old *National Geographic* article by Matt Stirling describing his foray into San Lorenzo almost 20 years before, there was a full-page color plate of his camp cook, Domatila González, preparing *empanadas* (meat turnovers). Since he described her as the best cook he had seen in eight seasons of fieldwork, one of my first steps was to find her and hire her. Over the course of the next three years, Domatila proved Matt to have been right, serving us up all sorts of local game (such as *jabalí* – peccary – and even roast armadillo), fish, green corn tamales, and other delicacies. She was a remarkable woman, with a host of children by different fathers. At one time in her life, she had been a *milpa* farmer all on her own, and had once hunted jaguars.

Domatila, her family, and everybody in the village were *jarochos*, the resilient, fiercely independent people of southern Veracruz, who spoke an Andalusian Spanish that even Paco had a hard time following. Some of them were corn farmers, others were fishermen or hunters, and even others followed all three ways of life simultaneously. During the rainy season the river flooded all the low-lying land, and tarpon would spawn over what was otherwise *potrero*, cattle pasture. Domatila loved to recount how she and her dwarf brother once harpooned a giant tarpon from their small dugout canoe, and how it towed them for a complete night before they finally could kill it.

I thought of them as worthy successors to the Olmecs: if we studied them and their ways of making a living in this environment, we might find out why and how that ancient civilization had flourished here in the first place.

𑀢

How old *was* San Lorenzo? How could one date the monuments that Stirling had found on the surface or lying in ravines that cut into the plateau? During our first season, Dick and Paula began laying out trenches in the middle of San Lorenzo, and Paco and Ramón on one of its ridges on the northeast. With most of camp finished, it wasn't long before Ray began his detailed mapping of San Lorenzo with plane table and alidade; when completed the next year, it was the only accurate map ever produced for an Olmec site (when I once asked Matt if he had made a map, he said "I thought Phil had made a map"; on asking Drucker about this, he replied "I thought Matt had made one"). La Venta had been so thoroughly destroyed by the operation of PEMEX, the national oil company, that any map made there would have been unrepresentative of what it was like before the bulldozers came.

Even during the first season, it had become clear to us that the main period of occupation at the site was during what we called the San Lorenzo phase, and it was during this time that almost all the monuments were carved and set in place – Colossal Heads, so-called "altars" (actually thrones as David Grove proved), and figural sculptures. The Río Chiquito, an arm of the Coatzacoalcos, had cut through a San Lorenzo village deposit at a place the locals called El Remolino, "the whirlpool," and one could see occupation layers with pottery, clay figurines, and charcoal-filled hearths. I began excavating here at once. My previous experience with the well-preserved Early Formative ceramics of Guatemala's Pacific coast helped me understand what I was getting, for the surfaces of pottery in Olmec sites were often eaten away by the highly acid soil conditions. Here I was also getting *tecomates* and carved bowls almost identical to those of the Cuadros phase of the Pacific coast, along with the white-ware, "baby-face" figurines so typical of Olmec art and culture. I rushed the charcoal samples to Yale's radiocarbon lab, and the dates came out to be between 1200 and 900 BC.

My conclusion: the great Olmec center of San Lorenzo and its carved monuments were not Late, but *Early* Formative. Older even than La Venta, San Lorenzo represented the very beginning of civilization in Mesoamerica.

↯

Our day usually began at dawn. After breakfast, Dick would muster the workmen and our horses, reading out the roll call. Then all of us would go in procession south to San Lorenzo, Domatila's dwarf brother leading the way, holding a machete almost longer than he was high. Before now, Dick had hardly ever been on horseback, and like the tyro he was, he decided one morning to take a fast gallop over the stump-strewn San Lorenzo mesa. The horse threw him – he was basically unhurt, but he learned his lesson. I had selected as foreman Agustín Camaño, a skinny, highly intelligent native of Tenochtitlán; Agustín worked directly with me, and he became so good at the job that he could set up excavation cuts himself, and could often detect subtle stratigraphic changes better than I. He was the best field archaeologist I have ever known, and a fascinating man in his own right.

The staff and I began bringing what Domatila thought were sandwiches out to the site, but these were not her forte, and we ended up having nothing more for lunch than sweetened *atole* (maize gruel) drunk out of a bottle. While at work, we would listen to the workmen gossiping about doings in the village, and query them minutely about farming, hunting, and fishing. As they recounted it, life along the Coatzacoalcos River system had elements of Greek tragedy: a father who shot his criminal son to death and then fled to live by himself in the forest, mothers who disposed of unwanted children down a well, and like matters. Everyone who could afford it had more than one wife, and the village head had three, disposed in three locations along the Río Chiquito.

We would return to camp in mid-afternoon. Ray had set up a solar-heated shower, and had also installed what was the only flush toilet on the middle Coatzacoalcos.

After a leisurely hour drinking beer from the village store, or something stronger, we would enjoy Domatila's cooking in our dining room. More than a few of our workmen were expert musicians, and might show up in camp in the evening to drink a few beers and play their guitars and sing in the wonderful *jarocho* style of southern Veracruz.

～

As the 1967 dry season wore on, the weather became hotter and more oppressive. Gone by March were the wet, chilly *nortes* that had plagued us earlier in the year. Each morning the orange sun rose in the haze formed by dozens of *milpa* fires. By the end of each sweaty day's work we looked forward to darkness and relative coolness, and especially to Domatila's cooking.

By way of preface to the strange event that occurred one March night, the San Lorenzo plateau had various ridges jutting out from it on the north, west, and south, with deep ravines between them. It was often in these ravines, or at their head, that Matt Stirling and ourselves had come across Olmec monuments. A pair of such ridges extended out from the west side of the mesa; when Ray Krotser mapped them, they proved to be mirror images of each other, a mound or bump in one matching the same feature in the other. On one of these – the Group D Ridge – could be seen a partly buried but upright stone slab; although plain on both sides, I felt that it would be worthwhile to put a trench here at right angles to the ridge's orientation, in hopes of finding a cache or offering at the base of the stone.

With his customary aplomb, Agustín Camaño, my foreman and by now a highly competent digger (he had many other talents, as will be later related) set up the stakes and strings, and work began.

Let us now move north to our camp on the edge of the village, and to the building that housed our dining room and Domatila's kitchen. I have no idea what we were eating that evening, but it could have been game such as venison or *jabalí* (peccary), or gar fish, or green corn tamales. Whatever it was, it was sure to be good. We lingered talking, and finally got up to return to our respective sleeping quarters, still chatting. As Dick, Paco and I stepped out into the darkness, all three of us noticed a brilliant white light directly over the San Lorenzo plateau.

"Do you see what I see?" one of us asked.

Yes, we all saw it. As we watched for the next 15 minutes, it moved slightly sideways and up and down.

Now you must know that there were absolutely no people living on the San Lorenzo plateau at this time. Anyway, it was far too bright to have been a flashlight. There were no roads, only simple trails, and thus no vehicular traffic. It could not have been a star or planet, since it moved. Could it have been the headlight from a locomotive of the trans-Isthmian railway? This was impossible, as the rail line lay far to the west.

So what was it? To this day I don't know.

But the following morning, as the work force and ourselves were mustering for the walk and horseback ride south to San Lorenzo, I told Agustín about what we had seen.

"*Claro*, doctor, it was a sign."

"A sign for what?"

"A sign that very soon you are going to discover something very important."

"And where will that be?"

"Right under where the light was."

Now, it so happened that the light was in a direct line that would have taken one to the Group D Ridge where we had been digging.

So, the next morning I was back again to the upright stone slab. It soon became quite clear that the square that I had set up to dig down to the hoped-for cache was too restrictive for Agustín to work properly, so I set up another square just south of that one, and went off a bit looking for other such stones on the surface. In about an hour Agustín excitedly called me back: "*Doctor*, I've come down on an upside-down stone cart! Complete with wheels!" This would have indeed been something new to science, as wheeled vehicles were absent in Pre-Columbian America – they were known only as small, clay toys in the Classic period on the Veracruz coast. I rushed over to take a look. In truth, the tops of two wheel-like stone disks were projecting from the fill. I had no idea what this was, and got to work with my trowel. In the space of about five hours we managed to clear most of Monument 34, one of the most extraordinary Olmec sculptures ever found, and certainly the most spectacular object I've ever wrested from Mesoamerican soil.

What we had here was a slightly over-life-sized basalt representation of a royal ballplayer, resting on one knee. His arms, probably originally of wood but now missing, had fitted into socketed disks placed at the shoulders – in other words, these arms had been movable. The fine relief on the statue showed that on his chest had been one of the concave iron-ore mirrors that are a hallmark of Olmec civilization. Sadly, his head was also missing – the usual case with such monuments, struck off when the statue had been mutilated and buried by hands unknown about 900 BC, when San Lorenzo was destroyed.

That night there was additional excitement at dinner, since Paco had been excavating a strange and very early basalt column bearing a relief of clasping human arms. While were talking, an unsettling rumor reached our ears: gunmen from Acayúcan, the local rail center and a haunt of criminals and other low types, had been planning to come to San Lorenzo and remove "my" monument by force. Agustín and his *compadre* volunteered to go out to the site immediately with their hammocks and spend the night guarding the sculpture, which would have to be transported the next day to the Tenochtitlán schoolhouse for safekeeping.

But just as we were unwinding from our long day's work, hopeful of going early to bed, another messenger arrived from the village with more unwelcome news:

"Your guests have just arrived!"

"What guests?" we asked ourselves. These visitors were totally unexpected. They turned out to be two large dugout-loads of students, male and female, from the University of Veracruz in Jalapa, along with their mentor, a well-known social anthropologist. They had to be fed, housed, and entertained; and horses had to be ordered for the grand tour of the site the next day. Exhausted as we all were, we were obligated to offer hospitality, regardless of the fact that Paco was not on very good terms with their professor.

So, I asked the musicians among our work crew to come with their guitars, and ordered beer and several bottles of tequila from the local *tienda* to be sent to our camp. Paco, Dick and I had just about had it, and the three of us proceeded to get completely inebriated, so much so that I was unable to touch alcohol for at least a month afterward.

The Mexican term *crudo* means "hangover," and it vividly describes the way I felt the following morning. Regardless, we had to get that sculpture into the school. Don Perfecto, the *cacique* (village boss), took charge of the operation. Like their distant Olmec ancestors, these people were past masters at transporting very large burdens without the benefit of wheels or any power other than human muscle. I already knew this, since on a moonlit night we had foolishly driven our two-ton Land Rover up onto the San Lorenzo mesa, where the vehicle's electrical system inconveniently shorted. No problem said the workmen; the next day about 20 of them carried it on their shoulders one-and-a-half miles through forest and swampy ground to our camp.

Don Perfecto's strategy for the monument was to lash together two eight-inch tree trunks as carrying poles, and to suspend the royal ballplayer from them by ropes. It wasn't long before 16 men, eight on each side, had the ancient masterpiece safely under lock and key. But the ancient ruler's journeys were not to end in this remote Veracruz village. In later years he has been put on exhibition not only in Mexico City, but also in Washington's National Gallery, and even in the Palazzo Grassi on Venice's Grand Canal.

⁂

There was great excitement in the village when they heard that "Don Estirlin" (Matt) and "Doña Mariana" (Marion) were coming to visit. Many of their former workmen were still alive, and some were with our project. To gain their confidence the year before, I had passed myself off as Matt's nephew. One can learn a lot about archaeologists by listening to what their employees say about them; in the case of Matt and Marion, the feeling was one of love and veneration.

They arrived at a most opportune time, for we were hitting pay-dirt as far as new monuments were concerned, and we had a lot more to show them than just pieces of broken pottery. When we took them out to the site on horseback, it was scorching hot, and I was worried about Matt as he was by then an elderly person, but neither had one word of complaint. Luckily, Agustín (who was only a boy when they were last here) had the bright idea of bringing succulent watermelons out to San Lorenzo, and these saved the day.

That evening, people who had known the Stirlings streamed in from other villages along the river, and we threw a *pachanga*, a party. In the heat of the night, the musicians tuned up their guitars, and improvised song after song in their honor, expressing their love for their old friends. All of us archaeologists, Mexican and *gringo* alike, felt that some great cycle of time had come to a perfect closure.

ॐ

I never brought Sophie and the children to the camp while the project was going on, for the simple reason that the older children were in school in New Haven, and anyway I didn't want to expose any of them to the multiple diseases that they might catch in such a place. We did everything possible while we were there to persuade the government to send the village a *pasante*, a recently graduated medical student, but this never happened and the area was completely without any medical attention other than the dubious injections administered by the local storekeeper. With two exceptions, no one in our camp ever got sick, as I had persuaded Domatila to boil all water and observe a degree of cleanliness in the kitchen. The exceptions were the two Krotsers; Paula had the idea that they both could eat a local yogurt with impunity, since the yogurt process "would kill all germs." This naturally proved to be far from the case.

By season number three, Dick had returned to Penn State to finish his dissertation on Teotihuacan for Bill Sanders, and we entered a new phase of research. I had started a very large, complex program with NSF funding that would take an area of 75 square kilometers centered on San Lorenzo Tenochtitlán as our sample, map it in total detail by means of aerial photography, and, in combination with ground checking and ethnographic research, come up with the total carrying capacity of this part of the heartland. In this, I was influenced by the work that my Yale colleague Hal Conklin had done as a young anthropologist in the Philippines (I had brought his classic *Hanunóo Agriculture* with me as a kind of Bible). For this research, we fielded a team of soil scientists from the agronomy school at Chapingo, near Mexico City, and a team of botanists from the University of Veracruz.

Every weekend I would spend endless hours recording on tape what Agustín and his friends had to tell me about corn farming, hunting, fishing, and a host of other things – including unsettling stories of how one could be bewitched and lose one's way in the jungle through the malevolence of *chanecos*, supernatural dwarfs. Most enjoyable were the expeditions that he and I would take so he could show me how he hunted, and the lagoons in which he fished; being a (former) hunter and a (present) fisherman myself, I was fascinated with his knowledge. So was the world expert on Mexican fishes, Robert Rush Miller of the University of Michigan: he was astonished to find that Agustín knew that some small, inconspicuous fish were egg bearers, but others similar to it were live bearers.

On one occasion, Agustín shot a yellow-headed parrot that had perched in a tree.

"Agustín," I pontificated, "you should never shoot anything you can't eat."

"Who says you can't eat it?" he replied.

When we brought the dead bird into camp, Domatila plucked it and cooked it. That night, my artist Felipe Dávalos and I ate it, being the only ones in the camp at that time. It was pretty tough going, in spite of our cook's culinary know-how. The next morning we arrived haggard at the breakfast table. Both of us had nightmares all night about that wretched bird. But I saved its feathers, smuggled them back to the United States, and gave them to my friend Alfonso Ortiz, the distinguished Tewa anthropologist. Alfonso in turn gave them to his uncle, the Hunt Chief of San Juan Pueblo, so that they could be worn by dancers in the Winter Clan rituals; to the Tewa, parrot and macaw feathers symbolize the heat and productive qualities of the tropical lands to the south, an idea that would have pleased the Olmec.

By the end of my stay in the land of the Olmec, Dick and I had worked out a scenario for the rise of civilization here at San Lorenzo. This had to do with the rise and fall of the river as wet season was followed by dry season, and wet season again. Each time the river rose with the coming of the rains, it would inundate all of the low-lying land including the naturally raised levee lands along its banks. At this time of the year, only the higher elevations could be cultivated for corn and other crops. Then, with the onset of the dry season (actually not all that dry as northers brought rain for much of it) the river began to fall, exposing the levees, now covered with their new, rich layer of silt. These were the most productive soils in all Mexico, and during our time there were entirely in the hands not of the *ejido* but of a pair of brothers who were the richest men in the village and who held all offices within it.

So, we had here a Nile-like situation. Over three millennia ago what had originally been an egalitarian society was radically transformed as one militarily powerful group within it seized control of these levee lands and set themselves up as paramount rulers. The great stone monuments, fashioned from huge basalt boulders laboriously brought from their source over 50 miles away, were testimonies to their overlordship. The Colossal Heads were their own portraits, and the "altars" their thrones. San Lorenzo was, we now know, as big as a modest-sized city, at a point in time when the Maya to their east were still in a pre-pottery stage, and living mainly by primitive hunting and gathering. This was, as Caso and Covarrubias and Bernal had been telling us all along, the "mother culture" of Mesoamerica.

ℒ

Ignacio Bernal was by now Director of INAH, a job which he confessed to me that he hated, as he found himself the target of a left-wing and very vocal younger generation within the institution. Several times we discussed what to do about the Yale camp when we left. I knew that there was a lot more to be done there; in particular, we had been very successful in finding buried Olmec monuments with a magnetometer, and I suggested that many more still lay under the surface. Why not send down a team of young Mexican researchers to take over? I would be willing to go down there from New Haven to "show them the ropes" and ease the way with our many friends in the village.

He agreed, and assigned the job to a young archaeologist of German name and heritage, and an equally young Belgian woman. When I got to the camp, it was clear that things were not happy there. While everybody liked her, *he* had managed to infuriate Domatila and our workmen, and arrogantly announced to me that as "typical Americans" we had spoiled all these people by paying them too much. "I'm sure that you haven't made a map," he announced to me. It so happened that Ray's beautiful map of San Lorenzo had just been printed, as well as the land use, topographical, and soil maps made on the basis of aerial photography. I handed him a set, which he accepted with ill grace.

The next day I made a long horseback trip with Agustín to a distant stretch of forest which I hadn't previously seen. On the way back we came across a troop of howler monkeys in some trees, and my companion instantly shot the old bearded patriarch. Once back in camp, the howler was skinned that night, right outside my house, various interested onlookers in attendance. The now fur-less simian looked amazingly like a human baby. "*Es puro cristiano*," exclaimed one of the men, that is, "he's a real human being."

I was going to leave downstream for Minatitlán and my plane to Mexico City at dawn the next morning. Domatila insisted on making me breakfast, and guess what the main course was: roast howler monkey! I can hardly choke down a boiled egg at that hour, but I chewed manfully on. Then I kissed Domatila goodbye for the last time, and got into the waiting dugout. As the sun was peeking above the eastern horizon, many of my friends were on the river bank to bid me farewell. Then Don Perfecto, the village's headman, asked me this question:

"In the last big war, which of these countries won, Germany or the United States?"

"The United States!" I answered, and they all cheered.

The much-detested archaeologist later went on to new triumphs at Yaxchilan, the beautiful Classic Maya city on the banks of the Usumacinta River, where he managed to have a gigantic tree dropped on one of the buildings. For this, he was banished by the Governor of Chiapas, the state in which Yaxchilan is located.

CHAPTER 12

A Farm in the Hills

"Did I ever tell you about my farm in Massachusetts?" This was asked me in April 1968 by Gillett Griffin as we were bouncing along a cobble-strewn river bed in his rented Volkswagen Bug. The temperature was about 100 degrees Fahrenheit in the shade, and Gillett was my guide on this exploration of the wilds of Guerrero, his favorite part of Mexico. He had already taken me to explore the amazing and very deep cave of Juxtlahuaca with its polychrome Olmec murals, which he and his Italian friend Carlo Gay had made known to the world a few years before. "No, Gillett, tell me."

He described his place, located on a high hill in the township of Colrain, in northwestern Massachusetts. The house had been built about 1815, and had no running water, electricity, indoor plumbing, or central heating. The only way to keep warm in the ferocious winters was to get the ancient fireplaces going, and light the wood stove. It sounded fascinating. "I'll have to get you and Sophie and the children up there some day."

My family and I rented a very modern house that summer in Contreras, overlooking the soupy, polluted atmosphere of Mexico City. I was still working on the ceramics from San Lorenzo, while simultaneously writing a popular book on the Olmec (boldly entitled *America's First Civilization*) to be jointly published by American Heritage and the Smithsonian. My editor was David McCullough, and he came down with his wife in mid-summer so that we could write the haiku-like captions together. At the back of the book we had a section that was to be illustrated by wonderful drawings of Olmec objects made by Miguel Covarrubias before his death. The lawyers at American Heritage wanted to know who owned the rights to these, and that is a strange, convoluted story that might have been devised by O. Henry.

Here it is. Several years before his death, Covarrubias had split with his wife Rosa (who was still living that summer of 1968 in their Tizapán home), and had an apartment in downtown Mexico City. When he unexpectedly passed away in a government clinic, the contents of the apartment were raided by relatives and friends, including the colorful William Spratling, who made off with two notebooks filled with original drawings that Covarrubias had intended for a major work on the Olmec. Bill took them down to Taxco, Guerrero, where he had a workshop that turned out not only the silver that made this town famous throughout the world, but also a constant stream of fake Olmec pieces in jade, serpentine, and other stones (visitors to the town can see these displayed as real artifacts in INAH's "Museo Guillermo Spratling").

At some point, the notebooks were borrowed and photographed by the Mexico City-based dealer George Pepper, a former Hollywood film director who had fled the U.S. during the McCarthy era. It was from him that I borrowed the negatives, and had a set of prints made, and this is how the drawings got into the book. But where were the originals, and who really owned them? One night Spratling, a very heavy toper, had hit a tree and was instantly killed as he was driving from Taxco to Iguala. According to one story, the adolescent boys that he had in his workshop immediately stole the drawings. In his will they had been left to the beautiful Audrey Hepburn and her then husband Mel Ferrer, but when the lawyers checked with them, they knew nothing about it. As far as I know, the mysterious notebooks have never surfaced again.

There was a pleasant coda to the story. The lawyers concluded that Rosa Covarrubias was the owner of the rights. Through mutual friends, I contacted this remarkable woman, who had produced most of the photographs in Miguel's wonderful books. Rosa was notoriously strong-minded and strong-willed: Matt Stirling once said, "She's no rose, she's a tiger-lily!" I contacted her through mutual friends, and was invited to lunch one day – she was one of the best cooks in Mexico. After venting her rage at the people who had looted her husband's apartment, she graciously gave me the permission I had sought.

$$\mathcal{Q}$$

That summer in Mexico, and in fact in America and Europe, too, revolution was in the air. It was 1848 all over again. Student agitation against the sclerotic, corrupt, one-party system that had ruled Mexico since 1929 reached a climax just before the Olympics, when the police and armed forces massacred many hundreds of unarmed protesters at Tlatelolco, the Aztec ruins in the northern part of the city, and "disappeared" their bodies.

When we returned to New Haven for Yale's fall semester, the campus was entering a period of turmoil. Radical, long-haired students were demanding all sorts of changes, some logical and others illogical, backed up by sometimes irresponsible members of the faculty. It was at this point that I became chairman of the Anthropology Department, and I had plenty of problems on my hands. On the other hand, this was the most interesting and committed group of undergraduates I have ever seen, before or since.

Yale was a very different place than it had been when I was hired in 1960, and much of the transformation was due to Kingman Brewster. Before he took the reigns as provost and later as president, Yale had been little more than a "boys' finishing school," as Clyde Kluckhohn once put it to me. A complete blueblood and Yale graduate himself, the more antediluvian alumni considered Brewster to be a traitor to his class: he had made Yale coeducational, had turned the university's reputation for antisemitism upside down by hiring many Jewish faculty (some of whom rose high in his administration), cut down on the number of "legacy" students admitted as freshmen, and did all sorts of other things that didn't go down well with the Old Blues. In my eyes, Kingman was one of those born leaders who seem to radiate a visible aura: they are "Sun Kings" like Louis XIV. When they come into a room full of people, they are immediately recognizable, creating their own space. Ray Peers had been one of these. Sophie and I had stood with about a million others when John Kennedy, on a ceremonial visit to Mexico City, came down the Avenida Juárez in an open limousine – even from a great distance, he gave out a golden glow that drove the huge crowd to a paroxysm of enthusiasm. Alfonso Caso and perhaps even Gordon Willey had charisma of this sort.

Kingman kept in close touch with every department in the university through his astute graduate dean, John Perry Miller. He knew that Cornelius Osgood had been a disruptive and negative force both in my department and in the Peabody Museum, and one day, over lunch at Mory's, Kingman told me that he intended to remove him from the museum. I told him that this would be a mistake, and would be taken as interference by the Anthropology faculty; that the best way to deal with him would be to "kick him upstairs" into a powerless position in the museum. He agreed, but observed that my difficult colleague was what Franklin Roosevelt used to call "a revolving son of a bitch." When I asked what that was, Kingman replied, "a son-of-a-bitch no matter which way you look at him."

Actually, Osgood did a great turn for Yale, one that in my mind made up for all his sins. One day, he asked me if there were any good younger specialists in Far Eastern prehistory, as he thought that our department ought to have one. I immediately put forward the name of K. C. Chang, who was then getting his degree at Harvard with his idol Hal Movius. Osgood jumped at the suggestion, and saw that the appointment went through (of course it was actually Ben Rouse who did this, but Cornelius was the prime mover).

The revolutionary atmosphere at Yale and many other American universities (other than the Bible colleges of the South) really began heating up in the next academic year, and culminated for us in 1970 in the May Day strike and demonstration. From one day to the next I never knew what to expect. The ostensible *causus belli* was the forth-coming Black Panther trial: Bobby Seale and his fellow Panthers had been indicted for murdering a colleague, and dumping his body in the salt marshes near New Haven. The leader of the strike was actually an undergraduate Anthropology major, who had told me that "they" were cooking up some real trouble for me. I didn't know who "they" were, but I did find out that this young revolutionary had been the president of the Young Conservatives at his prep school; he behaved a little more responsibly when I told him that I knew this embarrassing fact. This was an altogether unsettling, strange, but exciting period well documented in Gary Trudeau's *Doonesbury* strip (the originals of "Ms. Caucus" and "Zonker" were also majors in our Department; in fact, I was "Zonker"'s advisor for his senior paper).

I refused to join in the strike, but quite a few faculty did. In my opinion, these so-called strikers were not real workers, who if they went out on the picket line would forfeit their paychecks. In any event, practically none of my students stayed away from my classes. On the eve of the fatal day, 1 May, many thousands of outsiders, including the Yippie gurus Abbie Hoffman and Jerry Rubin, streamed into New Haven in support of the Panthers, many with the avowed intention of tearing down Yale to its foundations. Helicopters thud-thudded overhead, while National Guard units were drawn up, one contingent arranged behind the Peabody Museum. I had three inflammable buildings in my charge, so a few days before I had identified and recruited those of our students who had some paramilitary training; these were posted each night with buckets of water and sand to put out any blazes. The tension rose when a rumor went around claiming that the Hell's Angels outlaw bikers were going to descend in force from nearby Wethersfield or Wallingford to commit mayhem on the demonstrators, but this turned out to be false.

Instead of indulging in confrontation, Kingman had brilliantly decided to open up the University gates to all of these outsiders as our guests. The dining halls fed them, and undergraduates and graduate students with white armbands acted as marshals. Two of my favorite students, Judy French and Bob Zeitlin, had so volunteered. Their wedding in a flowery meadow on a lovely day that June was a bright spot in what had otherwise been a very murky year. It all ended peacefully, a relief to Sophie and me as our house – and our children – were located not all that far from Yale and the New Haven Green. Kingman had won.

꒐

One bleak November day in 1968 we had taken up Gillett's offer to visit his antique farmhouse in Massachusetts. There was yet no snow in New Haven, but when we got on the dirt river road leading up to Gillett's place, our VW van was slithering in six inches of it. The wind howled at night as we buried ourselves under our quilt, while the children slept in Gillett's attic among a clutter of antiques left by the previous owners, a pair of old maids one of whom had a goatee (on the wall of our room was a wonderful oil portrait of her by Gillett). The moon came out at night from behind scudding clouds, the branches of the leafless trees were clattering against each other, and I had a strong feeling that we were part of a weird tale by H. P. Lovecraft. Sophie and I immediately fell in love with this forgotten part of New England. This love affair was renewed the next November (1969), when Gillett asked us up once more to his rural retreat.

In the following March, just as things were heating up at Yale, our oldest boy Nick, now 14, was invited by our neighbor, the Yale physicist Bill Bennett, to spend a weekend with him and his family at a place they had just bought in Colrain, of all places, only a mile or two from Gillett's farm. He came back raving about his stay, and I went into a real estate feeding frenzy. Sophie and I had previously contemplated buying a *pied à terre* in Mexico City, but I thank my stars we didn't. What we needed was our own farm as a second home, both for the children and for ourselves – and also just in case the predicted revolution *did* happen. Within a week I had arranged with real estate agents in the town of Greenfield, not far from Colrain, to show my two boys Nick and Andy, and myself, farms that were up for sale.

The three of us spent two exhausting days looking for something suitable. By March, there is hardly ever any snow left in New Haven, but this was Franklin County, and we slogged through drifts that were up to our hips. Near the end of the second day I was getting discouraged, as there was something wrong with every piece of property or house that we had seen. Then the agent said that in Heath – one of the highest townships in the state, just south of the Vermont line – there was a farm for sale with an early 19th-century house on it in bad condition, but that the owner, old Mrs. Crowningshield, would only sell a few acres of land with it.

It was getting darker as we pushed our way through the deep snow on the abandoned dirt road. This led us up across an open field, then through a forest of beech and hemlock, until we finally came out on top of the hill and into another much larger field. In its midst was an ancient, dilapidated house, from which one could see 25 miles of undulating woodland, and not another dwelling in sight. Inside the house, underneath all of the usual linoleum wall covering, and in spite of the

Sears Roebuck metal shelving and circular fluorescent light fixtures, I could see that its central chimney stack and fireplace mantels were intact: it was a genuine, if neglected, antique of about 1810 vintage. On the front of a gambrel-roofed red barn was a white signboard with wooden letters telling us that this was "Skyline Farm." I almost fell on my knees. As Brigham Young said when he first sighted the valley of the Great Salt Lake, "this is the place."

Back down the hill we went, to a sugarhouse from which maple-flavored steam was pouring forth at a great rate. There was Mrs. Mildred Crowningshield herself, an apple-cheeked old lady. As soon as I had cleared my steamed-up glasses, we began to talk. I was the first non-hippie in several years that had come to ask about her place on the hill, and I made it clear to her that I'd buy the house, but I had to have the acreage, too. Her conditions were 1. that her son Fred could continue to hay the land, 2. that Fred could keep his Ayrshire cows in the south pasture, and 3. that Fred could tap the sugar maples every year. I agreed wholeheartedly with these, and she said she'd think it over and I'd have a reply the next day. On my return to New Haven that night, Sophie went along with me, even though the place for her was a pig in a poke. I could hardly sleep that night, thinking about Skyline Farm.

The next day the farm in Heath was ours, revolution or no revolution.

That summer we virtually camped out in our antique home, while I went to work stripping off linoleum and old paint layers, and we planted our first vegetable garden. It was a wonderful time – with five children, and armed with that hippie Bible, the *Whole Earth Catalogue*, we were a little like back-to-the-land hippies ourselves. As a matter of fact, there had once been a Heath Commune. I came across its last, bedraggled members on a Heath roadside in April; they had run out of firewood, and were deserting their chilly Utopia. I gave them their final ride out to the real world.

After an extensive title search in the Greenfield courthouse, I found that our little house had been built in 1810 by a poor farmer named Samuel Kendrick. He had died, leaving his wife and children nearly destitute. An inventory had been made of the place, and it makes sad reading; for instance he had only one pair of trousers and two shirts to his name. His widow by necessity remarried a short time later.

❧

In 1970, there were 16 dairy farms in the town of Heath; 35 years later, only one remained – the farm of my friend and neighbor Fred Crowningshield. Being anthropologists, Sophie and I soon found out how this community of about 400 persons was organized. It was basically divided into a pair of moieties, like so many tribes described by anthropologists, for instance Alfonso Ortiz's San Juan Pueblo. One moiety consisted of the old-time, Yankee farming families, some of whom had been in Heath since the mid-18th century. These included the Dickinsons; their distant cousin was the poetess Emily, and Miss Esther Dickinson, the postmistress, looked just like her famous relative.

The other moiety was made up of Summer People – second-home owners like ourselves. During the first part of the 20th century many of these were Episcopalian clergymen and their families. Bishop Angus Dun of Washington was such a Summer Person. I had remembered him preaching the Sunday sermon at St. Paul's; when he held up his hand in the pulpit, a finger was missing, just like the villain in *The Thirty-Nine Steps*. But several of this moiety had been even more distinguished: Justice Felix Frankfurter, and the Reverend Reinhold Niehbur, often considered America's greatest theologian (his Heath friends called him "Reiny").

Again, like any other tribe, there were organizations catering to the various needs of these two populations, and an annual ceremonial round. The old-timers had the Grange and the Ladies Aid Fair. Most of the Summer People but few of the old-timers belonged to the Heath Historical Society; I eventually became its President. The one time of the year when both moieties worked together was during the Heath Fair, held every August in a high field in the center of Heath. This is one of the last and still one of the best agricultural fairs in the northern Berkshires. Sophie and the children began exhibiting at the fair every year, carrying off all sorts of blue ribbons, none of which ever seem to have brought prizes worth more than three dollars.

It once was customary at the fair to have "The Speaking" – chairs were set up under a tent, and some person, distinguished or not, would address the listeners on some educational or uplifting subject. I was the very last person invited to do this. The weather was awful, the fairgrounds being enveloped in a thick fog like cotton wool, and thunder was rolling in the distance. I was standing at a microphone and holding forth on local archaeology. As the lightning strikes got closer and closer, all I could think of was not prehistory, but that the microphone probably would be a very good lightning conductor. I cut my sermon short.

Sophie had a real feel for gardening, and was a superb cook as well as embroiderer. It wasn't long before the Heath ladies asked her to help in the exhibits hall, and for every one of her final 16 years they put her in total charge, along with her friend Alli Thane, the wife of a Heath farmer. We had become "Heathens."

⁂

A few years after I came to Yale, I created a new course on field archaeology, which was intended to teach both undergraduates and graduate students many of the basic skills that the Anthropology Department at Harvard had neglected to teach *its* students, for example, how to make a map. Every Saturday during the fall semester we dug a prehistoric site in Farmington, Connecticut, in a field next to the old Farmington Canal. With an occupation that extended all the way from the Archaic through the Early Woodland periods, say from about 3000 to 800 BC, it was fairly rich in artifacts by Connecticut standards, but I still felt I had to offer a jug of cider to any student who found a whole projectile point, as an incentive.

Then I discovered the joys, intellectual and otherwise, of historical archaeology. The field course turned its attention away from sites like the one in Farmington to the Colonial-period Morris House owned by the New Haven Historical Society, and to the remains of the gun factory that had been built by Eli Whitney in nearby Hamden. Not only did student interest shoot up, since there were now thousands of artifacts turning up in their excavation units, instead of measly dozens, but there were mountains of documents to go with the sites, written by real people about real people. One semester, in searching for documents about the Morrises in New Haven's City Hall, they discovered a large cache of records from the 17th-century New Haven Colony that had been thrown into a back room of the welfare office; among these were divorce proceedings from these so-called Puritans, and they made very steamy reading, indeed.

It was therefore exciting to find that the Heath Historical Society owned the site of Fort Shirley, one of an east–west line of forts that had been built in 1744 to protect the New England frontier and the village of Deerfield from attack by the French and Indians marauding down the Deerfield River from Canada. These were relatively small block-houses constructed of horizontally laid timbers, surrounded by palisades. The only indication that such a structure had once stood on the site was a large, inscribed boulder placed there about 1901.

I rounded up a digging team that consisted of Yale undergraduate volunteers and local enthusiasts, and began excavating in June 1974. My foreman was Jack Kloppenburg (now a full professor of rural studies at the University of Wisconsin). It seemed to never stop raining that summer, and the shallow site of the fort was underlain with impervious clay hardpan, so I sometimes felt that we were excavating an underwater site; this was soggy going, worse than what I had experienced either in Tennessee or at San Lorenzo. Nevertheless, we did recover the musket balls, gunflints, clay pipe stems, broken rum bottles and other artifacts that proved this was indeed all that was left of the fort. What made it additionally interesting was that Governor Shirley had ordered it to be decommissioned in 1754, so that we had an extremely short occupation of ten years.

Next, I found out that in Rowe, the next township west of Heath, Dan Ingersoll of the University of Massachusetts had been running a field school at the exactly contemporary Fort Pelham, and it was now in its second and final summer. Dan's team had turned up far more mid-18th-century artifacts than we had, and since he was about to leave UMass, he very kindly agreed to turn over these and all his field notes to me. What immediately struck me about this material was that virtually all of it – knives, forks, medicine flasks, brass buttons, white salt-glazed teacups and saucers, churchwarden pipes, and so on – had been made in England. This was not the "age of homespun" by any means, but represented the impressive world of consumers that the British had created in their American colonies.

Finally, I discovered that these militiamen and their officers were incredibly well documented in local libraries and in the archives of the Massachusetts Historical Society. Not only did we have all the muster rolls for the period, but a large number of account books from the store-keeper and military commissary in Deerfield who had been supplying the Line of Forts. In them were thousands of transactions, in effect, the complete material culture of the Massachusetts frontier at a critical time in its history. The really interesting part of the story was that far from being any kind of democracy, everything in Massachusetts west of the Connecticut River was in the hands of an oligarchy of elite families whose offspring had been to Harvard or Yale, and who had total con-trol of the forts – including the ones that Dan and I had dug. These were known to their contemporaries in Boston as the "River Gods," and they were all of that.

It was overwhelming: I had bitten off far more than I could chew in a few years, and it has taken me more than 25 years to bring the project to its rightful conclusion: a final report.

No Native Americans had been seen in Franklin County since the close of the French and Indian War, which was brought to an end by the British conquest of Canada and by the Treaty of Paris in 1763. The only exception that I knew about was a friendly Navajo horse-breaker who lived down the road from us for a few years.

During the ferment of the 1960s and 1970s, Princeton had actively recruited many Native Americans under a program that was conceived and run by Alfonso Ortiz, who was now on their Anthropology faculty. I thought this to be a great idea, because every other year I had taught the undergraduate North American Indian course at Yale, and Sophie and I had been "Indian buffs" ever since our honeymoon days in the Southwestern deserts. Even more of a lover of Native American cul-ture than we were, if possible, was our friend Alfred Bush, the curator of Western Americana in the Princeton Library.

I had gotten to know the Princeton scene quite well from the semester during which Gillett and Alfred had me give a guest course on

Pre-Columbian art in their Department of Art and Archaeology. Gillett's house on Stockton Street was filled with great art from every ancient culture imaginable, and it was there at a party that I first met Princeton's Native American contingent. This occasion was memorable, since supper was cooked by young women students from the pueblos along the Río Grande. After the meal, when Gillett and I threw the food remains into the trash, they carefully extracted the corncobs and ceremonially buried them out in back.

One weekend in early fall, with his usual impetuous generosity, Gillett invited them all up to his house in Colrain. We had two house guests in Heath at that time, my old friend from Taiwan days Leo Pappas, and his wife Mildred, and we took them over to Gillett's party. When we and the children arrived, this had been going on for some time, but I quickly saw that Alfonso wasn't there – this definitely was not a good sign. The Indian guests had divided into two groups, the traditional Indians (mainly from pueblos like Santo Domingo) and the urban ones, largely of mixed origin. The former were sitting near the broad fireplace in Gillett's living room, and were clearly unhappy with what was going on elsewhere. I don't blame them. The "urbanites" were out in the front room, had been imbibing vodka screwdrivers alternating with wine, and were beating a drum while singing anti-White songs – in English, as they had no knowledge of their native tongues.

I was given the job of broiling the steaks on a grill suspended in the fireplace, while Mildred, who hailed from a family of Serb origin, was vainly trying to interest a "traditional" in the beauties of the Dalmatian coast. Finally, exhausted, I sat down for a while, only to feel a pair of large hands around my neck. "Guess who?" this inebriated giant asked; Gillett still swears that this "urbanite" had picked me up by the neck and that my feet were kicking in the air, while my children were tugging at them and crying "Daddy, Daddy!" but I don't think this was right. At one point this individual had tried to set the house alight with a kerosene lamp, but Gillett slugged him and he subsided.

The next day they all left for the south, the "traditionals" going back to Princeton, but the hung-over "urbanites" to the nation's capital, where they joined like-minded discontents in thoroughly trashing the Bureau of Indian Affairs.

CHAPTER 13

Life Among the Glyphs

From the day that I had been presented with *The Book of a Thousand Tongues* as a prize in Sacred Studies at St. Paul's School, I had been fascinated by exotic peoples, their languages, and their writing systems. I doubt that the sincere Christians who had published this wonderful volume would have approved, but this was my introduction to the subversive science of anthropology, long before I knew what anthropology was. When I actually became an anthropology major on my way to becoming a Mayanist, it was therefore a bit disappointing to find out how little was then known about Maya hieroglyphic writing. The Egyptian hieroglyphs and the cuneiform writing of Mesopotamia had been deciphered early in the 19th century. Why not the Maya script, too? It will be remembered that I had a copy of Eric Thompson's *Maya Hieroglyphic Writing: An Introduction* with me on White Dog Island, but after reading every bit of this huge tome, I still didn't understand how the system worked – or perhaps it wasn't even a codified system, a pessimistic opinion that Thompson nurtured to the day of his death.

My new mentor Gordon Willey had little interest in the glyphs, but a few of my fellow graduate students did. Chief among these was Dave Kelley, who had been a disciple of Alfred Tozzer rather than of Eric Thompson. Tozzer had long been convinced that there was a strong phonetic element in the non-calendrical hieroglyphs, and had sponsored the publication of a heretical monograph on this subject by the late linguist Benjamin Whorf, a work that was scathingly dismissed by Thompson.

But Dave had already heard about something far more heretical than Whorf's foray into decipherment, as I had, too: in 1952, a young Russian linguist and ethnologist named Yuri Valentinovich Knorosov had published an article in the journal *Sovyetskaya Etnografiya* (*Soviet Ethnography*). Appearing among a plethora of anthropological studies

praising Marx, Engels, Stalin and other official icons, Knorosov's contribution claimed that he had solved the problem of how to decipher
this script. Basically, in his view it was a mixed system consisting of
what we now call "logographs" (signs expressing meaning) and "syl-
labograms" (phonetic signs standing for syllables, each consisting of a
consonant followed by a vowel). And finally, using a so-called "alphabet" that was given in a 16th-century account of the Yucatan Maya by
Bishop Diego de Landa, Knorosov said he was able to decipher a signif-
icant number of the syllabic signs that had appeared in the Dresden
Codex.

Eric had heard about this only by second-hand reports based upon
Soviet propaganda handouts, and, at least on the surface, he had nothing but bitingly sarcastic remarks to say about this "Red" upstart.
Underneath, however, he must have been deeply disturbed; that's the
only way I can explain his decades-long campaign against Knorosov
and his ideas. But for the early part of the preceding summer, before I
went to Wyoming, I had taken an intensive course in beginning Japanese at the Georgetown School of Languages, and I was struck by the
similarity between Knorosov's proposed system and Japanese. Both
scripts eclectically combined logographs (Japanese *kanji*, signs derived
from Chinese) with syllabic signs (Japanese *kana*). I managed to get
copies of several of Knorosov's articles from Soviet publications, and
Sophie began translating these for Dave and me – of course, Tania
Proskouriakoff could have done this, too, but I think she was leery of
angering Eric.

In all events, I immediately entered into a written correspondence
with Knorosov. For how this interchange developed over the years into
a gradually growing acceptance on the part of most American epigraphers that Knorosov was right, and Thompson and his followers wrong,
I refer the reader to my *Breaking the Maya Code*. What I want to tell you
about now is how and why Sophie and I first met Knorosov.

It was complete madness on both our parts. When I'd completed *America's First Civilization* for the Smithsonian and American Heritage in

November 1968, a quite large and welcome check arrived. To my surprise (having forgotten the terms of the contract) I was generously rewarded as the photographer for many of the plates, while as author I got very little money for the text. I turned to Sophie.

"Let's blow it on a trip to Russia. Let's spend Christmas and New Year there. Let's see if we can meet Knorosov."

"Why not?"

Both sets of parents thought we were crazy, but Sophie's mother Natasha looked forward to us contacting her brother Alexander Sivertsev and his family, with whom all correspondence had been broken off during the 1930s by the Soviet authorities when Sophie's parents refused to return to a country dominated by Stalin. As for my parents, they invited our children Nick and Sarah to spend Christmas with them to their winter home in Florida. We took the two others with us on our mad odyssey, nine-year-old Andy and four-year-old Peter.

The whole affair was something of a gamble, for the U.S.S.R. was then in the hands of the thoroughly Stalinist *apparatchik* Leonid Brezhnev. Sophie's father had been placed *in absentia* under a sentence of death as a non-returnee, and the regime had generally refused to recognize the offspring of exiles as anything other than Soviet citizens, whether born in the U.S. or not. I was a little uneasy due to my early career with the Agency, but the U.S.S.R. was on such bad terms with China at that time that perhaps they would see me as an ally of some sort.

We arrived in Moscow on an Aeroflot flight from Amsterdam, on Christmas Eve, 1968, all four of us totally exhausted and jet-lagged. In the darkness and swirling snow, we were whisked by an Intourist car from Sheremetyevo Airport into the center of Moscow, past the Kremlin walls and towers surmounted by glowing red stars, and to the nearby and venerable Metropole Hotel, a monument of Russian *art nouveau*. Both Sophie and I were in total culture shock, which I would describe as an overwhelming feeling that one has landed in an alien, incomprehensible universe, and that one must be in a dream or hallucinating. Until then, the only times I had experienced such feelings were two: the first in 1950, on arrival late at night in the pouring rain at London's Waterloo Station via the boat train from Southampton, and the second when I stepped off the plane in Taipei a few years later.

Our chilly room in this hotel was enormous, with what seemed to be 20-foot ceilings. On this floor as on every floor there was a so-called concierge, a formidable, middle-aged female who we were sure was a KGB colonel, and who must have been in close touch with everything that went on in our room through wire taps. That made her a great babysitter, so we had no worries about our small boys when the two of us took in the ballet at the Bolshoi Theatre one evening.

Our Intourist handler eventually put us on the Red Arrow Express for Leningrad. This great train, left over from Tsarist days, departed Moscow at 10 PM, and arrived in Leningrad at 9 AM the next morning; the schedule had been set so that pre-Revolutionary Moscow merchants could get to St. Petersburg when it was just getting light. We had our own sleeping compartment, all red plush and polished brass. In the corridor was a samovar, so we could have a glass of tea whenever we wanted. As the train rolled along, I couldn't resist opening the shade a bit and peeking out at the moonlit forests of white birch; at station stops I also couldn't help thinking of Anna Karenina.

Once established in the Astoria Hotel, another relic from the Tsarist past, we met up with Sophie's aunt and uncle in their apartment on Bolshoi Prospekt, the exact same flat that her parents had occupied before they left Russia forever. Sophie's first cousin Irina and her husband Gennadi Ditmar ("Genya"), had their own flat elsewhere; both were field geologists with the Soviet Academy of Sciences, and their small son Pavel was Peter's age. Uncle Alexander had survived the Battle of Berlin as a Red Army soldier, and he gave me a large, brass nail that he had taken off a Reichstag door. But his wife Anna Andreyevna and Irina were also survivors: they had managed to live through the terrible Siege of Leningrad, when the city had been completely cut off by encircling German forces for 872 days, and hundreds of thousands died of starvation.

On a bitterly cold but clear New Year's Eve Irina and Genya took us to a nightclub on Nevsky Prospekt, where we drank vodka and listened to the Soviet version of a jazz band. After several hours of this, Sophie and I thought we had better return to the Astoria and our small boys, and Irina directed us to where a trolley could take us to St. Isaak's Square, where the hotel was located. The tram duly arrived; its windows were so fogged up that it wasn't until too late that we realized it was packed to capacity. The door opened, and someone hauled Sophie inside, and the tram took off into the night, leaving me behind. Sophie's cousins had disappeared, and unlike Sophie, who was bilingual in the language, I knew only a few words of Russian. I also have no sense of direction. But, convinced that this was all just a dream, I began walking along a frozen canal in the moonlight, thinking it might lead me home. On the way I passed a drunk lying on the snow, being systematically beaten up by the police. Miraculously, after about an hour, there was the golden dome of St. Isaak's looming up in front of me. Saved!

๑

Sophie had come to see her family, but I had come to Leningrad to meet Yuri Valentinovich Knorosov. We crossed a bridge over the Neva ice to Peter the Great's baroque Ethnographic Museum, now the Ethnographic Institute. His office was on the second floor, but only about a quarter of it was his territory, the rest being occupied by four or five other researchers, both male and female. He, however, had the best view, over the frozen Neva, across to the golden Admiralty spire celebrated by Pushkin. Those who have seen the now-famous photograph of Knorosov holding his Siamese cat will be familiar with the black hair parted in the middle, turning to white above the ears, his beetling eyebrows, and penetrating eyes – unnervingly recalling the features of the terrible monk Grigory Rasputin, whose noble assassins had finally finished him off by shoving the monster through a hole in the Neva ice not far from where we were sitting. It was the quality of Knorosov's eyes that struck me most forcefully, for they were sapphire blue and full of intelligence.

Yuri Valentinovich had been an artillery officer during the war, and proudly wore the medals that he won during the conflict. Like Sophie's uncle, he also had been in the final attack on Berlin, and survived. I later discovered that he was a cigarette addict, but in deference to us he would do all his smoking outside the building.

With Sophie interpreting, we had long discussions about the glyphs and about Thompson, whom he admired for his work on the calendar but for little else. I could see that he had taken a great liking to Sophie and our small boys, who were kept busy by his female colleagues eating various kinds of cakes and sweets. Next he took us on a tour of historic St. Petersburg, on which he was clearly an expert, telling us one anecdote after another; his favorite pieces of historical gossip were about Grigory Potemkin, Catherine the Great's corrupt prime minister and lover. Knorosov insisted on carrying little Peter throughout our walk, and to my astonishment he took all four of us to dine in the faculty club of the University of Leningrad.

Eric had written off Knorosov as some kind of minor Communist *apparatchik* whose claim to have deciphered the Maya script was laughable. We found instead a deeply sympathetic person with an immense knowledge and understanding of human history and, even more to the point, a comparative approach to ancient civilizations that Eric totally lacked. To Thompson, writing systems like the Chinese, Japanese, Egyptian, and Mesopotamian ones were completely irrelevant to the problem; to Knorosov they were not.

For two decades the only persons outside the U.S.S.R. who believed that Yuri Valentinovich had been the Champollion of the Maya decipherment were Dave Kelley, Floyd Lounsbury, and Sophie and me. Tania Proskouriakoff probably thought this, too, but she was so worried about Eric's possible reaction that she didn't dare put it in print. Our initial visit to the U.S.S.R. convinced me that we had been right all along.

But all was not exactly sweetness and light in the U.S.S.R. during the "period of stagnation," as the oppressive years of Leonid Brezhnev's rule were later to be called. Theodosius Dobzhansky had been condemned for his opposition to the autocrat of Soviet biology Trofim Lysenko, and this evil charlatan who had sent so many of Dobzhansky's former colleagues to the Gulag still had many adherents, including Brezhnev himself. When we went by ourselves to the Natural History Museum, several researchers appeared from the shadows and pressed messages into Sophie's hand to take back to her father in New York. We were sure that we were followed and bugged in both Moscow and Leningrad, and had to watch what we said. As we stepped off our plane in Brussels on our way back home, we looked at each other and said "Whew!"

The atmosphere was very different when we returned to the U.S.S.R. some two decades later, on an exchange fellowship between the U.S. National Academy of Sciences and its Soviet counterpart. This was the era of Gorbachev's *perestroika*, and freedom was in the air. I came to Leningrad bringing with me a sizeable pile of reprints and articles by Linda Schele, Dave Stuart, and others, representing the very latest in U.S. research on the glyphs – which in many respects had in its origin been based on Knorosov's approach. My project was for Sophie and me to set up a kind of dialogue between Yuri Valentinovich and his students, on the one hand, and Linda's people, on the other.

This was a great idea, but I'm afraid to say that it didn't get very far. The basic problem was this. In his 1952 paper, and in those written shortly later, Knorosov had shown that Bishop Landa's famous ABC was a syllabary, not an alphabet; all of his readings based on that fact have turned out to be 100 percent correct, and it is that *that* has been the key to "breaking the Maya code." But later on he also proposed readings for many other glyphs in the codices that were not clearly phonetic, but probably mostly logographic. Here he was on no better grounds than his antagonist Thompson had been. Sophie and I did our best to show him that Floyd, Linda, Dave, and others had worked out a methodology to "crack" the logographs: to identify places in the ancient texts where the scribes had substituted phonetic signs, or added phonetic signs to clarify or complement the reading. After a couple of sessions in our friend's office – unchanged after 20 years – it was clear that he and his two young students didn't want to hear anything about this. And there is nothing more stubborn than a stubborn Russian!

So, how do I think about Yuri Valentinovich now? I think that he was the Einstein of the Maya decipherment. Remember that Einstein had changed our view of the universe in five papers completed and published by the time he had reached 37 years of age. Other than his prediction of Bose-Einstein condensation made eight years later, the rest of his long and rightly honored life was spent basically treading water, during which he had failed to recognize the validity of quantum physics. Knorosov was only 30 when his ground-breaking article was published, and it, with a couple of more papers brought out in the next few years, contains everything that has been proved to be valid about his work. The rest of it was also treading water. After Eric's demise in 1975, the world of Pre-Columbian studies finally recognized Knorosov's genius, and he died as the respected founding father of archaeology's last great decipherment. I count it an honor to have known him.

I believe it was the beautiful Raquel Welch who, when asked by a nosy reporter to name her most erogenous zone, replied "the brain." For me, many of the most exciting adventures in archaeology have taken place not through pick and shovel (and trowel) digging in jungle or desert, but in the mind – for instance Michael Ventris's "cracking" of the Linear B script. There are two ways that enlightenment is achieved in the study of the human past. One is to deliberately seek it out patiently and (it is hoped) logically, step by step. This is what I had done in my research on the Guatemalan coast, in Costa Rica, and at San Lorenzo. The second is to have it descend on one like the Holy Spirit did on St. Paul on his road to Damascus: the scales would fall from one's eyes, and the truth would be revealed in a blaze of recognition. Call it intuition or playing one's hunches, or call it what you will, the blinding flash of insight can and does happen in archaeology. But mental adventures of this kind will seldom get you a mention in the *New York Times* or membership in the Explorers' Club. Nevertheless, I would like to tell you about such an adventure that happened three decades ago.

On a day in August 1968, Sophie and the children and I were standing among a crowd of Native Americans on one side of the broad, dusty plaza in the midst of Santo Domingo Pueblo. This was the day of the eponymous Saint Dominic, and the pounding feet of two long lines of dancers – over four hundred in all – made the ground shake. They were performing their annual Corn Dance, and the rhythmic drumming and dancing were believed to invoke the beneficent rain clouds. At first the sky was completely blue, with a blazing sun. But over the distant Jemez Mountains we could see a cloud "no bigger than a man's fist," and as the morning progressed, it grew bigger. As we left the pueblo that afternoon, a huge thunderstorm with driving rain was in progress.

197

During the dance, our friends Alfred Bush of the Princeton Library and Douglas Ewing told me that they were both members of the Grolier Club in New York (a club devoted to the collecting and study of old books), and that they both thought that it was time to do an exhibit there devoted to Maya writing. I agreed, but assured them that there was no chance that the institutions that owned the three known Maya manuscripts (the codices in Dresden, Paris, and Madrid) would let them out of their respective countries. However, by borrowing some painted or carved vases with writing on them from public and private collections, along with a few inscribed stone monuments that I knew existed in the country, I could put together something meaningful. I had no inkling of where all this would lead.

A short while later, I found myself invited to the Mexico City house of Dr. Josué Saenz and his wife Jacqueline, along with Betty Benson of Dumbarton Oaks in Washington. They had one of the world's largest and finest collections of Mesoamerican art; the walls of their dining room were lined with Maya stelae. But we were there to look at the amazing clay figurines and vessels from the Olmec site of Las Bocas in the state of Puebla. I had heard from others that Dr. Saenz had bought what purported to be a Maya codex, and I asked to see it, although I was almost certain it would be a fake. Back at Yale, I had a file containing many dozens of photos of false Maya codices, and with no exceptions these were sorry productions by persons with no real knowledge of how Maya writing worked. The minute I saw Saenz's codex, I knew it was something else.

It was on bark paper (most fake Maya codices are on leather), and consisted of ten pages of what was once a 20-page Venus calendar, painted in a Toltec-Maya style typical of the 12th-century AD. Dr. Saenz gave me photos of the manuscript, which I brought back to New Haven and showed to Floyd Lounsbury. After considerable study, we both concluded that this was the fourth known Maya manuscript. I then asked its owner if we could borrow it for the show, and he said yes.

The next step was to see where we could find Classic Maya vases with hieroglyphic writing on them. Up to now, nobody had really bothered about the texts painted or carved on these objects, since Eric had declared them to be mere decoration, carried out by illiterate peasant artists. A real problem lay in the fact that so few of these inscribed vases had been dug up by archaeologists – and even fewer actually published – that one could say very little else about them to counter Thompson. I would have to look into private collections.

I had heard that William Palmer, the owner of Bar Harbor Airlines, had a very large number of these vases in his Portland, Maine, home, and when I contacted him, he sent down his private plane (piloted by a retired Air Force colonel) to pick me up. Palmer turned out to be a real eccentric, a bit like Howard Hughes, but on a less extravagant scale, and far more generous. He was a pack-rat type collector with not one, but two homes in the area; lying outside one of these were about a dozen gigantic totem poles from the Northwest Coast. In the basement of another, with its own curator, was a quarter century's worth of old numbers of the *New York Times*, *Newsweek*, and other newspapers and journals. He told me "I just want to look things up when I feel like it." I discovered that he had also been at St. Paul's, a few classes below mine, but like so many others had been kicked out by Rev. Norman Burdett Nash. Sadly, he died relatively young; his entire collection was left to the University of Maine's Hudson Museum.

I flew back to New Haven with the colonel, along with 15 or so Maya vases and bowls packed in popcorn (against breakage). We temporarily stored them on a ping pong table in my basement, and I had a good chance to examine them. I discovered on several of the polychrome vases the figure of a handsome young Maya noble, with a back-sloping, tonsured head and lots of jade jewelry. All well and good, but why were there not one, but two of these youths on each vase? It was there standing by the ping pong table that I thought of the story of the Hero Twins in the *Popol Vuh*, the great creation epic of the Quiché Maya people, which had been written down using Roman script in the early Colonial period.

The *Popol Vuh* is a vast poetic work that begins with the Maya creation myth and ends with the Spanish Conquest. There had been previous worlds to ours, created and then destroyed by the gods. At the close of the last one, the sky had fallen upon the earth, and everything was in darkness; this interregnum was a time of mystic doings, when the gods brought forth a pair of handsome twins to rid the world of monstrosities, to overcome death. In brief, here is their story. Their father and uncle, also twins, were named One Hunahpu and Seven Hunahpu; they were great ballplayers, but their noisy game angered the lords of Xibalba, the underworld, where they were defeated and sacrificed by decapitation. Hun Hunahpu's head was hung up in a tree. One day the daughter of one of Xibalba's lords spoke to it, whereupon the head spat into her hand, making her pregnant. The disgraced girl was expelled to the earth's surface, where she gave birth to Hunahpu and Xbalanque, the Hero Twins of the story.

These two are also summoned to the netherworld after a ball game, but they turn the table on their adversaries (the personifications of mortal diseases and corruption), and eventually overcome them following a series of ordeals and a magical ball game. The Hero Twins reach apotheosis in the sky as the sun and the moon, but before they do, they resurrect their father Hun Hunahpu. You will see the significance of this act of filial piety later on in my tale.

So, I thought I had here in visible form the Twins themselves, in Late Classic times, 700 years before the extant version of the *Popol Vuh* was put in written form. According to Panovsky and Kubler's "Principle of Disjunction" this could not be, but I never believed this, anyway. Nor was I bothered by the fact that Thompson had never even mentioned the *Popol Vuh* in his massive *Maya Hieroglyphic Writing: An Introduction*, although everything else got in there including the poetry of minor Laureates.

When the day came actually to mount the exhibit at the Grolier Club, I had many other Classic vases in my hands, and I thought I could see all sorts of *Popol Vuh* imagery on some of these, too. For instance, on one polychrome vase from the Princeton Art Museum there was a "Young Lord" (this is what I was labeling these apparent twins) holding a knife behind his back, pulling an old god out of a snail shell. This suggested to me one of the final episodes in the epic, when the Hero Twins, after their apparent demise reappear in the court of the death gods and perform acts of legerdemain: at one point, one twin cuts the other up into pieces, and then brings him back to life, and this is repeated by the other. Their sinister hosts ask that this be done to *them*, and the Twins comply, but neglect to resurrect them.

Incidentally, thanks to Dr. Saenz's generosity, we put the new manuscript on show, naming it the Grolier Codex, since we could think of no other name. This aroused the immense displeasure of the ayatollahs who now ruled INAH in Mexico City. Invoking not the Koran like their Iranian counterparts but *Das Kapital*, which most of them had never read, they had eased my aristocratic friend Ignacio Bernal into what they hoped would be obscurity. Once the manuscript was returned to Mexico, Saenz loaned it to the Museum of Anthropology which immediately locked it into a vault, where it still languishes. The enraged authorities have ever since been torn between hurt pride at not having themselves recognized this as a major find, and an unquenchable desire to prove it a fake. It must still annoy them mightily that all competent Maya epigraphers regard it as real, a conclusion backed up by the radiocarbon date that I ran on the bark paper from which it is made.

It eventually came time to prepare a catalogue, to be published by the Grolier Club. The overall design was assigned to Norman Ives, who taught at Yale and had been a student and colleague of Josef Albers. The photography was to be done by Justin Kerr, whom I met for the first time; here the problem we were faced with was how to make a flat image of the curved surface of a cylindrical object. I wasn't happy with the idea of stitching together a lot of individual photos taken as the vase was turned, but this is what we ended up with here. Within a few years, Justin developed his rollout camera, and the study of Maya iconography through the vases was revolutionized. By this means, a whole world of *Popol Vuh* and other mythological imagery was revealed. With not just a few dozen but well over 1,000 Maya vases now photographically rolled out in black and white and in color, serious study of Classic art and culture could now begin.

What about the written or carved texts on these vases? Eric had proclaimed that they were meaningless, just mere decoration. But I had seen on the vases in the Grolier show some glyphs that seemed to recur over and over. Back in New Haven, I went through all the excavation reports that had pictures of excavated, inscribed pots, and I saw these same glyphs. Why were they there? Remember that I had no rollouts to work with, which would have made everything far easier, so I took as many photos as I could of these texts with a Polaroid camera, and copied other texts on a Xerox machine. That summer I took all of these with me to our farm in Heath, and cut them up into individual glyphs. In a local stationery store I bought long sheets of graph paper, which I laid on the floor of our living room. It soon became apparent that there were two kinds of text on a vase or bowl. The first was always in a primary position, usually around the rim, and this was the one that had all the repetition. The second usually appeared within the scene on the pot, and I guessed referred in some way to what was going on. So I concentrated on the primary one, putting like glyphs above and below each other in the same column.

It wasn't long before I had a kind of grid for my primary text, and this almost always began with what I called the Initial Sign (although this might be preceded by a date in the 52-year Calendar Round). Next in line was a glyph the main part of which was the head of the Old God N, whom I had identified as one of the underworld deities in the *Popol Vuh*; and so on through about 15 or 20 other glyphs, ending in what were obviously the names and titles of real people. I called the whole reconstructed text the Primary Standard Sequence (generally referred to by today's epigraphers as the PSS), but emphasized that the whole text might not always be given, but just an abbreviated version.

Just as I had figured it all out, to my great delight Dave Kelley came to visit us in our Heath home, and I was able to show him what I had discovered.

I had no real knowledge of what this PSS meant, but it clearly was of immense importance to the Maya of the Late Classic. I did know, however, that most or all of these vases had been found in tombs, and hazarded a guess that it was some kind of repetitious funerary chant listing gods of Xibalba that the defunct might meet. Here I was about 100 percent wrong! In later years, younger epigraphers got to work on this – Nikolai Grube in Germany (who wrote his doctoral thesis on the PSS), Barbara McLeod, David Stuart, Steve Houston, and Karl Taube, among others. Although not every glyph in it has yet been read, it is now certain that the PSS has four parts: 1. a dedicatory introduction; 2. a description of the vessel's surface, and its carving or painting (sometimes giving the name of the scribal artist); 3. a description of the

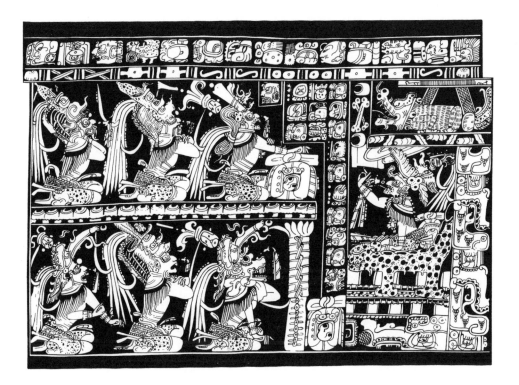

Artist's rollout of a cylindrical Maya vase of the eighth century AD, depicting seven Maya gods seated in the underworld. Just below the rim is a Primary Standard Sequence, here telling us that the vase once held the chocolate drink, along with the name and titles of the patron.

vessel itself and its contents, usually the chocolate drink; and 4. the name and title of the owner or patron.

That, and my reading of the name glyph of the old God N – the aged individual in the snail shell – as "Pauahtun" (a god mentioned in Landa's *Relación de las Cosas de Yucatán*), have been my only original contributions to the decipherment. As far as "breaking the Maya code" is concerned, I have always felt more like a Boswell than a Dr. Johnson.

When I first met her in Palenque in 1973, I never would have thought Linda Schele would be the one to revolutionize Maya studies. A heavy-set young woman in faded jeans, a Bohemian artist and teacher, totally oblivious to what she was wearing, and with a ribald sense of humor and salty language to go with it, she certainly didn't look or act the part. In many ways, she was the antithesis of the demure, ladylike, careful, and always nervous Tania Proskouriakoff. The venue was the now famous Primera Mesa Redonda de Palenque, the First Palenque Round Table (in recent years INAH has taken over this series of Maya conferences and pronounced it their "*Mesa Redonda*," but we all know what was really the first).

It was one of the most exciting intellectual events of my life, held in what has to be the most beautiful Maya site. Here is where iconographers and artists like Linda and our hostess, Merle Robertson, met up with epigraphers like my linguist colleague Floyd Lounsbury and Peter Mathews, and with art historians like Betty Benson. Betty was Curator of the great Pre-Columbian art collection at Dumbarton Oaks in Washington, and I had been advisor to the collection since 1963. The two of us set up the program and publication series in Pre-Columbian studies (we both left in 1979). With me were two Yale students, David Joralemon and Larry Bardawil, both of whom had been in my advanced seminars on Mesoamerican thought and culture. The highlight of the conference was when Floyd, Peter, and Linda worked out for the first time, before our very eyes, a complete dynastic history for Palenque. David's contribution was the iconography of the horrific royal rite of bloodletting by piercing the penis, while Larry gave us the definitive study of what he called the "Principal Bird Deity." You'll hear more about these in Chapter 14, when I come to San Bartolo.

The "dirt" archaeologists were quick to belittle the achievements of those who had been there at the Palenque dawn. Most of them knew nothing of the glyphs, and many still don't seem to believe that the script has been deciphered. But this is where it all came together for the first time – for the first time we were seeing the ancient Maya through their own eyes. And Thompson had been right about one thing: while the principal preoccupation of the Classic Maya may have been corn agriculture and the coming of the rains, it was mediated through an even greater preoccupation with religion.

Linda went on to get her doctorate at the University of Texas, writing her thesis on the epigraphy of the Maya verb – a long way from her previous métier, teaching painting in the University of South Alabama. But she was eclectic and holistic by nature – in her person, she brought together all the different threads that would tell us about the Maya. After she was hired by Texas, she brought her young protégé David Stuart to work with her on the inscriptions and iconography of that other lovely Classic site, Copán, by this time undergoing an amazing program of excavation, restoration, and deep tunneling by Bob Sharer of the University of Pennsylvania and by Bill Fash, then of the University of Southern Illinois, two "dirt" archaeologists who really understood what was going on in these fields.

I digress at such length about this amazing woman since she touched on my own life and that of my students in so many ways. She was very close to Floyd, whom she rightly worshipped – I think because she stood in awe of his intellect and of the painstaking thoroughness in everything he did. Linda could be sloppy, and often was, rushing into print long before all the data were in, and not all of her readings and interpretations have stood up to the test of time. But she was usually right.

I had been getting deeper and deeper into native Mesoamerican religion and thought ever since the early 1960s, through seminars that I taught every year at Yale, often using as texts native books such as the magnificent Borgia Codex from central Mexico. One might think this illogical for someone who had lost his own religion when a teenager, but I was convinced that no ancient people ever lived by bread alone. At the same time, I believed that it was necessary for anyone doing this kind of work to learn at least one Mesoamerican language, instead of having always to read about the indigenous civilizations through the filter of Spanish, the tongue of the conquistadores and missionaries. I put this into practice by beginning a study of Nahuatl (Aztec) with Gordon Whittaker, an amazing and thoroughly polyglot student from Australia (and now a Professor at the University of Tübingen). It was a wonderful language! I also sat in on a course in Yucatec Maya given by social anthropologist Paul Sullivan, which provided me with the linguistic background to write my book Breaking the Maya Code.

We now had a powerful Mesoamerican program going at Yale, and began attracting many students of the highest caliber. Peter Mathews came to study with Floyd, and Gillett had sent his student Mary Miller from Princeton; although she was at Yale to get her degree with George Kubler, she was allowed by the great man to take my seminars. Mary went on to collaborate with Linda on the pathbreaking *The Blood of Kings*, considered by many the greatest Maya exhibit of all time, and took Kubler's place in History of Art when he retired. These decades were magical times for me. At one point I had in my class three superstars: Steve Houston, Karl Taube, and Louise Burkhart. Louise is now the preeminent scholar of Aztec literature in the U.S. (Mary and I once sat in on her Nahuatl-language course). I can't say that I taught these young people anything; I just sat back and listened.

It was Karl who took the *Popol Vuh* Hero Twin legend into a new dimension, proving that the "Young Lords" on the pots were *not* Hunahpu and Xbalanque – the Hero Twins – but their father and uncle. And further, that this father, Hun Hunahpu, was none other than the Maize God. It follows that the very basis of Maya religion turns out to be a myth of the death and resurrection of maize: just as Hun Hunahpu goes into Xibalba, so does the Maya maize farmer drop his seeds into a hole in the ground, and just as the Twins bring their father to life again (one plate shows them actually watering him from a pot), so does the coming of the rains germinate the maize.

By the time he came to Yale, Steve was already in the front ranks of epigraphers, and he and Karl formed a wonderful intellectual partnership that continues today. With the collaboration of Dave Stuart, it was they who worked out what my PSS *really* stands for: it is an elaborate case of what they call "name-tagging," the Maya custom of writing the name of an object *on* that same object, and then giving the owner's name. Above and beyond his many new readings, Steve has been the theoretician of the great decipherment.

All of these discoveries came one after the other in a seemingly endless procession. But an end had to come, eventually, at least in Yale's Anthropology Department. I retired in 1994, and Floyd passed away in 1998. If there ever had been a "Yale School" of Maya iconography and epigraphy, it was pretty much over. It had been great fun while it lasted.

CHAPTER 14

Parallel Worlds

My long-planned retirement from Yale at age 65 sadly coincided with Sophie's death from a cancer that was detected far too late by her doctors to be cured – the greatest loss and sorrow I have ever suffered. For almost four decades we had been true partners in everything, so close to each other in feeling and thought that we often knew in advance what the other would say at any time; we enjoyed the same music, the same books, the same art, the same love of travel to exotic places, the same food, the same love of all things Italian – especially Rome and Venice. I think that most happy marriages are based either upon the unity of complementary opposites, or upon total likeness; the latter was the case with us. Believe it or not, we never had an argument about anything.

In the last ten years of her life, with our five children largely grown up and flown from the nest, Sophie became more and more involved with the world of food scholarship: the history and anthropology of the cuisines of ancient America. Like her Russian mother, she was a great cook, as I have said, and could prepare food not only in the Russian and American tradition, but in the styles of many countries – even in Shanghai style, taught her by Vivian Wu, her closest friend in New Haven. Every autumn she would attend the Oxford Symposium on Food and Cookery, the brainchild of the retired British diplomat Alan Davidson, whose scientific and insightful approach to the subject she greatly admired.

When her book *America's First Cuisines* was published by the University of Texas Press, she realized that she'd not done full justice to chocolate, an invention of ancient Mexico that played such an important role in all Mesoamerican cultures, and later on in the western world, so she planned a new book on the subject. Back we went to Rome on my final Yale triennial leave, and there she did a great deal of her research, and blocked out the chapters for the book. My Roman cousin Tino Vitetti was then Vice-Consul for Ecuador (of all things), and I would spend mornings in his consular office, typing out the manuscript of the fourth, revised edition of my book *Mexico*, while Sophie explored the libraries of Rome and the Vatican. We would meet every day at some fine restaurant for lunch.

The following January, Sophie fell seriously ill in New Haven, and spent the last four months of her life bedridden in our home on St. Ronan Street, the quietest neighborhood in the city. It became quite clear that she could never get beyond the first chapter and half, but I promised her I'd finish it, using her notes and research. Throughout her four-month-long ordeal, even when she was in great pain, she never once complained. I think that she was more worried about what would happen to me after she passed away than about her own end. Sophie died that May, and my children and I scattered her ashes in the lagoon of Venice, the city that she loved above all others.

Not long afterwards, with the help and encouragement of Alan and Jane Davidson and Harlan Walker, I established the Sophie Coe Prize in Food History, awarded annually at the Oxford Symposium, and now in its tenth year.

And Sophie need not have worried. During the past decade, I've been kept busy and reasonably happy living in four parallel universes: fly fishing, Planting Fields, Angkor, and the Classic Maya.

☙

I've been fishing ever since I was about six, when my parents' butler would take me out on his day off onto a usually rainy Long Island Sound in a rented rowboat. Our bait consisted of a cardboard box of sandworms crawling around in brown seaweed; the equipment was fishing line wrapped around a small board, and a hook and sinker. We caught vast quantities of flounder, and sometimes terrifyingly wriggly and slimy eels. I loved it.

You've already heard about the trout fishing on Irma Lake at our Cody ranch. As a boy, I excelled in angling with grasshoppers, which I would catch and keep in an empty pipe tobacco tin, but my grandfather used only the fly rod. At dusk, I would paddle him around the lake in a canoe; the lake's surface would be covered with the circles left by rising trout, and he would sometimes hook two fish at the same time with two flies. This looked like great fun, but he never taught *me* how to do it.

For years I was a spin fisherman, and took a spinning rod on all my archaeological expeditions. My best luck was on the Pacific coasts of Guatemala and Costa Rica, where I would cast from the beach for the evening meal after the day's digging was done. When my grandfather died in 1955, I inherited that same split-cane fly rod, but it sat unused in my attic for many years. Finally, I'd had enough of this, and traveled with it and my 13-year-old son Andy up to the Orvis School in Manchester, Vermont, and took their course in fly casting. I've never looked back.

My fishing experiences would make another book. I've caught fish on the fly all over the United States and the world, in places that I never dreamed I'd ever see: Arctic char with the Inuit near Hudson's Bay, bonefish in Mexico and the Bahamas, barramundi in Australia near the Arafura Sea, huge taimen (the world's largest member of the trout-salmon family) in Mongolia, rainbow trout in Siberia's Kamchatka Peninsula, Pacific sailfish on the Guatemalan coast (not far from where I once excavated!), peacock bass and pirhanas in the Amazon, and giant brown trout in Patagonia. Every June I am to be found at Homossasa, on Florida's west coast, fly fishing for industrial-strength-sized tarpon. But nothing compares to the sheer excitement and feeling of accomplishment as I stand in a lovely river in back-country New England, and watch a feeding trout take my tiny, artificial dry fly as it drifts down the current! Some enthusiasts claim that this is the only thing better than sex.

I've met some amazing people in this particular parallel world, both professional guides and fellow anglers. My favorite bonefish guide in Mexico is a pure Maya Indian named Lemus; while we are stalking this skittish and almost invisible fish in the shallows, he teaches me Yucatec Maya. When the sun is obscured, and the bonefish become even more difficult to spot, he mutters *muyal* ("cloud"); when sunlight strikes the water, Lemus exclaims *k'in* ("sun!"). In return, I tell him how to write Maya glyphs, beginning with the numbers.

༄

Even if my grandfather had left it to them in his will, none of his children or grandchildren could ever have afforded to maintain his Long Island estate, Planting Fields. The taxes alone on the 65-room house, the greenhouses, and the grounds would be beyond all of us. Wisely, before his death he deeded the whole place to the State of New York, with the understanding that it would be maintained as an arboretum for the enjoyment of the public, and as a horticultural center. But Governor Nelson Rockefeller had other ideas, and took it as a temporary campus for one of his state universities. Thus began a dark period of deterioration for this lovely place, with the state closing it down completely after the university departed for other quarters. One of the state bureaucrats of the period was overheard expressing a wish that the house would burn down, otherwise he would have to bulldoze it.

This never happened. Planting Fields was saved thanks to an active Friends organization, and to the Planting Fields Foundation that had been set up by my grandfather as a support organization. At first the Foundation was under the thumb of the formidable Miss Marguerite Pettet, who had been the old man's accountant and part-time secretary for years, having come to work for him as a good-looking young woman of 17. Since she had known me from infancy, she still treated me as a helpless infant, even when I became the Foundation's president and chairman. Miss Pettet's idea of saving the house would be to "fix it up" as a kind of memorial to the glory of the Coe family. I knew that this would never work. One night in Rome, I convinced my Uncle Bob Coe and Aunt Natalie Vitetti that the only solution was to turn the house into a museum, restore it, and open it to the public, on the order of the stately homes controlled by Britain's National Trust. They accepted my idea, and we began, with the full cooperation of the state.

On the advice of Florence and Charles Montgomery (Professor of Art History and American Studies at Yale), we contacted Charles Peterson of Philadelphia to put together a study team to plan the restoration. "Pete" Peterson was the grand old man of the restoration field in the United States. But Marguerite would have nothing to do with this project, and blocked it at every turn. On the team was Elizabeth "Liz" Watson, a historic furnishings expert who helped us with the house interior; she was also the wife of that same Jim Watson, whom you have met with his MG Midget in Chapter 8. Another team member was a young, bright architect, a Vietnam War veteran with psychological problems. It was not long before I discovered that Marguerite had turned his head, and he was not doing the job for which he had been hired. One day in late spring, I made a special trip down to Long Island from New Haven to admonish Miss Pettet (many years my senior, mind you), and to sack her young protégé.

I was to spend the night in this huge house, something I hadn't done since I was seven years old. By now no one lived in it, but Marguerite told me that I could stay in the former governess' bedroom. It was nighttime by the time I had completed my mission and eaten a solitary meal at a local restaurant. Lightning was flashing through the windows of the darkened mansion as I made my way to the second floor, thunder rolled, and a strong wind howled dismally outside. Just as I had reached the door to my room, it banged shut. My suitcase was inside, and I had no key to the Yale lock! I found a sofa in an office occupied in the daytime by Marguerite's cigar-smoking companion Joe Burkhart, and spent a sleepless night on it. I may not have much religion, but I'm very superstitious, and the eerie creaks emitted by the house and its furniture made me think of ancestral ghosts.

I survived and the house survived. Planting Fields has been saved as a whole for the people of Long Island and New York State, as the best preserved of the "Gold Coast" mansions of a long-past era. Thanks to a wonderful staff, and especially to the unflappable Director of the Foundation, Lorraine Gilligan, we now have conducted tours and children's educational programs in a place that was once the private home of an unabashed plutocrat who listed his profession in Who's Who as "capitalist." I think my grandfather would be pleased, but I'm not so sure about Miss Pettet!

ᘒ

In my long years as a Mayanist, I had never forgotten that magical visit in 1954 to the magnificent ruined city of Angkor. I had always intended to return there some day, but given the terrible violence that was inflicted upon Cambodia by the Vietnam War and by the Khmer Rouge, it seemed that that day might never come. Then, following the liberation of that unhappy country from the Khmer Rouge terror, ironically by the army of Communist Vietnam, peace of a sort finally came. In April 1993, on the eve of the UN-supervised elections, Sophie and I found ourselves in Siem Reap, on a two-person tour arranged by the firm of Abercrombie and Kent. Blue-helmeted troops were everywhere, but foreign tourists were understandably in short supply, as several had recently been killed by Khmer Rouge remnants.

It seems strange, but the Khmer Rouge had pretty much left Angkor alone – they needed it to give themselves some kind of legitimacy, and they needed the towers of Angkor Wat on their flag. Given the sheer size of the city – something over 100 square kilometers – war damage was minimal, except for the Phnom Bakheng (the hill temple complex at Angkor's center) and one of Angkor Wat's sculpted galleries. Armed Cambodian soldiers, sometimes labeled "police" by their arm badges, were present at every part of this huge site, and we could hear mortar fire and machine guns in the distance: the conflict was still going on about ten miles away, as it had been when I was last there in 1954. I had hoped that we could get to the diminutive Banteay Srei, the rose-pink "Citadel of Women" just northeast of Angkor, but that most beautiful of all temple complexes in Southeast Asia was still in Khmer Rouge hands.

Cambodia's capital city, Phnom Penh, combined euphoria with pandemonium. The Vietnamese-installed government had allowed its population, forcibly removed by the Khmer Rouge fanatics at huge human cost, to stream back in, and squatters occupied all of the lovely old villas and crowded the garbage-strewn streets. Everyone was in a hurry to catch up, to make a living, and even to learn English. The fine old museum was in a sorry state, with thousands of bats occupying the spaces in its roof and covering the unique sculpture collection with their pungent droppings. Nonetheless, it was wonderful to be back here, and Sophie was as delighted with Cambodia and Angkor as I had long been.

There was then no one book in English on Khmer culture history that was comparable to any of the volumes in Thames & Hudson's

"Ancient Peoples and Places" series, and I felt that I could do one. Almost all of the older scholarly literature was in French, and this was a language that had been drilled into me from First Grade through boarding school. I had also never stopped collecting books on Angkorian subjects, especially the classic reports of the *École Française d'Extrême-Orient*, the institution that had excavated and restored the ruined city. I came back to Angkor again and again over the next decade, often as a lecturer with the tour company Far Horizons. This was during a time when modern archaeological projects under the auspices of many institutions and countries had been discovering aspects of Angkorian culture that had been overlooked by the older generation. Not the least of these was the idea of this as a city in which people had actually lived: what was the settlement pattern of Classic Angkor, and how did it compare with that of that other monsoon-forest civilization, the Classic Maya?

By not rushing into print right away, I was able to write a better and more complete book. I have never had a chance to dig into Cambodia's past except as an armchair scholar, but in part my dream of 50 years ago has at last come partially true.

❧

On the other side of the globe, the world of Maya scholarship has entered a new and incredibly exciting phase. The fact that we can now actually read a Maya history that extends back to the third century AD is now rather "old hat," and accepted by all, but what came before that? What kind of Big Bang got Maya civilization started in the first place? Did the Olmec civilization turn into Maya civilization?

It was the last week of April 2004, at the height of the dry season in the Maya lowlands, and our sleek, blue helicopter was descending onto a cleared area in the northeastern corner of Guatemala's Department of Petén. Here, three years before, courtesy of Dame Fortune, a young Harvard-trained archaeologist named Bill Saturno had literally stumbled into making one of the greatest Maya discoveries of all time. Thirsty, hot, and tired, he had taken refuge from the sun in a looter's tunnel that had been run into a pyramidal structure in the small but very early site of San Bartolo. Looking up, he saw that part of a splendid polychrome mural was visible above his head. This has turned out to be the oldest Maya wall painting known, once covering the upper part of the four walls of a room that had been filled in and abandoned in ancient times.

When two intact wall surfaces had been photographed and then copied in half-scale watercolor by the expedition artist, the immensely talented Yale graduate student Heather Hurst (receiver of a MacArthur "genius prize" in 2004), the world of Maya scholarship was electrified. Bill had brought in Karl Taube as his iconographer and David Stuart as epigrapher. What was shown on the north wall in brilliant colors was the birth and resurrection of the Maize God – the Hun Hunahpu of the *Popol Vuh* – attended by beautiful maidens bringing him food and water. Even though this mural had been painted about 100 BC, three centuries after the demise of Olmec civilization, Hun Hunahpu's face was depicted as an Olmec Maize God mask in profile, a clear indication that much of Maya high culture was derived from Olmec roots. Once again, goodbye to Kubler's "Principle of Disjunction"!

I was being taken to San Bartolo by one of the principal angels of the project, my friend Leon Reinhart, a San Diego banker who had once been in charge of Citibank in Mexico, and a longtime archaeological *aficionado*. With us were my old friend Dr. Guillermo ("Billy") Mata Amado, whose Guatemala city house I had rented during the second field season on the Pacific coast, his son Estuardo, now the President of the capital's wonderful Museo *Popol Vuh*, and John Clark of the NWAF.

Shortly after our helicopter landed, stirring up a storm of dust and debris, in came the Presidential helicopter, with Vice President Eduardo Stein and his group. A film crew from NASA was already on the spot, since part of Bill's project included satellite-generated mapping and analysis of the entire San Bartolo region. In groups of four or five, Bill led us into the excavation tunnels. We took in the wonders of the north wall – the Maize God and his attendants, standing on a serpent "floor" emerging from the monstrous maw of an anthropomorphic mountain; then a scene of an early Maya ruler on a scaffold, being offered the diadem of accession; and, finally, the west wall.

It was the west wall that left me gaping in amazement. Three decades earlier, when I had been working on the Grolier Club exhibit of Maya vases, I had proposed that some of the imagery of Classic Maya pictorial ceramics reflected a mythology that survived into the early Colonial period, where it could be fund in the 16th-century *Popol Vuh*. In 1989, in Justin and Barbara Kerr's *Maya Vase Book*, I was able to show that of the Maize God's two sons (the Hero Twins), Hunahpu could be identified by black spots on his face and body, and his brother Xbalanque by patches of jaguar hide. Here in this tunnel were revealed not one but *four* Hunahpus, each standing before a world-direction tree, all Hunahpus bloodily piercing their penises with huge perforators. Atop each tree was a gigantic raptor, the Principal Bird Deity of Maya iconography, to be identified with Vucub Caquix of the *Popol Vuh* – the bird monster slain by the Hero Twins.

So here was the *Popol Vuh* in spades, a wonderful vindication of the idea that there had always been a single tradition in Maya culture history, leading from the Olmec of 3,000 years ago, through the Late Preclassic in centers like San Bartolo, and extending from the Classic and Post-Classic beyond the Colonial period to the living Maya of today.

As I write this, amazing new discoveries continue to be made by the Saturno team at San Bartolo, including what seems to be the earliest Maya writing known thus far, and even earlier murals. Hardly a fortnight goes by without e-mail messages hinting at ever newer findings. Yet this small site cannot be alone as a testimony to the precocity of Maya civilization. For instance, the Mirador Basin to the west has ancient cities even larger than Tikal, and it is in that zone at the site of El Mirador that one finds the world's largest pyramid in terms of sheer bulk. Some day even more spectacular evidence for the splendors of Preclassic Maya culture is going to be found there, I am sure.

The great age of Maya archaeology is far from over. In fact, it's just beginning.

Envoi

❧

Thus far, I've had a generally lucky and good life, even in the highly unsettled world of the last seven decades, and I have no complaints – although who knows what the future may hold. The great Maya calendrical cycle that has been running unbroken for over 5,000 years will end on 23 December, 2012. Will I live beyond it? I'm not worried, but others may be. I've had a wonderful life with Sophie and our five children, and I was indeed fortunate with two sets of loving parents – both Sophie's and my own.

So much of my life has been a series of happy accidents totally beyond my control, and I often ask myself, what if that high-school biology teacher had *not* gone on leave?

What has been of continuing satisfaction to me has been the opportunity of discovering something that was previously unknown, and sometimes not even guessed at, for instance a distant, ancient culture like that of Guatemala's Pacific coast; or – without digging at all – to figure out the inscriptions and iconography on Maya vases. Much of my life has been dedicated to following the lure of the unknown, and to imparting something of the excitement of that quest to my students and readers and listeners. In one and the same profession, I've been able to do all sorts of truly interesting things, such as: to study the art of people like the Olmec, to collaborate with natural scientists in the investigation of ancient remains, to bring written documents to bear on the investigation of New England people contemporary with Bach and Handel, to read Maya inscriptions, and – above all – to write for an educated public (remember, I'm a frustrated writer as well as a frustrated biologist).

Hindus and Buddhists believe in *samsara*, the cycle of reincarnations, and that one's fortune and happiness in this life depends on one's good and/or bad actions in the life just past. I don't, but if I did, I would have to think that I could not have been very bad in my last incarnation, otherwise that silver spoon would never have been in my mouth when I was born into this one. I hope they're not right about *samsara*, as I can't but think it would be all downhill after this one.

In ancient Hindu mythology, the god Vishnu – the Preserver of the Universe – had ten incarnations or avatars, each time coming down to earth to save humans from different calamities. In one of these, he is born as Rama, prince of Ayodhya. When he grows up, the handsome, wise, and compassionate prince takes as his wife the beautiful Sita, princess of an allied kingdom. Through the machinations of an evil stepmother, Rama and his bride, along with his faithful brother Lakshmana, are banished for 14 years to wander in the forest as hermits, during which time Sita is abducted by the powerful ogre king Ravana, the ten-headed embodiment of everything evil in the world, and taken to Lanka, his island to the south of India.

Eventually Rama and Lakshmana, with the aid of a great army of monkey-men, invade the island; this is the great Battle of Lanka seen on a bas-relief at Angkor Wat. Ravana is defeated, and Sita brought back to Ayodhya, where Rama claims his throne, which has been temporarily occupied by another brother, Bharata.

This, in brief, is the plot of the *Ramayana*, the great mythic epic that is still celebrated throughout the Hindu-Buddhist world, where Rama has always been seen as the perfect prince and king, and the embodiment of all that is meant by the word *dharma* – duty, fate, what is right in the universe. While Rama is in exile, Bharata tries to persuade him to come back and take the throne, but Rama says that he (Rama) must act out his *dharma*, and turns down his invitation, while saying:

> Think of time, Bharata: how she carries us along, helpless, on her
> mysterious currents. Her ways and her purposes are always
> secret, and just hers to know. What is gathered today is scattered
> without warning tomorrow...
> Nothing except change is permanent in our lives, and nothing
> but death is final in this world. Death walks at our side on every
> trail; he wrinkles our skin and turns our hair white. We delight
> in each sunrise and sunset, and forget that our lives are
> shortened by every one. The seasons come, each with its own

allurements; but they take great slices of our lives with them. The relations of men are like ships passing each other on the ocean; whether with fathers, mothers, or children. We meet and are briefly together, only to part inevitably; if not in life, then surely in death. We must not make too much of our sorrow; it is nature's way. And who are we to question the wisdom of fate?

The *Ramayana*, retold by Ramesh Menon (North Point Press, 2003), p. 142

Principal Publications

Books and monographs only

1961, *La Victoria: An Early Site on the Pacific Coast of Guatemala*. Papers of the Peabody Museum, Harvard University, Vol. 53. Cambridge, MA.

1962, *Mexico* (Ancient Peoples and Places). London: Thames & Hudson. (4 subsequent editions.)

1965, *The Jaguar's Children: Pre-Classic Central Mexico*. New York: Museum of Primitive Art.

1966, *The Maya* (Ancient Peoples and Places). London: Thames & Hudson. (6 subsequent editions.)

1967, *Early Cultures and Human Ecology in South Coastal Guatemala* (with Kent V. Flannery). Smithsonian Contributions to Anthropology, Vol. 3. Washington, D.C.

1968, *America's First Civilization: Discovering the Olmec*. New York: American Heritage Press.

1973, *The Maya Scribe and His World*. New York: The Grolier Club.

1978, *Lords of the Underworld: Masterpieces of Classic Maya Ceramics*. Princeton University Press.

1980, *In the Land of the Olmec* (with Richard A. Diehl). 2 vols.
Vol. 1: *The Archaeology of San Lorenzo Tenochtitlán*.
Vol. 2: *The People of the River*. University of Texas Press.

1983, *Aztec Sorcerers in 17th Century Mexico: The Treatise on Superstitions* by Hernando Ruiz de Alarcón (with Gordon Whittaker). Albany: Institute for Mesoamerican Studies.

1986, *Atlas of Ancient America* (with Dean Snow and Elizabeth P. Benson). New York: Facts on File.

1992, *Breaking the Maya Code*. London & New York: Thames & Hudson. (Revised edition 1999.)

1996, *The True History of Chocolate* (with Sophie D. Coe). London & New York: Thames & Hudson.

1997, *The Art of the Maya Scribe* (with Justin Kerr). London: Thames & Hudson. New York: Abrams (1998).

2001, *Reading the Maya Glyphs* (with Mark Van Stone). London & New York: Thames and Hudson. (2nd edition 2005.)

2003, *Angkor and the Khmer Civilization* (Ancient Peoples and Places). London & New York: Thames & Hudson.

Sources of Illustrations

TEXT FIGURES: pp. **38–39** Ben Plumridge; p. **77** Ben Plumridge; p. **119** Drawing by Michael D. Coe; p. **123** Drawing by Antonio Oliveros C.; p. **163** Ben Plumridge after R. Diehl *The Olmecs* (Thames & Hudson 2004), ill. 2; p. **203** Drawing by Diane Griffiths Peck.

PLATES: All Michael D. Coe or Collection Michael D. Coe except: **4** Courtesy The Mark Twain Papers & Project, University of California; **6** Courtesy Planting Fields Foundation; **7** Courtesy Planting Fields Foundation; **8** Courtesy Fay School; **9** Courtesy Planting Fields Foundation; **11** Courtesy Planting Fields Foundation; **32** Courtesy Gillett G. Griffin.

Index